The Synergy Effect™
The Advisor's Guide

Doug Warren, CLU

The Synergy Effect™ The Advisor's Guide

Copyright © 2013 by Doug Warren

For more information, email Doug Warren at
doug.salesart@gmail.com.

Printed in the United States of America.

For Cheryl, Stephanie and Blake—
my enduring motivation

Also by Doug Warren, CLU

Advanced Annuity Strategies

The Great Roth-Rush

Indexed Universal Life Unleashed

About the Author

Doug Warren, CLU

With over 40 years of experience as an insurance professional and a recognized expert in life insurance, annuities, and Roth IRA conversion, Doug leverages his wealth of knowledge and practical sales experience to show you how to simplify complex concepts and help your clients understand the unparalleled power of *the Synergy Effect*™ of integrating life insurance, annuities, Roth IRAs, and Social Security claiming strategies, to boost spendable retirement income the way traditional planning can't.

The Synergy Effect:™ *The Advisor's Guide* is Doug's fourth book. His first book, *Advanced Annuity Strategies,* was the result of hundreds of hours of exclusive interviews with over 50 top annuity producers. It provided a first-ever look into the minds of mega-producers, allowing readers to "eavesdrop" as the top guns revealed their strategies and secrets. Doug's second book, *The Great Roth-Rush*, provided specific techniques for using Roth conversion strategies to gain more clients and transact more business. The popularity of this book helped Doug become the number one choice of leading insurance and annuity marketing organizations for Roth conversion training. Thousands of agents across the country have benefited from attending his live training sessions. In these dynamic sessions, he reveals proven techniques for pivoting from the Roth conversion discussion to a compelling presentation on the power of the indexed universal life insurance product. The popularity of these concepts led to his third book, *Indexed Universal Life Unleashed.*

I'd like to hear from you!

I would like to hear your comments. To stay competitive, we really want you, as a life insurance professional, to let us know what you like or dislike about this book or our other products. Feel free to contact me at; **doug.salesart@gmail.com** to share your opinions of this book.

Doug Warren, CLU

Find tools, articles, webinars, live training,
case studies and more resources devoted
to the Synergy Effect™
at *Doug-Warren.com*

Contents

Introduction

The Sky Really Is Falling

This is the Voice of Doom speaking! Special bulletin! Flash! The sky is falling! A piece of it just hit you on the head! Now be calm. Don't get panicky. Run for your life!

From Disney's original, 1943 version of *Chicken Little*

The first thing important to understand is that no one is driving this economic train that we are all riding on. Look inside the locomotive pulling this out-of-control train, and you won't find the U.S. president, the Congress, the Federal Reserve chairman or any elected or appointed bureaucrat:

> America greeted 2013 numbed to the absurdity of 0%
> interest rates, endless Federal Reserve bond purchases and
> $1 trillion deficits. President Obama imposed a January
> fiscal deal that added $4 trillion to the projected national
> debt, on the surreal claim that the U.S. government
> doesn't have a spending problem. His Cabinet and policy

choices show satisfaction with the status quo and a state of denial over the dangers ahead.[1]

There simply couldn't be anyone driving this economic train, or we would have changed direction a long time ago. Now, it is simply too late. We are moving too fast, and the decline is too steep. Ahead is a lot of pain and suffering that will be shared by all of us. But some will endure more misery than others. These will be the people who insist on following the old financial strategies that developed during different times, to deal with different issues, than those we will all face in the future.

People following these outdated strategies will continue to believe that as long as they do what they, their parents, their neighbors and their co-workers are doing and have always done, that they will one day achieve financial security.

And well before the last baby boomer has died, we will know that these old methods have failed a large portion of these people.

Who's at fault? Is it the politicians, who sold out our futures by incurring more debt than any sane and rational person would ever rack up? Is it the Wall Streeters, who have peddled low-performing, high-fee investments that are designed more to make them rich than to profit the clients they serve? Is it the bankers, who destine millions of people to a life of virtual servitude, as ever-increasing amounts of their wealth are lost to finance charges, credit card payments and student loans? Or, is the people themselves, who see no value in saving for a rainy day when they can enjoy the sunshine now as they ride their Sea-Doos and go on vacations?

While there is plenty of blame to be shared, there is no point in spending too much time in finding who is most at fault.

---

[1] David Malpass. "The Battle to Limit Government America Needs to Win Now" *Forbes* 11 February 2013.

This book was written for the financial professional who makes his or her living helping clients plan for the future. And the one thing that neither we nor our clients have much of is *time*!

The challenges our clients face are either upon us, or are rapidly approaching.

Challenge #1: Our country is already bankrupt

I am not an economist, so I lack the formal qualifications to suggest that our country is already bankrupt. But Boston University economics professor Laurence J. Kotlikoff is a very well-respected economist, and in a recent article he summarized our current situation by saying:

> *Let's get real. The U.S. is bankrupt.*

Professor Kotlikoff took a close look at the Congressional Budget Office data, and calculated that the U.S. government is facing a fiscal gap of $202 trillion.

The reason that his number is so much greater than the $16 trillion dollars of debt that most politicians will admit to is that Professor Kotlikoff's total includes all of the unfunded future liabilities that the U.S. government has already committed to. (Unfortunately, by the time you read this, the $16 trillion will be exceeded by a large margin, so check the U.S. National Debt Clock at www.usdebtclock.org to get an update on the bad news.)

To put that into perspective, consider that if the government sold all of the gold in Fort Knox (estimated to be 147.3 million ounces) at the current (and historically high) price of $1,776 per ounce, the total proceeds would amount to $261.6 billion.

If there was such a thing as a billion-dollar bill, you would need 1,000 of them to equal one trillion dollars; so $261.6 billion would hardly put a dent in the $202 trillion dollar debt. Even if we could sell all of the gold that has ever been mined in the history of man (estimated at

185,000 tons) at $1,776 per ounce, we would only end up with $10.5 trillion dollars. That would be only enough to pay off about 5 percent of what Professor Kotlikoff estimates as the total U.S. debt.

According to the U.S. Census Bureau, there are a total of about 113 million households in the U.S. If we divide the $202 trillion debt among the total households, each household's share amounts to over $1,787,611.

There are about 300 million people in America, so if we divide the total estimated debt by this number, it comes to a much more manageable $673,333. Unfortunately, that means that if you are married with two children, your gang's total share is a little under $2.7 million.

Prior to World War II it was generally considered to be immoral to leave debt for the next generation to pay. Evidently, morality has changed since then to such a degree that today we give little thought to saddling our children, grandchildren and great-grandchildren with a good deal of debt.

Our country is indeed bankrupt; most of us just don't know it yet. So who is going to help the aging baby boomers who run out of money and can't pay for their food, rent and medical bills?

Challenge #2: The cost of our county's entitlement programs is growing exponentially

Social Security and Medicare currently eat up about one-third of the current federal budget. If that isn't frightening enough, consider that this share is expected to grow *exponentially* over the next 25 years.

The significance of exponential growth can be difficult to grasp. It means starting at one, then increasing to two, and then going to four, eight, 16, 32, and so on. Instead of increasing by a certain percentage, exponential growth means doubling and then doubling again and again.

Look at it this way: Assume a person has a pound of peanuts. He wants them to last a long time, so he decides he will eat only one peanut today, but then double that number each following day. The next day he eats two peanuts, then the day after that, he eats four, and so on.

By day ten, the original pound of peanuts is gone. In fact, to keep on schedule, he must consume a total of two pounds on the tenth day alone. By day 15, he would have to eat 32 pounds of peanuts. On the 21st day, he must consume a full ton (2,000 pounds) of peanuts. And, only 30 days later, he would need to eat 500 tons of peanuts to stay on schedule.

Certainly the costs of Social Security, Medicare and our other entitlements aren't doubling every day or every year, but their rate of growth is far from peanuts. It is so significant that the financial rating agencies have started sounding the alarm:

> We lowered our long-term rating on the U.S. because we believe that the prolonged controversy over raising the statutory debt ceiling and the related fiscal policy debate indicate that further near-term progress containing the growth in public spending, especially on entitlements, or on reaching an agreement on raising revenues is less likely than we previously assumed and will remain a contentious and fitful process.[2]

If these programs continue their current trajectory, it will be mathematically impossible for our country to pay for them. So what do our leaders do? They spend even more money on new entitlements.

---

[2] Arthur B. Laffer. "Get Ready for Inflation and Higher Interest Rates" *The Wall Street Journal* 11 June 2009.
<http://online.wsj.com/article/SB124458888993599879.html>

Challenge #3: The 401(k) disaster

Over the past three decades, almost every business entity in America has replaced its defined benefit pension plan with a 401(k) or similar defined contribution plan. It is safe to assume that a large reason for this massive change was simply that business leaders realized it was a lot cheaper to provide a 401(k) matching fund than it was to fund a true pension plan that provided a lifetime of guaranteed retirement income.

This no doubt retained billions in corporate profits, but at the price of sending a great many loyal employees down a path in which they will have only a fraction of what they will need at retirement.

According to the Employee Benefits Research Institute (EBRI), the average person approaching retirement today has a total balance in his 401(k) and other retirement plans of only about three times his annual salary.

Without any other savings and only the additional income from Social Security, most baby boomers' meager 401(k) balances will be completely exhausted in just seven or eight years following retirement.

What then?

Challenge #4: Staggering health care costs after retirement

In 2006, Fidelity Investments did a study to learn how much savings a typical retired couple without any form of employer-sponsored retirement health insurance might need to pay for their out-of-pocket lifetime health care expenses. These expenses included things like Medicare premiums and co-pays, but did not include long-term care. The estimated amount was over $200,000.

In order to save this much money in a 401(k) growing at an average rate of six percent per year, a person 15 years from retirement would need to contribute more than $8,000 annually.

In August 2011, Fidelity Investments reported that the average annual contribution participants made to their 401(k) plans was $5,790. No doubt these participants are assuming that these contributions will provide them with future retirement income. They will, but instead of using that income to pay for food, shelter, golf and gifts for the grandkids, these people will need it all and more just to pay the estimated cost of their health care.

Challenge #5: An expected rapid climb in inflation rates will hit retirees hard

For the past few decades, the rate of inflation has been at historical lows. The government's consumer price index has increased an average of 2.8 percent annually for the past 20 years.

But many experts expect that these low rates of inflation won't last much longer. Consider the massive amounts of money our government has thrown at our current financial woes, and then add the even-greater amounts that will be necessary to keep step with the exponential growth of our social safety net entitlement programs, and it is no wonder that many experts expect a rapid climb in the future rate of inflation:

> It's difficult to estimate the magnitude of the inflationary and interest-rate consequences of the Fed's actions because, frankly, we haven't ever seen anything like this in the U.S. to date. What's happened is potentially far more inflationary than were the monetary policies of the 1970s, when the prime interest rate peaked at 21.5% and inflation peaked in the low double digits.[3]

If the baby boomers are forced to contend with even a four percent inflation rate during their retirement years, their cost of living will

---

[3] Arthur B. Laffer. "Get Ready for Inflation and Higher Interest Rates" *The Wall Street Journal* 11 June 2009.
<http://online.wsj.com/article/SB124458888993599879.html>

double in just 19 years. This means that the purchasing power of whatever meager income they have at the time will drop by half.

Challenge #6: Our politicians lack courage and leadership

> The choices facing the 112th Congress come at a time when the federal government's debt has increased dramatically in the past few years and when large annual budget deficits are projected to continue indefinitely under current laws or policies. If current laws remain unchanged, deficits will total $7 trillion over the next 10 years, the Congressional Budget Office (CBO) projects; if certain policies that are scheduled to expire under current law are extended instead, deficits may be much larger. Beyond the coming decade, the aging of the U.S. population and rising health care costs will put increasing pressure on the budget. If federal debt continues to expand faster than the economy—as it has since 2007—the growth of people's income will slow, the share of federal spending devoted to paying interest on the debt will rise more quickly, and the risk of a fiscal crisis will increase.[4]

If you listen to the vast majority of politicians today, no matter if they are Republican, Democrat or Independent, it becomes painfully obvious that they are either idiots or they are more interested in their political futures then the future of the country. When did we last hear intelligent, courageous and honest words of warning from any politician about the painful steps that must be taken today if we have any hope of minimizing the suffering that will be felt by many in the future?

---

[4] Congressional Budget Office. "Reducing the Deficit: Spending and Revenue Options" March 2011.
<http://www.cbo.gov/sites/default/files/cbofiles/ftpdocs/120xx/doc12085/03-10-reducingthedeficit.pdf>

For decades now, all we have really heard are the sounds made when these politicians just kick the can full of problems farther down the road.

Consider the cowardice of Congress when in August 2011 it concocted the Select Committee on Deficit Reduction, euphemistically referred to as the "Super Committee."

By forming this committee, what the Senate and House members did was to tell the American public that our elected officials did not have the courage to do their jobs and address this issue themselves. They were such cowards that instead of taking a stand that might cost them the loss of a future election, they turned the problem over to a committee of non-elected past politicians.

Consider that even if the Super Committee had succeeded in its goal of cutting $1.2 trillion over the next decade (they did not), even this would have fallen short of the $4 trillion reduction that many experts said was necessary to come close to solving the problem.

The Congress kicked the can to the Super Committee, which kicked it back to the 112th Congress. This Congress kicked the can down the road until after the 2012 elections, for the 113th session of Congress to deal with.

Challenge #7: Our economy, the driver of our country's wealth, will slow considerably in the future

When you combine the previously-stated challenges, one thing should become clear. The standard of living enjoyed by Americans today will decline in the future. It has to.

A greater percentage of our population will stop working as this giant baby boomer generation enters retirement. With insufficient savings in their 401(k)s, the baby boomers will have no option but to cut back their retirement spending to a bare minimum. Those still working will be taxed even more. With less of their paychecks remaining after taxes, people will have less to spend on cars, clothing, appliances, gadgets, toys and everything else we now spend our money on. Businesses that make these products will cut employment. There will be fewer people working to pay the taxes needed to support the spending the government requires, which means that those still working will in turn be taxed even more. They will have less to spend and consumption will drop further. It is a vicious cycle that is already in motion.

Neither we nor our political leaders seem to posses the wisdom or the will to break this cycle now and thus limit the suffering. So we all continue to sit back waiting for *someone* to do *something* while this cycle continues to spin out of control, until one day it will fracture by its own momentum.

In the process, we will all be forced to endure pain, but some will suffer far less than others.

Those who suffer least will be the ones who realize now that the future will be much different than the past. And because of this, they will be wise enough to adopt the **new strategies that will be required to cope with these coming challenges.** The strategies needed are those that marshal all of a person's resources in ways that make those resources work harder to boost lifetime spendable income, while at the same time protecting those resources from volatile financial markets and higher taxes and inflation.

The old methods tell individuals and advisors that retirement will be built on the three-legged stool of Social Security, personal savings and pensions (now 401(k)s, IRAs, etc.). According to these methods, at age 65 people retire, claim their Social Security, and supplement this income as best they can by withdrawing first from any personal savings. Once this money is gone, they'll replace it with distributions from their qualified plans.

Unfortunately, by doing this, they ultimately expose themselves to the potential to have their income hit with the highest possible taxation and risk. Not only are their qualified plan distributions taxable, but as much as 85 percent of their Social Security will be as well. To pay these taxes, many will be forced to withdraw even greater amounts from their taxable qualified plans in order to net the after-tax amount required to meet their spending needs. If these withdrawals are coming from a portfolio of stocks during a period when the market is down, they will lock in losses that can never be recovered.

This is not only risky, but for many it will also be very tax-inefficient as well.

Instead, by precisely combining the right Social Security claiming strategy, the judicial use of annuities within the qualified plan, a partial Roth conversions tactic, a properly-structured indexed universal life insurance policy and other financial instruments, a synergistic effect can be created that could minimize exposure to market risk, assure the continuation of tax efficient income, significantly increase the after-tax amounts received from Social Security and much more.

No present-day politician, whether a member of Congress, a member of the Senate, or the president can come close to doing this for your clients. Only one person can help these people: you. This is, of course, assuming that you are an advisor who clearly sees the coming challenges, who knows how to implement new-age strategies to meet them and who cares enough about your clients that you are willing to serve them regardless of what it does to your bottom line.

This is the heart of *the Synergy Effect*™.

Chapter 1

The Great 401(k) Catastrophe

"A long habit of not thinking a thing wrong
gives it a superficial appearance of being right."
Thomas Paine

Baby boomers have been the primary mice used in the great 401(k) retirement experiment. We know precisely the date that the experiment first started. It was 1978 when politicians in Congress decided to reengineer retirement plans for the *benefit of workers* and passed the 1978 Tax Revenue Act. The date that the experiment will end, however, is less clear. Most likely, it will be sometime around 2030, when the oldest members of the Baby Boomer generation — born during the last days of World War II — turn 85.

There is much evidence that by that time, the results of this experiment will show that many will have benefited from the 401(k) plan. Unfortunately, few of them will be the retirees that relied on this plan for retirement security.

Who are those who benefited? Well, certainly Wall Street and the others who promoted high-fee funds will have come out pretty well. And let's not forget about the corporations that got billions of dollars of future liability off the books by shifting the obligations of funding and administering the old defined benefit pensions over to employees with their new 401(k)s.

But what about the plan participants? How well will history say they did?

The Accumulation-Phase Failure

Baby boomers are the first generation that has been forced to deal with the widespread transition from defined benefit retirement plans to the do-it-yourself plans like 401(k)s, IRAs, 457s and other defined contribution plans. It is appropriate to characterize them as do-it-yourself plans because with them, for the first time participants were faced with the responsibility of making investment decisions relating to their plan's assets. Tragically, when it comes to do-it-yourself investing in stocks and bonds, there is a great deal of evidence showing that many boomers have failed miserably.

Some of it is not their fault. So far at least, timing has not exactly been on their side. The period from January 2000 to December 2009 has been called the "Lost Decade" for stocks for a very good reason:

> $100,000 invested in an S&P 500 index fund in January 2000 would have been worth $89,072 by mid-December of 2009. Adjusted for inflation, the returns are even worse. That initial $100,000 becomes $69,114 at the end of the decade known as the "aughts."[5]

Unfortunately, the do-it-yourself investor, which typically defines 401(k) participants, appears to have done much worse.

---

[5]Burstyn, Gerald. "A Lost Decade for Advisors?" *Research Magazine* Nov 2011

"You must never ever, gamble with your hard earned money......That's my job!"

DALBAR Inc., a respected market research firm located in Boston, has been reporting the annual results of its Quantitative Analysis of Investor Behavior research for almost two decades, and the results consistently show that individual investors consistently underperform both the equities and bond markets by a wide margin during both good and poor economic periods.

Their report covering the 20-year period ending with the particularly devastating year of 2008 is even more disturbing, saying, "Equity fund investors lost 41.6% last year, compared with 37.7% for the S&P 500 Index."[6]

So during a year when the stock market was down 37.7 percent, the individual investor actually lost an even greater *41.6 percent.*

How does the individual investor do during years when the stock market performs better? The average return of the Standard & Poor's 500 Index during the 20-year period ending in 2010 was 9.1 percent. Not bad. But according to the DALBAR research, the average return actually earned by individual investors during this period was a paltry 3.8 percent.[7]

Consider what these statistics might mean for a participant who had his entire 401(k) balance invested in equities. Assume that at the beginning of 1991, he had contributed $10,000 into his 401(k), and continued

---

[6] DALBAR press release, 9 March 2009
[7] DALBAR press release, 1 April 2011

making the same contributions every year for the next 20 years. If this money had been invested in such a way that he had captured the 9.14 percent return of the S&P 500, his balance at the end of 2010 would be $567,211. Subtract the $200,000 in total contributions, and the he is left with a gain of $367,211. Not bad.

However, if he instead averaged only 3.83 percent, his 401(k) balance after 20 years would be only $303,789. This represents a gain over contributions of only $103,789.

The difference between the two is over $263,422. Where did this money go?

Of course, some went to fees and the other charges deducted from the 401(k). Depending on the size of the plan, the all-in fees, including mutual fund investment options are reported as averaging between one percent and 1.9 percent annually.[8]

If we used an average of 1.45 percent, fees would account for a total of $33,438 over the 20 years.

There are many people who argue that these fees are reasonable, and there are others who strongly disagree. But if you get too caught up in this argument, you miss the real significance of the DALBAR research.

On the Internet, you will find articles from numerous financial commentators that reference the DALBAR research and attempt to explain the causes for such poor performance. While you will find many different versions, essentially they all come to the same basic conclusion: that it is the individual's *emotions* that get in the way of successful investing.

One of the most useless yet often-asked questions that investment advisors pose to their clients is, "What is your tolerance to market

[8] Lieber, Ron. "Revealing Excessive 401(k) Fees." *The New York Times* 3 June 2011 <www.nytimes.com/2011/06/04/your-money/401ks-and-similar-plans/04money.html>

risk?" The reason it is a useless question is because the answer undoubtedly changes as markets move:

> During the times and periods stock markets are in positive territory and increasing in value, the masses believe they are risk tolerant. Then, in the next week, month, or year when markets decline sharply, they decide they are risk averse and can't handle the volatility. They sell out, liquidate, and miss-time the market. Their attitude to financial risk is more fickle than the markets themselves, and risk-aversion becomes an elusive temperament without a solid foundation. It is, therefore, almost meaningless to ask people what their risk attitude is. It changes based on yesterday's market, today's mood, and even tomorrow's weather. How can one make investment decisions regarding hundreds of thousands of dollars based on the answer to a question that changes daily?[9]

"And in the event of a sudden drop in the market, oxygen masks will drop from above your seats."

The emotions of the typical individual investor cause him to buy and sell at the wrong time, just like they cause the participant to reallocate his 401(k) investments at the wrong times.

---

[9] Milevsky, Moshe A. *Are You A Stock Or A Bond?: Identify Your Own Human Capital for a Secure Financial Future* FT Press, 1 October 2012.

The undeniable truth is that the majority of participants are not prepared for the do-it-yourself investment challenges necessary with 401(k)s and other defined contribution retirement plans. These plans have caused scores of investment experts, mutual fund promoters and even politicians to advance opinions and theories as to how to solve this problem.

Unfortunately, while everyone speculates on a solution, the entire baby boomer generation is now at the doorstep of retirement. And they are woefully unprepared:

> The median household headed by a person aged 60 to 62 with a 401(k) account has less than one-quarter of what is needed in that account to maintain its standard of living in retirement, according to data compiled by the Federal Reserve and analyzed by the Center for Retirement Research at Boston College for The Wall Street Journal.[10]

And if the challenges of investing this money have proven to be difficult, wait until these boomers stop working and are forced to figure out how to take the relatively small balances in their 401(k)s and turn them into incomes large enough to meet their needs over their entire lifetimes.

The challenges that boomers face during the do-it-yourself distribution phase of their 401(k) plans will make their do-it-yourself investment challenges look small by comparison.

The Coming Distribution-Phase Failure

Most retirement planners are well aware of the fact that Americans are expected to live longer than ever before. What should be of particular interest to advisors is an Associated Press-LifeGoesStrong.com poll in

---

[10] Browning, E.S. "Retiring Boomers Find 401(k) Plans Fall Short" *Wall Street Journal Online* 19 February 2011.

June of 2011 that found that more than one in four adults expects to live to at least 90, including nearly half of those currently 65 or older.

Many 401(k) participants are starting to understand that they now face the even-greater challenge of coming up with a distribution strategy so that their do-it-yourself 401(k)s can provide the income they will need over the next two, three or possibly four decades.

"Those were years of such ambitious plans
... before the money ran out."

The more meager their 401(k) balances, the more likely they are to throw up their hands and conclude that their only option is to work as long as they are able, and then to finish their lives in some degree of poverty.

But consider the more fortunate boomer who reaches retirement with a seemingly large 401(k) balance. She still faces the challenge of balancing her need to make withdraws sufficient to support the lifestyle she desires while at the same time minimizing the risk that she might ever run out of money.

If her annual withdrawals are too conservative, she may not be able to enjoy her retirement the way she had always dreamed. At her death, there might remain a larger balance to pass on the heirs than she really wanted. If she withdraws too liberally, she might enjoy her retirement early on, but at the risk of one day fearing that she might live too long and run out of money.

People facing this dilemma often receive the advice from their advisors, planners or financial commentators in the media that with a well-diversified portfolio of stocks and bonds, they *should* be able to safely withdraw four to five percent of their balances each year with minimal risk of ever exhausting the balance.

This four to five percent *safe-withdrawal* rate can be traced back to what is commonly referred to as the Trinity Study. The study's name comes from that fact that it was conducted by three Trinity University professors. The three professors used historical data published by Ibbotson Associates to examine the impacts of various withdrawal rates from three to 12 percent on portfolios with different combinations of stocks and bonds investments. Using these parameters, they determined the chances of running out of money over all rolling withdrawal periods of 15, 20, 25, and 30 years from 1926 through 1995. Among other things, this study revealed that withdrawal rates that exceeded five percent would increase the probability that a person would go broke before they reached life expectancy.

Let's assume for a moment that five percent is in fact a valid safe withdrawal rate. For every $10,000 of annual income that a retiree needs to generate, her 401(k) would need a balance of $200,000 if she limited her withdrawal to five percent of the balance. If a total of $50,000 of income is needed from the 401(k), the balance required would be $1,000,000. While there are certainly a large number of people retiring who will need at least $50,000 in annual withdrawals, what percentage of them will have the $1,000,000 balance to support those withdrawals?

But what makes this even worse is that there are more problems with relying on these so-called safe withdrawal rates.

In April of 2001, an article appeared in *Financial Planning Journal* that argued that there was a flaw in the research conducted to support these safe-withdrawal rates. The flaw was that while it was assumed that clients would earn the same returns as a stock market index, the research ignored the taxes and investment expenses that clients actually must pay.

This article showed that if only the investment expenses were considered, "withdrawing 3.5 percent of the initial value of the portfolio has about the same sustainability as a 4 percent withdrawal with no expenses."

In other words, if a safe-withdrawal rate had been assumed to be four percent, one-half of one percent (or possibly more) should not be considered available for consumption, because this amount would likely already have been withdrawn by the investment firm managing the portfolio to pay the fees they charge.

Regarding taxes, the article shows that when the entire withdrawal is subject to income taxes, as is typically the case when the withdrawals are coming from a 401(k), "the available consumption is obtained by reducing the withdrawal by the average applicable income tax rate." In order to estimate the impact of taxes on the withdrawal rate, you need to know the individual's tax rate. But regardless of the specific rates, the author of this article concluded that "the reduction required in withdrawal rates for taxes and expenses is likely to be significant."[11]

What many retirees are destined to discover is that their income needs at retirement will force them to withdraw more than these safe-withdrawal rates. The higher the actual withdrawal rate, the greater the risk of depleting the nest egg prior to death.

Morningstar Inc. published a study that showed how the risks of depleting a retirement portfolio over a 25-year period increased as withdrawal rates increased. Assuming the portfolio was invested 50 percent in bonds and 50 percent in stocks, the study showed that as long as the withdrawal percentage was limited to 4 percent, the individual enjoyed a 96 percent chance of not depleting the portfolio.

---

[11] Pye, Gordon B. "Adjusting Withdrawal Rates for Taxes and Expenses" *Financial Planning Journal* April 2001.

However, when the withdrawal percentage increased to 6 percent, the individual's rate of success in terms of not depleting the portfolio reduced to just 57 percent. Far worse, individuals only have a 13 percent chance of not depleting the portfolio when an eight percent withdrawal rate is assumed.

The advice to anyone facing retirement is clear: if you don't want to run out of money, you'd better keep your withdrawals at four percent or less.

Reconsider the quote referenced earlier from the Wall Street Journal article: "The median household headed by a person aged 60 to 62 with a 401(k) account has less than one-quarter of what is needed in that account to maintain his standard of living in retirement." If this is accurate, then how realistic is the assumption that these people can limit withdrawals to four percent? At this rate, a $250,000 nest egg would likely not generate an income of more than $833 a month. (Assuming no investment fees had been subtracted first.) Add this to the 2012 average monthly Social Security benefit of $1,230, and you have a total monthly income of $2,063. While this is above what is considered the poverty level in this country, it does not exactly provide for a retirement that is either enjoyable or very secure.

A more likely reality is that instead of consistently limiting withdrawals to four percent, many individuals will either be forced to periodically increase withdrawals to meet some unexpected emergency, or in a moment of weakness, they will pull more money out so they can go on a vacation or buy some gifts for the grandkids. Regardless of the reason, even a temporary increase in withdrawals, combined with the possibility of out-living life expectancy, can ultimately doom the nest egg. This will leave many dependent solely on Social Security and a remaining life where enjoyment and security are replaced with fear and poverty.

While the impact may not be apparent for another decade or two, as baby boomers age and their retirement plan balances shrink, ultimately it will be clear that this great 401(k) experiment was a catastrophe for a large number of people.

Find tools, articles, webinars, live training, case studies and more resources devoted to *the Synergy Effect*™ at *www.iSYNERGIZE.com.*

Chapter 2

Boosting Spendable
Retirement Income

*It's not how much retirement income a person has,
but how much they have to spend.*

The Synergy Effect™ is an innovative retirement income planning
strategy that precisely integrates four essential financial instruments —
indexed universal life insurance, income annuities, Roth IRA
conversions and Social Security claiming strategies — to **boost
spendable retirement income the way traditional planning can't**.

If you are a life insurance agent, your time has arrived. You have
exactly the right products, with precisely the features and benefits that
are needed in a world that has forever changed. To understand why, it is
important to know that the single greatest need most baby boomers will
face in the future can be described in one word:

Income

But there are a number of words that must be placed in front of the word "income" in order to truly appreciate the depth of the challenge in providing for this need:

Ample Income

Guaranteed Income

Lifetime Income

Inflation-Adjusted Income

Tax-Efficient Income

And perhaps the most important one of all:

Spendable Income

Only licensed insurance agents who fully understand permanent life insurance and income annuities have the essential financial instruments to *safely* boost spendable lifetime retirement income the way traditional financial planners can't.

You are in the right place at the right time

When clients go to a broker, CPA or money manager for traditional retirement planning, they're typically told that asset allocation, the right blend of equities and bonds, plus a so-called "safe" withdrawal rate will make their retirement more secure. If the financial meltdown of 2008 and 2009 proved anything, it was that traditional financial planning can not protect clients from losing money.

But even when the traditional methods did work to grow more retirement income, they also raised huge problems. The higher a person's retirement income received from "traditional" sources, the more of a target of government taxation that person becomes. And as our country's deficits grow, we can expect that more government benefits like Medicare, prescription drugs and even Social Security will be "means-tested."

In his 2013 State of the Union address, President Obama said, "We'll reduce taxpayer subsidies to prescription drug companies and ask more from the wealthiest seniors." Here's what the Washington Post said in response:

> What the Obama administration has proposed is essentially jacking up these income-related premiums by 15 percent, so they would pay a bigger chunk of their own health-care premium.[12]

The retiree with a large gross income could easily find that the spendable portion that remains after taxes and the loss of benefits won't come close to supporting the lifestyle that he or she worked so hard to achieve.

The fact is today, market losses and uncertainty, low or no interest on CDs coupled with predictable changes in taxation, increased medical and medical insurance costs, confusion of what's deductible and what's not and when to take social security, together with clients' risk aversion, threatens spendable income, and in most cases, crimps it all the way.

The old ways of retirement income planning are gone forever

Traditional financial planning simply doesn't address how the world has changed, and in fact, many so-called experts in the media continue to reject the only products and methods that have a chance of providing a stable and secure amount of spendable income that will last throughout a person's lifetime. Many of the people who insist on listening to these financial entertainers are stuck with products and

---

[12] Kilff, Sarah. "Three ways Obama wants to cut Medicare" *The Washington Post* 13 February 2013.
<http://www.washingtonpost.com/blogs/wonkblog/wp/2013/02/13/three-ways-obama-wants-to-cut-medicare/>

methods that ultimately can't deliver. Even financial planning that leans heavily on tax reduction alone can't do it.

Only the life insurance and annuity professional who fully understands IULs and income annuities, plus Roth IRA conversions and the profound impact they can have on reducing Social Security taxation and boosting spendable income, can do the job that millions of baby boomers need done.

Why is it that life insurance agents are now the most important members of financial planning teams? It's simple: they have the exact products needed for the changed financial world.

Clients want and need protection against market risk...
"Indexing" delivers

Clients want and need protection against taxes destroying not only their futures but also the legacies they leave their loved ones...
Life insurance contracts deliver

Clients want and need guaranteed lifetime incomes...
Income Annuities deliver

Clients want and need more predictable and greater spendable retirement incomes...
***The Synergy Effect*™ delivers**

The Synergy Effect™ strategy combines IULs, annuities, Roth IRAs and breakthrough Social Security claiming strategies to do what no planner can do without it.

Finding a safe way to achieve greater *spendable lifetime retirement income* is the primary objective. *The Synergy Effect*™ strategy explains that a good first step in that direction is to understand that with the right "claiming strategy," many people could significantly increase their lifetime Social Security retirement incomes. Instead of $23,000 a year, a married couple might be able to get $40,000 or more in annual retirement income.

The chapter in this book devoted to Social Security claiming strategies will show you how this is possible with proper planning.

While strategies to boost Social Security retirement income are moving in the right direction, they alone may not boost spendable income enough. Before a person can enjoy this increased income, he must find a way to reduce the taxes on that income.

Traditional financial planning doesn't do the job. Most often, it combines Social Security income with the wrong sources of other income, like distributions from traditional IRAs and 401(k)s, that only make the tax problem worse. And it isn't just higher taxes that are at stake; income from these sources is typically more exposed to the risk of being decimated by volatile stock markets.

Though this book focuses only on indexed universal life, income annuities, Roth IRAs and Social Security claiming strategies, the reader should not assume that other financial products and instruments aren't worthy of being included in your clients' retirement plans. And it certainly does not mean that clients should not also consider investing a portion of their money in bank CDs, bonds, real estate, stocks, mutual funds, exchange-traded funds, precious metals or other options that are available. There are logical places for a variety of financial instruments in your client's retirement portfolio.

However, the instruments that are the focus of this book each provide unique features and benefits that are particularly well-suited for meeting future financial challenges.

For example:

Income Annuities – At the heart of an annuity is its unique ability to provide a guaranteed income. It is the only financial vehicle that is able to pool the longevity risk to provide this guarantee until the very end of a client's life, no matter how long that might be. Lifetime income annuities can provide an income stream that is not only guaranteed, but can be greater than what might be provided by any alternative, due to the unique benefit of mortality credits.

Roth IRAs – *Roth IRAs* can transform the future growth of virtually any investment vehicle, whether it is stocks, bonds, precious metals or even real estate, from being tax-deferred to 100 percent tax-free. If a client's tax rates are higher in the future, the investments used inside the Roth IRAs will provide more spendable income than those very same investments would provide if the client held them outside of a Roth IRA.

Indexed Universal Life Insurance (IUL) – When properly structured, an IUL can serve the risk-averse client as a powerful way to both accumulate and transfer wealth. Properly accessed, this wealth can provide a supplemental income while the client is alive. It can also guarantee the continuation of an income stream to a surviving spouse or other heirs after death. But the real magic that a knowledgeable advisor can unlock for his clients can be found in the IUL's tremendous tax advantages and its cash value loan options.

Social Security – While there is no question that the long-term outlook for this government program may appear bleak, it will likely be around in one form or another for many decades to come. If the right strategies are used, Social Security might easily provide a significant source of tax-efficient, inflation-adjusted income for a long period of time.

What is very exciting to the knowledgeable advisor is that while each of these financial instruments has its own unique features and benefits, they all have the potential of becoming even more powerful when properly combined. This synergy can mean that 1 + 1 might equal more than two.

For example:

If future tax rates are higher:

Without the beneficial effects of *the Synergy Effect*™ strategy:

> **Taxable distributions from traditional 401(k)s or IRAs**
> **+ _Social Security retirement income_**
>
> *Can be like adding 1 + 1 and getting something <u>less</u> than two, because not only is the 401(k) or IRA money fully taxable, but depending on its amount, it can cause as much as 85 percent of the Social Security income to be taxable as well.*

With the beneficial effects of *the Synergy Effect*™ strategy:

> **Tax-free distributions from Roth IRAs or cash value loans**
> **+ _Social Security retirement income_**
>
> *Can be like adding 1 + 1 and getting something <u>greater</u> than two, because not only is the Roth IRA money not taxable income and the IUL cash value loans potentially not taxable income, but neither would go into the provisional income calculations to determine the taxable portion of the Social Security income. Depending on the client's other income sources, less of the Social Security income would be subject to taxation, or it could be entirely tax-free.*

If a person's retirement income is too low to be impacted by taxes:

Without the beneficial effects of *the Synergy Effect*™ strategy:

> **A 4% (so-called) safe withdrawal strategy**
> **+ _A portfolio of investments subject to market losses_**

> *Can be like adding 1 + 1 and getting something <u>less</u> than two, because if investments are liquidated during an extended period of market losses in order to provide the needed income, those losses are locked in and could cause the entire portfolio to be exhausted earlier in the person's lifetime.*

With the beneficial effects of *the Synergy Effect™* strategy:

> **A lifetime income annuity**
> **+ <u>A portfolio of investments subject to market losses</u>**

> *Can be like adding 1 + 1 and getting something <u>greater</u> than two. Because of mortality credits, less of the person's money would need to be allocated to an annuity designed to provide a level of income necessary to meet the client's basic, essential living expenses. The money not allocated to the annuity could be invested in any way that meets the person's risk tolerance. In good economic times, the overall income could be attractive. But no matter how bad the economy, the person enjoys a lifetime of guaranteed income.*

It is important to understand that *the Synergy Effect™* strategy will not always result in higher income. That may not be possible, or it may not always be the objective. However, *the Synergy Effect™* strategy does have the potential of providing a client with an increase in something. That increase may be greater security, greater peace of mind, greater protection against running out of money, greater protection from market volatility, a greater ability to combat inflation, or a greater ability to deal with many of the challenges that people face when it comes to protecting themselves from all forms of financial risk.

It bears repeating that it is a mistake for any reader to assume or believe that this book is suggesting that all of a client's money should be placed in annuities, indexed universal life insurance or Roth IRAs. Depending on a client's circumstances, investments in equities, bonds and other vehicles are likely not only warranted, but prudent. No matter how concerned a client is about the prospects of future tax rate increases, an important place remains for contributions into 401(k)s, IRAs and other tax-deferred retirement plans, especially when these plans provide employer matched contributions.

There is no perfect savings account or investment vehicle. Income annuities, indexed universal life, Roth IRAs and every other financial instrument have their weaknesses. However, income annuities, indexed universal life, and Roth IRAs have some very powerful and unique features that few financial instruments offer. The goal of *the Synergy Effect*™ strategy is to combine the strengths of these products with each other *and* the strengths unique to other financial instruments in a way that offsets the unique weaknesses they all have, so that the result is that our clients are in a much better position to deal with the challenges ahead.

Find tools, articles, webinars, live training,
case studies and more resources devoted
to *the Synergy Effect*™
at ***Doug-Warren.com***

Chapter 3

Social Security Claiming Strategies

This chapter is based on the current rules of the Social Security system and the implied promises that have been made to participants. No one knows how future legislation may change Social Security or its benefits. Based on intuition and recent proposals, it is the author's opinion that Social Security likely will change little for current retirees and those soon to retire. Consequently, strategies outlined here may best serve individuals in this target audience. Nevertheless, it is important to note this limitation. Finally, the rules pertaining to Social Security are full of exceptions and nuance that are beyond the scope of this chapter. Readers should do their own research. For additional details, see the Social Security Administration Web site at http://www.socialsecurity.gov/.

The Synergy Effect™ strategy is all about boosting spendable retirement income. If ever there was a vehicle with the potential to accomplish this objective, it is the Social Security retirement benefit. Unfortunately, the decisions made by the majority of Americans today regarding when to start their Social Security retirement benefits, and how to coordinate those benefits with their other sources of retirement income are not only misguided, but will likely prove to be disastrous for their long-term financial security.

There are literally thousands of different choices as to the dates a married couple can choose to start their Social Security retirement benefits. Most people make the wrong choices, and because of them, they forfeit tens, or even hundreds of thousands of dollars in benefits.

In a nutshell, the conflicting strategies concern whether it's better for a person to:

*Start Social Security at an early age
and by doing so, receive a smaller monthly benefit.*

Or:

*Delay the start of Social Security to an older age
and by doing, so receive a larger monthly benefit.*

Before continuing, it is important to state that many people will have no choice other than to start receiving Social Security at an early age. They might be forced to do so because of financial or health considerations. Much of what is discussed in this chapter applies to people who expect to live to normal life expectancy or beyond, and who have sufficient financial resources so that, with proper planning, they have the option of delaying the start of their Social Security retirement benefit.

Prior to 2000, the majority of Social Security participants believed that starting benefits as early as possible was the best strategy, as evidenced by the fact that 60 percent of eligible workers decided to collect their retirement benefits prior to reaching their full retirement age.[13]

---

[13] Leonesio, Michael V., Vaughan, Denton R., and Wixon, Bernard. "ORES Working Paper Series, Number 86: Early Retirees Under Social Security: Health Status and Economic Resources" *Social Security Administration Office of Policy* August 2000.

It used to be that the position of taking benefits as early as possible was supported and encouraged by the many leading financial experts at the time:

> Robert Hey wastes no time informing readers of "Benefit Puzzle: Take the Money at 65, or Wait?" (AARP Bulletin, November 2000) that "many financial advisors have no trouble making a strong recommendation: Take the money now." Hey explains that individuals that wait until age 70 to begin receiving benefits must live until age 86 to recoup the benefits they lose between 65 and 70. Hey briefly mentions that an individual's tax situation could affect the decision, but says that it is possible to come out ahead by waiting until age 70 to begin taking benefits only if the person lives a "very long life."

And:

> Humberto Cruz ("Age Weighs Heavy on Social Security Benefits," Corpus Christi Caller-Times, November 6, 2000) takes a slightly more cautious approach, but suggests that age 62 is probably the better time to begin receiving benefits. The article points out that retirees that do not need the money and plan to invest it may benefit more by taking early benefits.[14]

But more recently, a growing number of financial experts have changed their positions, and now believe that for many people, it is actually much better to delay the start of Social Security. Take for example the same Humberto Cruz quoted above. Mr. Cruz has been a highly regarded financial journalist for decades. His initial opinion that "age 62 is probably the better time to begin receiving benefits" had changed

---

[14] Van Zante, Neal R. "Choosing the Right Beginning Age for Social Security Benefits" *The CPA Journal Online* March 2002 <http://www.nysscpa.org/cpajournal/2002/0302/dept/302d56.htm>

significantly by 2008, when he wrote about when he and his wife Georgina were planning to take their own Social Security retirement benefits:

> Georgina will wait until her full retirement age of 66 in 2010 primarily because her earnings from freelance work would reduce her benefits until then. As the higher-earning spouse, I will then "file and suspend" when I reach my full retirement age of 66 in 2011.

> That means I will file for my full retirement benefits but immediately ask that they be voluntarily suspended, which can be done in the remarks section of the application, either on paper or online, said Dorothy Clark, a Social Security spokeswoman. I will then wait to collect until I am 70.[15]

Mr. Cruz, like many other experts, changed his opinion concerning the best age to claim Social Security retirement benefits in large part because so many things have changed over recent years:

> The full value of delaying Social Security has not been properly measured due to a lack of inclusion of the tax benefits, survivor benefits, projected Cost-of-Living-Adjustments (COLA) benefits, and spousal benefits available under the Social Security provisions and the Senior Citizens' Freedom to Work Act of 2000.[16]

But while scores of experts have changed their opinions and now believe that a better option for many people is to delay the start of their

[15] Cruz, Humberto. "Waiting on Social Security Benefits Can Pay Dividends" *Chicago Tribune online* 3 February 2008 <http://articles.chicagotribune.com/2008-02-03/business/0802010816_1_spousal-benefit-full-retirement-age-georgina>
[16] Mahaney, James, and Carlson, Peter. "Rethinking Social Security Claiming in a 401(k) World" *Pension Research Council Working Paper* August 2007, pg. 1. <http://www.planningtampabay.org/net/gallery/files/SocialSecurityWhitePaperbyCarlson_Peter.pdf>

Social Security, millions of Americans have not yet caught up with their advice. In fact, today, even more Americans are taking the benefits early:

> The experts we talked with frequently recommend that retirees delay taking Social Security to increase their lifetime retirement income, but most of today's retirees took Social Security before their full retirement age, which has committed many to substantially lower monthly benefits than if they had waited. Among those who were eligible to take benefits within 1 month after their 62nd birthday from 1997 through 2005, 43.1 percent did so, according to Social Security administrative data compiled by the Office of the Chief Actuary. An estimated 72.8 percent took benefits before age 65, and only 14.1 percent took benefits the month they reached their full retirement age, which varied from age 65 to age 66 depending on birth year. In addition, only about 2.8 percent took benefits after their 66th birthday. By taking the benefits on or before their 63rd birthday, 49.5 percent of beneficiaries born in 1943 passed up increases of at least 25 to 33 percent in monthly inflation-adjusted benefits that would have been available, had they waited until their full retirement age.[17]

In 1983, and again in 2000, Social Security was reformed in ways that seemed relatively minor at the time to many people. Today, the impact of these and other changes is more apparent, and so dramatic that it warrants a much different approach to financial planning.

The 1983 changes to Social Security phased in an increase to full retirement age (FRA) from age 65 to what today is now age 66 for most baby boomers, and age 67 for those born in 1960 or later. Of *major*

---

[17] US Government Accountability Office Report "Ensuring Income throughout Retirement Requires Difficult Choices" June 2011 < http://www.gao.gov/new.items/d11400.pdf >

significance is that this changed the penalty for starting Social Security at the earliest age from 20 percent to 25 percent.

This same 1983 legislation, and a later change in 1993, introduced and then increased income thresholds that when exceeded, caused up to 85 percent of Social Security to be included as taxable income. This is of *major* significance because these thresholds were not indexed to inflation — so we should expect that eventually, 100 percent of future recipients will be exposed to this taxation:

> The thresholds beyond which first 50 percent and then 85 percent of your Social Security benefits are subject to federal income taxation are explicitly NOT indexed for inflation. Hence, eventually, all Social Security recipients will be taxed on 85 percent of their Social Security benefits.[18]

And:

> By not providing for these bracket points to be indexed for inflation over time, Congress elected to allow for automatic increases in the taxation of Social Security benefits. As a matter of reference, had the threshold amounts been indexed to inflation in 1983, the amounts would be 2.28 times as much in 2011, according to the inflation calculator at the Bureau of Labor Statistics website; had the amounts been indexed beginning in 1993, they would be 1.57 times as much.[19]

Today, the fiscal problems facing the country are so profound that the likelihood is that tax rates will be higher in the future. Of *major*

---

[18] Kotlikoff, Laurence. "44 Social Security 'Secrets' All Baby Boomers and Millions of Current Recipients Need to Know - Revised!" *Forbes online* 3 July 2012. <http://www.forbes.com/sites/kotlikoff/2012/07/03/44-social-security-secrets-all-baby-boomers-and-millions-of-current-recipients-need-to-know/>
[19] VanZante, Neal R., and Fritzsch, Ralph B. "Senior Citizens and the 'Marriage Tax' on Social Security Benefits" *The CPA Journal* February 2012.

significance is that the unique tax treatment of permanent life insurance and Roth IRAs can be harnessed in a way that allows clients to significantly boost the lifetime spendable income they will receive from Social Security.

Few retirees who rush to start their Social Security recognize that they could potentially increase the amount of the income checks by at least 80 percent if they waited just eight years:

> Imagine you earned an average of $75,000 a year. If you retired early, at age 62, you'd receive $15,888 in Social Security annually from retirement until the end of your life. If you retired at your full retirement age (let's say it's 66), you'd receive $21,181 annually. If you waited to retire until age 70, you'd receive $28,821 annually, an 81% increase in monthly payments over claiming them at age 62.[20]

And depending on the amount of future cost of living increases (COLAs), the actual increase by waiting until age 70 could double the age 62 benefit:

> If you wait the eight years until age 70 to take benefits, the inflation-adjusted benefit you finally receive will be nearly double.[21]

And:

> A man born on January 2, 1948, who earns $80,200, he can expect a $2,157 a month from Social Security at his normal full retirement age of 66. But if he retires this year,

---

[20] Warner, Ralph. "When to Claim Social Security Benefits" *NOLO Law for All* < http://www.nolo.com/legal-encyclopedia/when-claim-social-security-benefits-29886.html>

[21] Burns, Scott. "Defer Social Security Benefits? No question." *Seattle Times online* 1 September 2012. <http://seattletimes.com/html/businesstechnology/2019032020_burns02xml.html>

at 62, he'll receive just $1,458 a month, about a third less. Using Social Security's assumptions, by waiting until 70, his checks will start at $3,303 — more than double what he'd get at 62.[22]

Think about that for a moment. In 2012, the maximum Social Security benefit when started at age 62 was approximately $22,600 annually. Depending on COLAs, this same recipient could easily receive over $44,000 per year by waiting until age 70 to start his benefit.

Most people do not understand that their benefit check has the potential to increase so dramatically, because they are unaware that the COLAs apply even in the period during which they are delaying the start of their benefit:

It is also unlikely that most individuals realize that even when they are delaying benefits, that they are receiving credit for COLAs during the period for which they are delaying the start of Social Security.[23]

The typical argument made by those who favor starting a lower benefit early, centers around the *time value of money* and the *lost opportunity cost* that comes when delaying the start of benefits. The logic is that a person could save and invest all of the monthly checks received between the earliest start age of 62 and the latest start age of 70, and accumulate an extra pool of funds that could be used to make up the difference in the higher income received that would result from delaying the start of Social Security. And there have been many break-even analyses completed that lend support to this position:

[22] Brenner, Lynn. "Double Your Social Security Benefits" *CBS MoneyWatch online* 10 May 2010. < http://finance.yahoo.com/news/pf_article_109492.html>
[23] Mahaney, James, and Carlson, Peter. "Rethinking Social Security Claiming in a 401(k) World" *Pension Research Council Working Paper* August 2007, pg. 7. <http://www.planningtampabay.org/net/gallery/files/SocialSecurityWhitePaperby Carlson_Peter.pdf>

Advisors advocating the use of annuities often believe that clients would be better off starting Social Security retirement benefits as early as possible and use a commercial annuity to make up the difference in income that the client would have received had they waited to claim their Social Security. Under market conditions at the time of the drafting of this report, we found that by delaying Social Security benefits an individual can gain additional retirement income at a lower cost than from an immediate annuity. While individuals may choose reduced Social Security benefits at the early eligibility age of 62, the payments they will receive at full retirement age (age 66 for those born from 1943 to 1954) will be higher, and continue to increase incrementally the longer they wait, up to age 70. The total estimated amount of benefits collected by electing to delay receipt of benefits from age 62 up to age 70 is intended to be approximately actuarially equivalent, but determinations of actuarial equivalence at any particular time depend on assumptions as to current and projected interest and mortality rates. The amount of money that a retiree would forego by waiting to start benefits until age 66 is less than the amount needed to purchase an annuity that would provide the additional monthly income available by waiting until full retirement age. If, for example, a person collects $12,000 per year at age 62 and every year thereafter (with yearly adjustments for inflation), they could wait until age 66 and collect $16,000 per year (33 percent more with additional adjustments for inflation from age 62 to 66) and every year thereafter. By beginning to collect benefits at age 62 they would have collected a total of $48,000 by age 66, and could then purchase an inflation-adjusted annuity to provide income to make up the difference. However, the cost of the annuity for a single male would be 47.4 percent

43

more than the $48,000 they could collect from age 62 through 65. (See fig. 3.)[24]

Figure 3: Delaying Social Security Is More Cost Effective than Purchasing an Annuity to Enhance Retirement Income

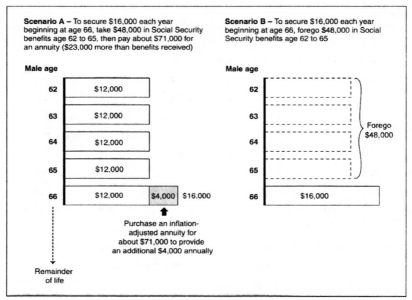

Source: GAO analysis based on formulas from SSA and an annuity quote from Income Solutions.

Notes: This is a quote for a single-life immediate annuity for a male resident in the State of Washington, currently aged 66, with no beneficiary. If the annuity were based on a female's life, the cost of the annuity would be more.

The Senior Citizens' Freedom to Work Act of 2000

Prior to 2000, married couples had much more limited options when it came to delaying the start of their Social Security retirement benefits. For example, if the husband was the worker, and he delayed his Social Security to get larger benefits, the wife would not be able to collect spousal benefits, and would also not receive *delayed retirement credits*.

---

[24] United States Government Accountability Office. "Report GAO-11-400: Ensuring Income throughout Retirement Requires Difficult Choices" *Report to the Chairman, Special Committee on Aging, U.S. Senate* June 2011. < http://www.gao.gov/new.items/d11400.pdf >

This lessened the value of delaying Social Security for many married couples.

The Senior Citizens' Freedom to Work Act of 2000 significantly changed this by allowing what is referred to as *file and suspend*. Now, a worker can file for benefits once reaching full retirement age, and immediately suspend those benefits. This allows the spouse to file for spousal benefits based on the worker's earnings record. Because the worker suspended benefits, the worker continues to accumulate delayed retirement benefits:

> File and suspend allows the primary wage earner to apply for benefits, then suspend collecting, while allowing the other spouse to start collecting spousal benefits immediately. Here's the best part: The primary wage-earning spouse can wait to claim benefits until age 70, which increases the future individual Social Security benefit by eight percent each year between ages 66 and 70.[25]

The decisions facing married couples regarding the most beneficial ages to start Social Security retirement benefits is complicated by the fact that many spouses qualify for benefits based upon their own work and earnings record, and/or a spouse benefit that is based on their spouse's work and earnings record. Combine this with the potential opportunities to claim either of these benefits at any age from 62 to 70, and you end up with literally thousands of possible options.

Not only will some of these options prove to be superior to others, but also Social Security imposes many rules that have the potential to place a person in a paradoxical situation in which solving one problem only creates another.

---

[25] Schlesinger, Jill. "Social Security: File and Suspend" *Chicago Times online* 16 August 2012. <http://articles.chicagotribune.com/2012-08-16/business/sns-201208161100--tms--retiresmctnrs-a20120816-20120816_1_spousal-benefit-full-retirement-age-social-security-benefit>

The most important consideration for many married couples is the *file and suspend* option:

> For married couples, there are some clever strategies to get higher payments without risk. In certain circumstances, a spouse can file a restricted application, earning a spousal benefit while his or her own benefit continues to grow. In other cases, a spouse filing and immediately suspending benefits allows the husband or wife to collect benefits.[26]

And:

> But there are also a few clever and perfectly legal ways to time the collection of your retirement benefits so that you increase their worth. Play your cards right and you'll increase your household income by thousands of dollars a year now, plus ensure larger benefits later.[27]

No matter how "clever" these strategies might appear, it is important to keep in mind that in practice, their true benefit, if any, will ultimately depend on the person's Social Security work and earnings history and how long he or she might live.

File and Suspend: *A strategy for high earners who can wait until age 70 to start Social Security*

The opportunity that file and suspend can provide is best seen by using an example. Consider Bill and Judy, a married couple who are both age 66 and who have a similar work and earnings history with Social Security. Both have retired, but they do not intend to start their

[26] Roth, Allan. "When should you take Social Security?" *CBS Money Watch online* 5 November 2012. <http://www.cbsnews.com/8301-505123_162-57543891/when-should-you-take-social-security/>
[27] Franklin, Mary Beth. "Getting a Bigger Check From Social Security" *Kiplinger online* December 2010. <http://www.kiplinger.com/magazine/archives/get-a-bigger-check-from-social-security.html>

respective Social Security benefits until they reach age 70, in order to take advantage of the maximum delayed retirement credits.

Because they currently are not receiving Social Security, they must take larger withdrawals from their IRAs to provide the income they need.

But now, because of the Senior Citizens Freedom to Work Act of 2000, Bill could file for his Social Security and immediately suspend the collection of his benefit. This would allow Judy to file for the Social Security *spousal* benefit. In this example, Judy is not filing for her own *worker's benefit,* instead, she is filing for the spousal benefit that she is eligible for based on Bill's work and earnings history.

Because Bill *filed and suspended* his own worker's benefit, he is still benefiting from all of the delayed retirement credits until he permanently files at age 70.

When Judy reaches age 70, she will file for her own much larger worker's benefit, and her spousal benefit will be dropped.

"I've found $40,000 under the cushion."

Effectively, the *file and suspend* strategy allowed Bill and Judy to receive four years of a spousal benefit prior to age 70. If the amount of that spousal benefit was $10,000 per year, they could receive $40,000 total. This is more or less free money that allows them to reduce the amount of withdrawals that they would otherwise need to take from their IRA until their larger Social Security benefits kick in at age 70.

Bill and Judy are like many people who would like to delay starting their Social Security to get larger retirement checks, but have the problem of how to get by until they start receiving those checks. To a degree, the file and suspend strategy can allow many married couples the opportunity to have their cake and eat it too.

Of course, the *spousal* benefit that Judy was able to start at age 66 would be smaller than what she and Bill would receive if they both started their worker's benefit at that age. But if they did start their worker's benefits at the earlier age they would also lose the delayed retirement credits they get by waiting until age 70.

The Potential Trap

File and suspend may seem like a fairly straightforward strategy, and it is when it is presented using the above example, but in practice, it can be more complicated and potentially put a married couple in a trap that they cannot get out of. The trap can occur if the couple attempts to do a file and suspend before the spouse reaches full retirement age. Prior to full retirement age, when a spouse applies for one benefit, she is deemed by Social Security to be applying for both benefits.

Assume the same circumstances with Bill and Judy as before, except consider the trap they could fall into if Judy was a year younger than Bill. At age 66, Bill *files and suspends* his Social security benefit. Judy, age 65, has not yet reached her full retirement age. She may think that she is filing for her *spousal* benefit, but Social Security deems that she is filing for both her *spousal* benefit and her *worker* benefit based on her own work and earnings history. In this example, the assumption is that Judy was a high-income earner during her working years, so her *worker* benefit would be greater than her *spousal* benefit. Social

Security will automatically pay the larger of the two, so Judy will receive the *worker's* benefit in this example. And because she is receiving her *worker's* benefit, she will no longer receive delayed retirement credits, even though her real intention was to delay starting this benefit.

Spousal benefits do not receive delayed retirement credits, so there is little advantage to waiting to collect them until *after* reaching full retirement age. But if they are applied for *before* reaching full retirement age, a person might unintentionally start receiving her *worker's* benefit instead of her *spousal* benefit.

It is important to keep in mind that married couples cannot both simultaneously collect free spousal benefits using the *file and suspend* strategy. However, this is different when a marriage has ended in divorce. In this case, both ex-spouses can collect free spousal benefits at the same time. *(See the section below regarding strategies for divorced spouses for a more complete explanation.)*

When there are two spouses who are each high income earners, and their goal is to both wait to age 70 to take full advantage of the delayed retirement credits, the *file and suspend* strategy can be a way to get free money between full retirement age and age 70. But for the *file and suspend* strategy to work as intended under these circumstances, it is critically important that each spouse waits until his or her full retirement age to apply.

File and Suspend: *A strategy for high and low earner spouses who need income at age 62*

Not every married couple is comprised of two higher income earners, or has the financial resources that allow them to wait until age 70 to start their Social Security benefits. These couples may still be able to take advantage of a *file and suspend* strategy, but utilized in a different way.

Consider the example of Ted and Alice, who are both age 62. Ted was a high-income earner over his working years, but Alice, like many women, left and reentered the work force in order to care for her young children and later to care for her aged parents. Because of her work and earnings history, Social Security will provide her with a much lower worker's benefit.

Ted and Alice would like to wait as long as they can to start their Social Security benefits in order to maximize those benefits, but they need some income now.

One strategy that they might consider is for Alice to claim her *worker's* benefit, not the *spousal* benefit starting at her age 62. Again, based on her work and earnings history with Social Security, this won't be a large benefit, but at least it will provide some immediate income. Once Ted reaches his full retirement age of 66, he could *file and suspend* his worker's benefit. This would allow Alice to file for her spousal benefit. Since she was a low income-earner, the assumption is that her spousal benefit would be the higher of the two, so that is the one that Social Security would change to at that time. Ted could possibly wait until sometime later to permanently file for his benefit, so that he receives some or all of the delayed retirement credits.

This strategy may seem to contradict what was stated in the prior example, and the potential trap that people using *file and suspend* can fall into. If you recall with the Bill and Judy example, because Judy filed for benefits prior to reaching her full retirement age, Social Security deemed that she was applying for both her worker's benefit and her spousal benefit. This is true, but only because Bill had filed for his worker's benefit at the same time.

In the Ted and Alice example, in which Alice is applying for the worker benefit at age 62, Ted had not applied for his benefit, so Social Security does not deem that Alice is applying for both. This allows her to collect her smaller worker's benefit between the ages of 62 and 66, and then change to the larger spousal benefit.

Whether or not this strategy provides the most lifetime benefits for a married couple will depend on their specific work and earnings history with Social Security. You not only have to consider both the husband and the wife, but what the higher-earning spouse intends to do with regards to his or her worker's benefit.

File and suspend also works well for many couples where one spouse does not qualify for any *worker's* benefit from Social Security:

> This strategy (file and suspend) works best for one-earner couples where one spouse worked full-time and the other spouse did not work outside the home or did not work long enough to qualify for Social Security retirement benefits.[28]

File and Suspend: *A strategy when a younger person is the higher earning spouse*

Assume a retired married couple, in which the husband Dean is currently age 68, and wife Debbie is age 66. Debbie has a higher work and earnings history with Social Security than Dean. And as of this point in time, neither has filed for Social Security. Their original plan was to each wait until they reached age 70 so that their respective *worker's* benefits would be increased by the largest possible delayed retirement credits.

Instead, they might consider having Dean (the lower earner in this example) *file and suspend* his *worker's* benefit. Since Debbie has reached her full retirement age, she could file for and receive only the *spousal* benefit. She could continue to delay filing for her *worker's* benefit until age 70 so that it would increase based upon the delayed retirement credits. When she then files for that higher *worker's* benefit, it will replace the lower *spousal* benefit that she had been receiving.

---

[28] AARP. "How to Maximize Your Social Security Benefits" *Ready for Retirement?* 2012.
<http://www.aarp.org/content/dam/aarp/money/budgeting_savings/2012-02/How-to-Maximize-Your-Social-Security-Benefits-AARP.pdf>

The Potential Trap

This can be a great strategy but the same trap exists here as discussed earlier. If Debbie tried to do this before reaching her full retirement age, Social Security would deem that she was applying for both her *worker's* and her *spousal* benefit. She would be paid the higher *worker's* benefit, which means that it would no longer earn delayed retirement credits.

Strategies for Divorced Spouse

In many ways, Social Security treats divorcees better than they do married couples. Because of this, there are specific strategies that should be considered for divorcees.

> If you are divorced, your ex-spouse may qualify for benefits on your earnings. In some situations, he or she may get benefits even if you are not receiving them. To qualify, a divorced spouse must:
>
> • Have been married to you for at least 10 years;
> • Have been divorced at least two years;
> • Be at least 62 years old;
> • Be unmarried; and
> • Not be eligible for an equal or higher benefit based on his or her own work or someone else's work.[29]

As long as the above qualifications are met, and the person has not remarried (unless that subsequent marriage ended by death or divorce), he can start collecting a *divorcee* benefit based upon his ex-spouse's work and earnings history.

---

[29] "Understanding the Benefits" *Social Security Administration publication no. 05-10024* March 2012, pg. 13.

One important difference with regards to how Social Security works with divorcees is that the ex-spouse does not need to apply for her own *worker's* benefit in order for the other spouse to start his *divorcee* benefit. As long as the ex-spouse qualifies for her *worker's* benefit, and the other qualifications listed above are met, the *divorcee* benefit can be collected:

> If your ex-spouse has not applied for retirement benefits, but can qualify for them, you can receive benefits on his or her record if you have been divorced for at least two years.[30]

The use of an example makes it easier to understand this distinction. Assume that Nick and Nancy's 12-year marriage ended in divorce. Both are age 66 (their full retirement age). Nick has remarried, but Nancy has not.

Nancy could apply for the Social Security *spousal* benefit based on Nick's work and earnings history with Social Security. Unlike with married couples, Nancy can apply for this benefit even though Nick has not applied for his worker's benefit. In the case of divorced couples Social Security automatically assumes that the worker has filed and suspended his or her benefit anytime one spouse attempts to claim the *spousal* benefit, and the other spouse has not yet filed for their own *worker's* benefit.

Because Nick remarried, he would not be able to apply for the Social Security *spousal* benefit based on Nancy's work and earnings history. But if Nick had not remarried, or if he did remarry but that marriage ended by death or divorce, then he could also apply for the Social Security *spousal* benefit based on Nancy's work and earnings history with Social Security. This means that, unlike the case with a currently-

---

[30] "Retirement Planner: If You Are Divorced" *Social Security Administration website* <http://www.ssa.gov/retire2/divspouse.htm>

married couple, divorcees have the potential to each collect a spousal benefit simultaneously. Again, all of the qualifications listed above would have to have been met.

The Potential Trap

If we assume that Nick and Nancy are both currently age 62, we can see some traps that can occur with divorced couples.

In this case, because Nancy has not reached her full retirement age, if she attempts to file for the *spousal* benefit based on Nick's work and earnings history, she will be forced to collect the greater of her *worker's* benefit and her *spousal* benefit.

This may be ok, but it will be a problem if her intent had been to wait to collect her *worker's* benefit so that it could be increased by the delayed retirement credits.

If Nancy waits until her full retirement age, she can specifically apply for and receive her *spousal* benefit. She can collect that benefit for four years, and then at age 70, she can apply for her *worker's* benefit that would have been significantly increased due to the delayed retirement credits. At this point, the *spousal* benefit would be dropped and replaced by the larger *worker's* benefit.

Just like with married couples, divorced spouses will need to wait until full retirement age when their objective is to collect only their *spousal* benefit.

If you have reached full retirement age and you are eligible for a *spousal* benefit **and** your own *worker's* benefit, you have a choice:

You can choose to receive only the divorced spouse's benefits now and delay receiving retirement benefits until a later date. If retirement benefits are delayed, a higher benefit may be received at a later date based on the effect of Delayed Retirement Credits.[31]

Again, since Nancy collected her *spousal* benefit for four years between the ages of 66 and 70, she more or less got *free* money.

If Nick and Nancy were each age 66, and they met the other qualifications listed above, they could each collect their *spousal* benefit and each receive this *free* money:

> The Social Security rules actually provide an incentive to get divorced. If you untie the knot at least two years before reaching full retirement age, you can both get "free" spousal benefits.[32]

The divorced spouse is entirely independent of his or her ex-spouse, or that ex-spouse's new spouse with regards to claiming *spousal* benefits. For example, assume that Nick has remarried and his new spouse's name is Linda. As long as Nancy has not remarried, she can claim a *spousal* benefit based on her ex-husband Nick's work and earnings history. Regardless of how much she collects, Social Security views Nancy as being completely independent from Nick and Linda, with regards to the benefits each is able to claim. So Linda can receive full *spousal* benefits based on Nick's work and earnings history, even though Nancy is also receiving *spousal* benefits as an ex-spouse, based on Nick's same work and earnings history. However, this assumes that

---

[31] "Retirement Planner: If You Are Divorced" *Social Security Administration website* <http://www.ssa.gov/retire2/divspouse.htm>

[32] Kotlikoff, Laurence. "Ten of the Worst Social Security 'Gotchas'" *PBS NEWSHOUR online* 18 September 2012. <http://www.pbs.org/newshour/rundown/2012/09/ten-of-the-worst-social-security-gotchas.html>

the divorced spouse meets all of the qualifications listed at the beginning of this section.

One of those qualifications is that the marriage must last a minimum of ten years. Financial advisors don't want to get into the marriage counseling business, but when dealing with clients who are contemplating divorce, it may be important to keep this minimum time period in mind. A couple who is close to, but not yet at that ten-year mark, may want to consider delaying the divorce if these *spousal* benefits will be important for their future financial security.

Widows and Widowers

COLAs and delayed retirement credits can have an even-greater impact on widows. To understand why, it is first important to be clear that delayed retirement credits (DRCs) impact *spousal* benefits, and *widows* benefit much differently, and this difference is often a source of confusion. It is easier to see the difference by using an example.

Jerry and Jennifer are a married couple both age 62. Jerry has a greater work and earnings history with Social Security, because Jennifer left the workforce for a period of time to care for their children. Because of this, her *spousal* benefit will also be larger than the *worker's* benefit she would collect based on her own work and earnings history with Social Security. And this will be the case regardless of when they decide to claim their benefits.

If Jerry and Jennifer each started their benefits prior to reaching full retirement age, both Jerry's *worker's* benefit and Jennifer's *spousal* benefit will be permanently reduced. If Jerry delayed starting his *worker's* benefit beyond full retirement age, he would receive an eight percent annual increase, plus any COLAs for each year that he waited until age 70. However, Jennifer's *spousal* benefit does not receive any delayed retirement credits. It will be 50 percent of Jerry's benefit, had he started that benefit at full retirement age, not 50 percent of Jerry's benefit if he delayed its start to age 70:

The benefits for your spouse do not include any delayed retirement credits you may receive.[33]

Upon learning this, many people mistakenly assume that delayed retirement credits (DRCs) also would not increase the *widows* benefit that a surviving spouse receives. This is not correct:

> Workers who postpone receipt of benefits past their FRA, or who prior to the repeal of the earnings test at the FRA in 2000 had benefits withheld because of the test, receive DRCs that are inherited by aged-widow beneficiaries, which again helps achieve parity between worker and widow benefit amounts.[34]

In general, *spousal* benefits while both spouses are alive provide the larger of the spouse's own *worker's* benefit, or 50 percent of their spouse's benefit (referred to as the *spousal* benefit). However, once one spouse dies, this changes so that the surviving spouse receives the larger of his or her own *worker's* benefit (including any COLAs) or 100 percent of the deceased spouse's benefit (including COLAs). As the above quote states, the surviving spouse "inherits" any delayed retirement credits (DRCs) that would have increased the deceased spouse's benefit.

This can be an enormous advantage for any couple that is concerned about the long-term financial security of a widow or widower.

For more information on benefits for widows and widowers, the reader should refer to the Social Security Handbook, which is available for download at the Social Security Administration's website.[35]

---

[33] *Social Security Administration website*
<http://www.ssa.gov/retire2/yourspouse.htm>
[34] Weaver, David A. "Widows and Social Security" *Social Security Bulletin vol. 70, no. 3* 2010.
[35] Download the Social Security Handbook at
<http://www.ssa.gov/OP_Home/handbook/>

The Windfall Elimination Provision

Special considerations must be given any time you have a client who has worked for an employer that does not withhold Social Security taxes from his or her salary. This could be the situation if the client had worked for a government agency or was employed in another country. In these circumstances, any pension your client might one day receive that was based on that work may reduce his or her Social Security benefits under the Windfall Elimination Provision (WEP).

This provision affects how retirement (and other Social Security benefits) are calculated when a pension is received from work for which Social Security taxes were not deducted from pay. Generally, the modified formula used to calculate the benefit amount results in a lower Social Security benefit than the person would otherwise receive.

For example, this provision would apply to individuals who worked for the federal government and were covered under the Civil Service Retirement System (CSRS).

However, the Windfall Elimination Provision (WEP) applies in other situations as well. Generally speaking, the provisions may apply if the person:

• Reached 62 after 1985, or

• Became disabled after 1985, and

• Became eligible for a monthly pension based on work where Social Security taxes were not paid

The reason behind the potential reduction in benefits under WEP is that Social Security is designed to provide a safety net that replaces only a portion of a person's income after he or she retires. The way that the Social Security benefit amount is calculated favors a lower-paid worker. It is designed to replace a larger percentage of a lower-paid worker's income and a smaller percentage of a higher-paid worker's income after retirement. For example, a lower-paid worker can receive a benefit from Social Security that represents as much as 55 percent of his or her pre-retirement income. A higher-paid worker's average benefit is approximately 25 percent of his or her pre-retirement income.

Congress passed the legislation that created WEP in 1983 because it had become apparent that some career government employees were retiring at relatively young ages and then continuing to work in jobs covered by Social Security. These individuals would then have a pension from their government service and were eligible to receive Social Security retirement benefits as well. But because they had a limited number of years in jobs covered by Social Security, their benefits were calculated as if they were long-term, low-wage workers.

The combination of the two provided a total retirement income that was often a much higher percentage of preretirement income even when the worker was a higher-paid employee.

The purpose of WEP is to reduce this percentage by lowering the amount of the Social Security benefit.

Another problem exists in that many people who will ultimately see their Social Security benefit reduced because of WEP aren't aware of it. In fact, you might say that they are unintentionally misled into believing that WEP will not affect them adversely. The reason is that the WEP reduction is not calculated until a person actually *applies* for his or her Social Security benefit. It is only at this time that the Social Security Administration checks to see if this person is entitled to a pension from an employer who did not withhold Social Security taxes. Prior to the application date, a person will receive paper or online statements from Social Security showing the projected amount of benefits without any WEP reduction.

These statements do say:

> "If you receive a pension from employment in which you did not pay Social Security taxes and you also qualify for your

own Social Security retirement or disability benefit, your
Social Security benefit may be reduced, but not eliminated,
by WEP."

Unfortunately, many people miss this warning and assume that the
benefit amount shown on the statement is what they will receive.

It is extremely important for advisors who intend to integrate Social
Security claiming strategies into retirement income planning to be
aware of this potential problem. When working with a client who will
be affected by WEP, the advisor should exercise caution before
assuming that the full benefit amount shown on the client's Social
Security statement will actually be available during retirement.

You can get additional information and see the maximum amount that a
benefit could be reduced under WEP by going to
www.socialsecurity.gov/retire2/wep-chart.htm.

Medicare

With regards to Medicare, it is important for the advisor to understand
that even though *full retirement age* has increased for many recipients,
Medicare eligibility is still set at age 65. Before the 1983 changes,
Social Security's *full retirement age* and Medicare's eligibility age were
the same: age 65. After 1983, these benefits are no longer *coupled* with
regards to age. This means that regardless of the age that a person
might choose at which to start Social Security, he or she should contact
the Social Security administration three months prior to turning age 65
for the purpose of possibly enrolling in Medicare.

Because this chapter has focused primarily on the *advantages* of
delaying Social Security, it is important to say that with regards to
Medicare, there could be *disadvantages* to following such a strategy.
One can occur during period of low inflation:

When inflation is low, like it is now, there is a
disadvantage to delaying until, say 70, collecting one's

retirement benefit. The disadvantage arises with respect to Medicare Part B premiums.   If you are collecting benefits (actually were collecting them last year), the increase in the Medicare premium this year will be limited to the increase in your Social Security check. This is referred to as being "held harmless." Hence, when inflation is low, the increase in your check due to the cost of living adjustment will be small; meaning the increase in your Medicare Part B premium will be limited. But, if you aren't collecting a benefit because you are waiting to collect a higher benefit later, tough noogies. You're Medicare Part B premium increase won't be limited. And that increase will be locked into every future year's Medicare Part B premium that you have to pay.   You can wait to join Medicare until, say, age 70, but if you aren't working for a large employer, the premiums you'll pay starting at 70 will be higher and stay higher forever.[36]

Working While Receiving Social Security: The Retirement Earnings Test (RET)

To complicate matters even more, under the Social Security Retirement Earnings Test (RET), the monthly benefit of a Social Security beneficiary who is below full retirement age (FRA) is reduced if he or she has earnings that exceed an annual threshold.

Much has been written that suggests that this earnings test results in *penalties* or *lost benefits*. This is not entirely true, because if some of a recipient's retirement benefits are withheld because of earnings, the recipient's benefits will be increased starting at his or her full retirement age to take into account those months in which benefits were withheld:

---

[36] Kotlikoff, Laurence. "44 Social Security 'Secrets' All Baby Boomers and Millions of Current Recipients Need to Know - Revised!" *Forbes online* 3 July 2012.<://www.forbes.com/sites/kotlikoff/2012/07/03/44-social-security-secrets-all-baby-boomers-and-millions-of-current-recipients-need-to-know/>

> If a beneficiary is affected by the RET, his or her monthly benefit is recomputed, and the dollar amount of the monthly benefit is increased, when he or she attains FRA. This feature of the RET, which allows beneficiaries to recoup benefits "lost" as a result of the RET, is not widely known or understood.[37]

And:

> But you don't "lose" money to the earnings test forever. Instead, your benefits will be recalculated at your full retirement age and increased to make up for the months when your benefits were withheld because of the earnings test.[38]

When a recipient is *under* his *full retirement age*, $1 will be *held back* from his benefit check for each $2 of earnings in excess of the specified limits of $15,120 (in 2013).

This will change the year that the recipient reaches his *full retirement age*. That year, the recipient will have $1 *held back* from his benefit check for each $3 of earnings in excess of $40,080 (in 2013). This means that from the month of January until the month before the recipient attains full retirement age, the recipient is allowed to earn up to $40,080 (in 2013), and still receive his or her full Social Security retirement check.

The $40,080 (in 2013) applies if the recipient reaches full retirement age on or before the last day of the taxable year. The $15,120 (in 2013)

---

[37] Nuschler, Dawn, and Shelton, Alison. "Social Security Retirement Earnings Test: How Earnings Affect Benefits" *Congressional Research Service Report R41242* 17 June 2010

[38] Lankford, Kimberly. "Understanding the Social Security Earnings Test for Early Retirees" *Kiplinger online* 27 February 2012.
<http://www.kiplinger.com/columns/ask/archive/social-security-earnings-test-early-retirees.html>

applies if the recipient does not reach full retirement age on or before the last day of the taxable year.

After the month when the recipient reaches his or her full retirement age, there is no longer any earnings limitation imposed. This means that a person can work beyond age 66 (for those born between 1943 and 1954), and regardless of the amount of the recipient's earnings, he will receive the full Social Security retirement benefit.

Assuming that a person reports earnings on a calendar-year basis, the following example would apply: Sally, a business owner, turns age 66 on July 20, 2012. The lower specified earnings limit applies for the calendar year 2011, and the higher limit applies from January through June for the calendar year 2012. After July 2012 (the month Sally attains full retirement age), the earnings limit no longer applies.

It is only earned income from wages and net income from self-employment that counts towards the specific earnings limit. Any unearned income from sources such as interest, dividends, distributions from IRAs, 401(k)s and other retirement plans, Roth IRAs, annuities or cash value loans from life insurance does not count towards the specified limits.

Income earned by one spouse may or may not be included in the earnings test of the other spouse, depending on the circumstances. For example, an older spouse might be retired and receiving Social Security based on his own work and earnings record, while the younger spouse continues employment, and receives no Social Security benefit. In this case, even though they file a joint return, the younger spouse's earnings would not be included in the older spouse's earnings test. If, however, a retired spouse was collecting benefits, not based on her own work and earnings record but as a spouse, then her working husband's earnings would be included in her earnings test.

Again, it is not entirely accurate to think of any reduction in benefits that results from employment as a penalty, because the amount deducted is actually added back to increase the recipient's benefit check after they reach full retirement age:

> Although this is often described as a penalty, the withheld benefits are added back to your benefits, after you reach 66, using a complex actuarial formula.[39]

Social Security provides an explanation with the following example:

> Let us say you claim retirement benefits upon turning 62 in 2012 and your payment is $750 per month. Then, you return to work and have 12 months of benefits withheld. We would recalculate your benefit at your full retirement age of 66 and pay you $800 a month (in today's dollars). Or, maybe you earn so much between the ages of 62 and 66 that all benefits in those years are withheld. In that case, we would pay you $1,000 a month starting at age 66.[40]

There are other ways that continuing to work can increase a recipient's benefits. As long as Social Security taxes are deducted from her pay, any additional earnings might potentially increase the amount of her monthly payment:

> Each year we review the records for all Social Security recipients who work. If your latest year of earnings turns out to be one of your highest years, we refigure your benefit and pay you any increase due. This is an automatic process and benefits are paid in December of the following year. For example, in December 2012, you should get an increase for your 2011 earnings if those

[39] Miller, Mark. "To maximize retirement benefits, know the rules" *REUTERS online* 18 January 2012. <http://www.reuters.com/article/2012/01/18/us-column-benefits-maximizing-idUSTRE80H1XO20120118>
[40] "How Work Affects Your Benefits" *Social Security Administration online, SSA Publication No. 05-10069, ICN 467005* March 2012. <http://www.socialsecurity.gov/pubs/10069.html#a0=5>

earnings raised your benefit. The increase would be retroactive to January 2012.[41]

It is important for people to understand how continuing to work while collecting benefits impacts their Social Security, because it can be expected that a large number of people will need to work well into their retirement years because they do not have adequate savings.

The Potential Impact of COLAs

Regardless of whether a worker is married or not, the potential impact of COLAs on benefits must be considered. Social Security cost-of-living adjustments are not guaranteed by law, but from a practical perspective, it may be difficult for any politician to support their removal, especially for people who today are in their 50s or older. Social Security COLAs can significantly impact the total lifetime benefits received.

Many financial professionals are aware that a person receives a *delayed retirement credit* of about eight percent for each year after his full retirement age that he waits to start his Social Security. What is often not as well understood is that COLAs can increase this percentage even more. Because of the COLA in 2012, the increase resulting from waiting just one year to start Social Security amounted to 11.6 percent for some recipients:

> The COLA for 2012 is 3.6 percent. If you turn 67 in 2012 and apply for benefits, your benefit would be 11.6 percent larger (the 8 percent delayed retirement credit plus the 3.6 percent COLA) than if you had applied for benefits at age 66 (when there was no COLA). In addition, the COLA is applied to the monthly benefit amount beginning when the

---

[41] "How Work Affects Your Benefits" *Social Security Administration online, SSA Publication No. 05-10069, ICN 467005* March 2012.
<http://www.socialsecurity.gov/pubs/10069.html#a0=5>

person turns age 62. This is true whether the person is actually receiving benefits at age 62 or not.[42]

The delayed retirement credit will boost the income amount by eight percent for each year that a person waits beyond his full retirement age. This is simple interest, so between the ages of 66 and 70, a person will see a 32 percent increase in the amount of his retirement check by waiting until age 70 to start his Social Security. Many people believe that their actual increase will be less, because they mistakenly assume that if they delayed the start of their benefit, they would miss out on any COLAs that they might have received had they started their benefit earlier.

As the above quote from AARP shows, this is simply not true. A person who delays the start of her benefit not only receives a delayed retirement credit of eight percent for each year she waits beyond her full retirement age, but her benefit is also increased by any COLAs applied during those years.

For example, assume that a person's Social Security statement shows an estimated future benefit amount of $1,708 per month at an early retirement age of 62, and a $3,018 monthly benefit if started at age 70. Again, neither of these amounts reflects any possible COLAs. Instead, they reflect only the *actuarial neutral* reduction for starting benefits early or the increase gained by delaying their start. If between the ages of 62 and 70, there were periodic COLA adjustments that totaled 15 percent, the $1,708 benefit would have increased to approximately $1,964 by the time the recipient reached age 70. But those same COLA adjustments would also serve to increase the age 70 benefit by the same percentage. And this increase is over and above the increase provided by the *delayed retirement credits*. So, assuming that the recipient is currently age 62, he could begin his benefit immediately, and start out

---

[42] "If you delay claiming beyond your full retirement age, do you also receive a COLA adjustment?" *AARP's Social Security Q&A Tool* 19 July 2012. <http://www.aarp.org/work/social-security/question-and-answer/delay-claiming-beyond-your-full-retirement-age-do-you-also-receive-a-cola-adjustment.html>

with a check in the amount of $1,708 per month, see that amount increase as COLAs were applied, and by age 70, his checks would have grown to $1,964. Or, he could delay the start of his benefit until age 70 and his actual check (including COLAs) would start out at a much greater $3,470 (in this example).

This is a significant difference, and not just because of the dollar amount of the increase in the monthly check. By delaying the benefit, the base amount that all future COLAs are applied to is much larger. For example, the increase at age 71 from a two percent COLA adjustment would only be about $40 ($1,964 X 2 percent = $39.28) for the person who started their benefit at age 62. Contrast this increase to what the same person would receive if he had waited until age 70 to start his benefit. His monthly check would increase by approximately $69 ($3,470 X 2 percent = $69.40). Over a lifetime, these COLAs could make a very large difference:

> A much higher initial benefit will receive much higher absolute dollar increases over time as the COLA rate is applied. Since these adjustments are compounding, the cumulative differences can be quite significant. Many individuals are likely not considering the impact of higher COLAs on a delayed benefit since the Social Security statement they receive does not illustrate the benefits of those higher COLAs. For example, in discussions with many retirees, we found that they use Excel spreadsheets to forecast their own break-even points and use the Social Security estimated benefits from the annual statement. By entering the age 66 amount and age 70 amounts (which are in current dollars) into a formula that measures future dollar values, the analysis becomes skewed. In nearly all break-even analysis, COLAs are ignored.[43]

---

[43] Mahaney, James, and Carlson, Peter. Rethinking Social Security Claiming in a 401(k) World" *Pension Research Council Working Paper* August 2007, pg 8.

Before any claiming strategy can be formulated, the first thing that an advisor needs to know is the estimated benefit the client is eligible to receive at his or her full retirement age.

There are several ways to obtain this benefit amount using free calculators on the Social Security Administration's website. Some of these calculators can be accessed at: http://www.ssa.gov/planners/benefitcalculators.htm

Social Security's Online Calculator and Detailed Calculator

Far more accurate results will come from using either the Social Security's *Online* or *Detailed* calculators, because they both use a person's actual work and earnings history to calculate benefits. The *Detailed* calculator is a program that can be downloaded and installed on the user's computer. And the Social Security Administration's website suggests that it will produce the most precise estimates.

One problem with both of these programs is that they are not linked to a person's earnings record, so they will require the user to input this data in order for the program to calculate the benefit. Before this can be done, the user must obtain the work and earnings history.

Obtaining the Work and Earnings History

There are two ways for a person to obtain his work and earnings history with Social Security. One is from the Social Security Statement that is prepared and sent by the Social Security administration. In February 2012, the Social Security Administration resumed mailing paper statements, but only to workers age 60 and older who are not yet receiving benefits. There has also been speculation that they might resume mailing paper statements to younger workers as well. But a second and perhaps more efficient way for a person to obtain his work

---

<http://www.planningtampabay.org/net/gallery/files/SocialSecurityWhitePaperby Carlson_Peter.pdf>

and earnings history is to access Social Security's new online statement:

> To get a personalized online *Statement*, people age 18 and older must be able to provide information about themselves that matches information already on file with Social Security. In addition, Social Security uses Experian, an external authentication service provider, for additional verification. People must provide their identifying information and answer security questions in order to pass this verification. Social Security will not share a person's Social Security number with Experian, but the identity check is an important part of this new, robust verification process.
>
> Once verified, people will create a "My Social Security" account with a unique user name and password to access their online *Statement*. In addition, the portal also includes links to information about other online services, such as applications for retirement, disability and Medicare.[44]

Before a person can get an online statement, he must first create an *account* at the Social Security website: http://www.socialsecurity.gov/mystatement/

Creating an account is relatively simple. It is done at this webpage: https://secure.ssa.gov/RIL/SiView.do

---

[44] "Social Security Statement Now Available Online at www.socialsecurity.gov" *Social Security Press Release* 1 May 2012.

Clicking this button will take you to a screen outlining the *Terms of Service*. Advisors should read these terms carefully and take note of the following statement:

> *"You can create an account only to gain access to your own personal information. Even with a person's written consent, you cannot use this online service to access the records of a person:*
> *- With whom you have a business relationship; or*
> *- For whom you are an appointed representative."*

It is clear that it is a violation to attempt to create an account to access anyone's personal information but his own. This means that your client must create and access his account, and then be willing to provide you with any information that is needed for planning purposes.

After agreeing to the Terms of Service, the applicant will arrive at a page where he enters his name, Social Security number, date of birth, home address and primary phone number.

The website uses the above information to immediately locate the applicant's Social Security file. The site will then ask the applicant to answer a few questions based on information in the file that only he would know.

The entire application process is surprisingly simple, and should take only a few minutes. After it is completed, the applicant is immediately taken to a screen that will show the *Estimated Benefit at Full Retirement age.*

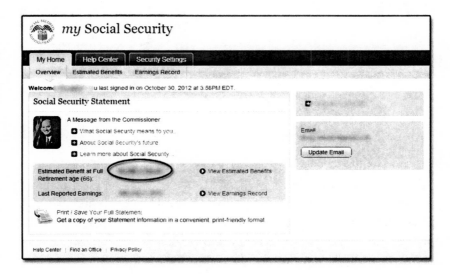

To the right of the benefit amount, there is a link to *View Estimated Benefits.*

The *View Estimated Benefits* screen will show the benefit amounts at full retirement age, at age 70 with the delayed retirement credits included, and the reduced amount if taken at the earliest possible age. Remember that these are not the only options as to ages that the benefit can be taken. Actually, a person can choose to start benefits in any month between early retirement age (age 62) and the oldest age of 70. The benefit amounts for each month will be different, but the three dates shown on this page provide a good range.

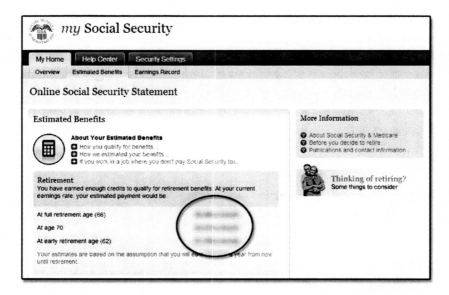

It is important to understand how the Social Security Administration estimates the benefits shown on the online statement. First, the benefits are based on the actual work and earnings history of the individual. And if that individual is younger than retirement age, the calculator assumes the individual will continue to work and earn about the same as he did in the previous year. Because of this, the further away a person is from retirement, the less accurate the estimated benefit will be.

A potentially more significant thing to understand is that the benefit amounts shown are NOT adjusted for cost-of-living increases. A valid argument can be made that because cost-of-living increases are not guaranteed, that they should not be reflected in the estimated benefits. While that may be a logical reason not to include COLAs, the problem is that by not including them, a person often does not see the full advantage of delaying the start of his benefits.

Any time you look at the difference in the estimated benefits based on different start ages that are provided by *any* Social Security calculator, or that appear on *any* statement provided, whether online or on the paper statement, it is important to realize that the benefit amounts

shown for delaying the start of Social Security are understated with
regards to the missing impact of likely COLAs.

Again, this can not only have a significant impact on the total benefits
received over a worker's lifetime, but can greatly impact the lifetime
benefits of a surviving spouse as well. It is important to always keep in
mind that the surviving spouse "inherits" any delayed retirement credits
that served to increase the deceased spouse's benefit.

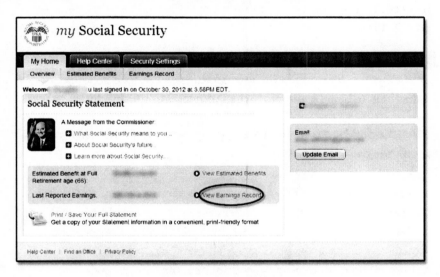

If you return to the previous screen from Social Security's online
statement, you will find a link that will allow you to view your work
and earnings history that Social Security has on file. It will be
important for the advisor to obtain the actual earnings history if he or
she intends to use any commercially-available software to develop
claiming strategies for a client.

Again, it is a violation of the Terms of Use of Social Security's online
statement for anyone but the account owner to access this information.
This means that the client will need to set up and access his or her
account, and then give this information to the advisor. Note that in the
lower left corner of the online calculator (see above), there is a button
that will allow the person to *Print / Save Your Statement*.

In addition to the online statement, and the calculators already discussed, there are other tools available from the Social Security Administration's website that are worthwhile for advisors to become familiar with.

There is a *Retirement Age* calculator, which will calculate and illustrate the reductions in benefit amounts if a person retires early. There is an *Earnings Limit* calculator that can be used to see how any earnings from continuing employment might impact Social Security benefits received prior to full retirement age.

AARP also has a couple of free calculators that are easy to use, and provide good information on how earnings can reduce benefits and reductions in benefit amounts when retiring prior to full retirement age.

Most Social Security software programs and calculators focus on the wrong thing

The problem with just about every software program and calculator that is available from the Social Security website or sold commercially is that they all focus on the wrong thing. What they do is provide projections of the *gross* amount of income that a person can expect to receive in the form of Social Security benefits.

Some may do a fairly good job of illustrating the benefits of delaying Social Security or from the use of strategies like *file and suspend.* The problem is that when they project benefit amounts, they only show *before tax* amounts of income.

One of the most powerful aspects of Social Security benefits is the potential tax advantage. As will be discussed in the next chapter, under current law, the maximum portion of Social Security that can be taxed is 85 percent, but with proper planning, in certain situations it may be possible to significantly reduce the taxable portion.

This tax advantage provides a tremendous opportunity to significantly boost spendable income throughout retirement. It makes one dollar from Social Security potentially worth much more than a dollar from an IRA or 401(k). Unfortunately, this opportunity simply cannot be demonstrated with the programs available from the Social Security website and most of the commercially-available software programs and calculators.

Most software programs and calculators are designed to do a *break-even* analysis or to show how much more total *gross income* would be provided by using one claiming strategy over another.

Before using any program or calculator that is based on an analysis of before tax benefits, advisors and even clients should read a report written by James Mahaney and Peter Carlson, "Rethinking Social Security Claiming in a 401(k) World."[45] It not only provides great insight as to claiming strategies, but it also exposes the flaws in most traditional analyses that tend to understate the potential value of delaying the start of benefits.

Find tools, articles, webinars, live training,
case studies and more resources devoted
to *the Synergy Effect*™
at ***Doug-Warren.com***

---

[45]<http://www.planningtampabay.org/net/gallery/files/SocialSecurityWhitePaper byCarlson_Peter.pdf>

Chapter 4

Trading IRA Dollars
for More Social Security Dollars
to Reduce Risk and Taxation

One extremely important factor that can favor delaying the start of
Social Security to receive a greater lifetime benefit has to with the
potential impact of income taxes:

> In general, taking taxation into account when planning the
> strategy for claiming Social Security may be a key factor
> in helping both single people and couples decide what to
> do.[46]

People complain that the income provided by Social Security
retirement benefits has lost much of its tax-favorable status over the
years. As most financial professionals are aware, at one time the entire

---

[46] Society of Actuaries. "Deciding When to Claim Social Security" 2012, pg 7.

income from this benefit was received tax-free. Today, many recipients must include up to 85 percent of this income as taxable income. Because of this, there is no question that these benefits are less tax-efficient today when compared to past benefits. But when you compare income from today's Social Security to most of the other traditional sources of retirement income, it must be recognized that income provided by Social Security continues to be very tax-efficient. And with proper planning, this efficiency can be significantly increased. An advisor who understands how to generate additional tax-efficient income using permanent life insurance cash value loans and/or distributions from Roth IRAs might be able to increase Social Security's tax-free portion to 50 percent or higher for many clients. How much higher? For some clients, certain strategies could cause all of the Social Security retirement income to be entirely free from income tax.

"I wonder if this will effect our social security checks."

The significance of this potential becomes more apparent when you consider just how much money might be involved. According to the Urban Institute:

> A two-earner couple, both turning age 65 in 2011 might expect to receive a total of $672,000 in lifetime Social Security benefits and another $357,000 in lifetime Medicare benefits. That's a total of $1,029,000 (in 2011 dollars).[47]

If a client might potentially receive $672,000 in lifetime Social Security retirement income, the tax treatment of that income could make a significant difference.

The key to increasing the total amount a person might receive from Social Security, while at the same time reducing the total taxes they might be required to pay on this income, starts with understanding the concept of trading IRA dollars for more Social Security dollars.

Anyone approaching retirement age that has an IRA has choices as to when he or she will start taking withdrawals from it (at least until required distributions start at age 70½). We also have choices regarding when we will start our Social Security retirement benefit.

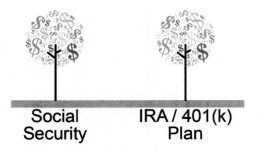

Social
Security

IRA / 401(k)
Plan

Assume we have a person who is retired and needs a single dollar. Like many people, this individual has two primary sources of retirement income: his IRA and Social Security. This means that he has at least two places that he can get the dollar he needs. He could take the dollar from the IRA and wait until a later date to start his Social Security. Or,

[47] Steuerle, C. Eugene, and Rennane, Stephanie. "Social Security and Medicare Taxes and Benefits Over a Lifetime" *Urban Institute* 20 June 2011. <http://www.urban.org/publications/412281.html>

he can leave the dollar in his IRA and instead start his Social Security immediately.

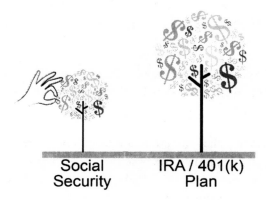

Past wisdom was that a person should take Social Security as soon as he might need a dollar so that he could leave his IRA dollars untouched, allowing them to grow. The logic was that because of the expected investment returns, the IRA could ultimately provide a greater number of dollars in the future.

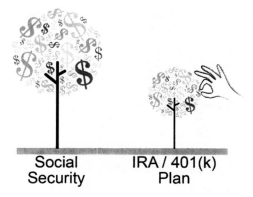

A new strategy has gained popularity. It recognizes that if a person starts withdrawing from his IRA as soon as he needs a dollar, he can delay claiming his Social Security, which means that it benefits from delayed retirement credits, which will allow it to provide more dollars in the future.

Looking at it this way puts the question of when to start Social Security in a different perspective. The only way that a lot of people can delay starting their Social Security is by withdrawing more money from their IRAs sooner, to make up for the retirement income they won't be getting from Social Security.

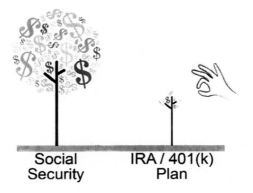

Social Security IRA / 401(k) Plan

Reducing the IRA balance sooner means that it will provide less income (perhaps no income) in the future. But, these people's Social Security income checks will be higher once they do start that benefit.

Conversely, when a person starts his Social Security early, the amount of each check will be smaller, but he won't need to withdraw as much from his IRA to generate the total amount of income he needs. The IRA balance will remain large, so the future income it provides should be greater.

This choice often involves trading IRA dollars for more Social Security dollars, which is often the effect of a person deciding to delay the start of Social Security, or trading Social Security dollars for more IRA dollars, which can be the effect of a person deciding to start Social Security early.

Which is better? Does one of these dollars have more value than the other?

Social   IRA / 401(k)
Security   Plan

From the perspective of income taxes, a Social Security dollar can be much more valuable than an IRA dollar. The tax treatment of each dollar is entirely different. And some people might find that they can significantly reduce their future income taxes by doing their retirement planning in ways that result in higher Social Security income and lower IRA income.

There are two tax advantages enjoyed by Social Security dollars that IRA dollars don't have. The first is that currently, a maximum of only 85 percent of Social Security dollars is considered taxable. The second is that only 50 percent of a person's Social Security income is used in the *provisional income calculations* to determine the taxable portion of the benefit.

100 Percent Taxable Dollars vs. 85 Percent Taxable Dollars

As most readers are aware, most IRA dollars will be 100 percent taxable when withdrawn. The maximum taxable portion of Social Security dollars will be 85 percent under current law.

This difference alone can make Social Security dollars more valuable than IRA dollars, and might warrant any planning strategy that exchanges IRA dollars for more Social Security dollars.

Better still, many recipients pay income taxes on less that 85 percent of their Social Security, and with planning, the taxable portion can be reduced for many more.

50 Percent Social Security Dollars vs. 100 Percent IRA Dollars Included in the Provisional Income Formula

If 100 percent of IRA dollars are used to calculate the taxable portion of Social Security, but only 50 percent of Social Security dollars are used in the same formula, then it stands to reason that a person might be able to receive twice the amount of income from Social Security than from an IRA, without paying greater tax on this income.

In chapter three it was shown that by delaying the start of Social Security to age 70, a recipient could expect to increase the amount of his or her monthly check by 80 percent to perhaps double (depending on COLAs) the amount he or she would receive if Social Security had been started at age 62. The ability to perhaps double the Social Security income check, combined with the fact that only 50 percent of it is used to determine the taxable portion, presents some very real opportunities for many people to reduce their income taxes. Again, we have choices regarding when we start withdrawals from our IRAs and the age at which we start Social Security that allow many of us to effectively trade IRA dollars for Social Security dollars to possibly gain a tax advantage.

This potential advantage is available for people with a wide range of retirement incomes, even those at the higher income levels. It is often mistakenly assumed that once a single person reaches the $34,000 threshold, or a married couple reaches the $44,000 threshold used in the provisional income formula, there is little that can be done to avoid having 85 percent of Social Security included as taxable income. However, this is actually a false assumption, because the provisional income formula actually uses three tests to calculate the taxable portion, and the actual amount is the lowest number generated by the three.

Taxable S.S. is the Lowest of Three Tests

Test #1 = 85 percent of the benefit

Test #2 = 50 percent of the benefit, plus 85 percent of amounts over the second threshold

Test #3 = 50 percent of amounts over the first threshold, plus 35 percent of amounts over the second threshold

As most financial professionals are aware, the income thresholds that the above tests refer to are as follows:

The First Threshold
(Social Security is tax-free up to these amounts)
Single Person = **$25,000** of provisional income
Married (Filing Jointly) = **$32,000** of provisional income
Up to 50 percent of Social Security is subject to tax,
but only on amounts exceeding the first threshold

The Second Threshold
Single Person = **$34,000** of provisional income
Married (Filing Jointly) = **$44,000** of provisional income
Up to 85 percent of Social Security is subject to tax,
but only on amounts exceeding the second threshold

Consider the example of a single person where the third test for determining taxable Social Security is applied. She could enjoy up to $50,000 of Social Security income before being required to pay any tax, because only $25,000 of this is included in the provisional income formula, assuming that that money was her sole source of income. On the other hand, she can only have $25,000 of income from an IRA before she would have to include a portion of her Social Security as taxable income.

Consider the example of a married couple filing a joint return that pass test #3. They could enjoy up to $64,000 of Social Security income before being required to pay any tax, because only $32,000 of this is included in the provisional income formula, assuming that it was their sole source of income. On the other hand, they can only have $32,000 of income from an IRA before they would have to include a portion of their Social Security as taxable income.

Even when IRA withdrawals and Social Security income combine to totals exceeding the first and even the second thresholds, there can be significant tax savings when more of that income comes from Social Security.

Consider the example of two married couples, Mr. and Mrs. Quick and Mr. and Mrs. Delay. Each couple has an identical pre-tax retirement income need of $80,000.

Mr. and Mrs. Quick's Taxable Income

Because the Quicks started their Social Security income early, their annual check is $30,000. They must withdraw $50,000 from the IRA in order to have the $80,000 of pre-tax income they desire. Their provisional income used in the formula to determine taxable Social Security would be $65,000.

Social Security Income at 50 percent = $15,000
+ IRA Income at 100 percent = <u>$50,000</u>
Provisional Income $65,000

Of the three provisional income tests, the following (the third test) results in the least taxable Social Security so it would be the one used.

Provisional Income = $65,000
Minus $32,000 *(first threshold)*

$33,000 *(amount over first threshold)*
50 percent

(A) **$16,500** *(taxable)*

Provisional Income = $65,000
Minus $44,000 *(second threshold)*

$21,000 *(amount over second threshold)*
35 percent

(B) **$7,350** *(taxable)*

The total amount of the Quicks' Social Security that will be included as taxable income is **$23,850** (A + B). They must add this to their total IRA income of $50,000 to arrive at their total taxable income of **$73,850.**

Mr. and Mrs. Delay's Taxable Income

Because the Delays postponed the start of their Social Security, their annual check is a higher $60,000, which means they must only withdraw $20,000 from the IRA in order to have the $80,000 of pre-tax income they desire. Their provisional income used in the formula to determine their taxable Social Security would be only $50,000.

Social Security Income at 50 percent = $30,000
+ IRA Income at 100 percent = $20,000
Provisional Income $50,000

Of the three provisional income tests, the following (the third test) results in the least taxable Social Security, so it is the one used.

Provisional Income = $50,000

        Minus   <u>$32,000</u> *(first threshold)*

               $18,000 *(amount over first threshold)*

                 <u>50</u> percent

          (A) **$9,000** *(taxable)*

Provisional Income = $50,000

        Minus   <u>$44,000</u> *(second threshold)*

               $6,000 *(amount over second threshold)*

                 <u>35</u> percent

          (B) **$2,100***(taxable)*

The total amount of the Delays' Social Security that will be included as taxable income is **$11,100** (A + B). They must add this to their total IRA income of $20,000 to arrive at their total taxable income of **$31,100.**

The Quicks' and the Delays' total incomes each equal $80,000, but because a larger portion of the Delays' income was from Social Security, their taxable income is $42,750 less ($73,850 - $31,100).

What is interesting to note is that the Quicks' Social Security is a lower $30,000, but of this amount, a much greater $23,850 must be included as taxable income. Compare this to the Delays' Social Security, which was a much greater $60,000, but of this amount only $11,100 must be included as taxable income.

The assumption behind the Delays receiving a much higher amount of Social Security is that they waited to start the benefit, and to be fair, we must consider that before this benefit started, their only source of income might have been from their IRA. During those years when they withdrew $80,000 from their IRA, their taxable income would have been the entire $80,000.

For example, assume that the Quicks and the Delays were all the same age, and both couples decided to retire at age 62. Also assume (as was the case in the prior example), that the Quicks' $80,000 of total income came from a combination of $30,000 of Social Security and $50,000 from their IRA. And, assume that from age 62 until age 69, 100 percent of the Delays' income was from their IRA, and then starting at age 70, the sources changed so that $60,000 came from Social Security and $20,000 from their IRA. Based on these assumptions, each couple's taxable income would have looked like this *(not considering COLAs)*:

Taxable Income

Age	Quicks'	Delays'
62	$73,850	$80,000
63	$73,850	$80,000
64	$73,850	$80,000
65	$73,850	$80,000
66	$73,850	$80,000
67	$73,850	$80,000
68	$73,850	$80,000
69	$73,850	$80,000
70	$73,850	$31,100
71	$73,850	$31,100
72	$73,850	$31,100
74	$73,850	$31,100
75	$73,850	$31,100
76	$73,850	$31,100
77	$73,850	$31,100
78	$73,850	$31,100
79	$73,850	$31,100
80 +	$73,850	$31,100

The Delays' taxable income is $6,150 more the first eight years, and then $42,750 less each year for the rest of their lives. *(Not considering COLAs.)*

Of course, if the Quicks and the Delays had also started with the same IRA balance, we would expect that the Delays' IRA balance to be significantly less after eight years, because of the increased withdrawals they would have taken.

In effect, what the Delays did was trade their IRA dollars for more Social Security dollars, and benefit from the significant difference in how these dollars are treated for tax purposes:

> Single individuals or couples impacted by these high marginal rates may want to consider special tax planning strategies. For example, a strategy of delaying Social Security to increase lifetime income may also carry beneficial tax effects. Say that Mary uses her 401(k) funds to bridge the gap from retirement to the claiming of Social Security. In that case, the funds she withdraws will be taxed at only the base marginal rate. Then, when Mary later claims Social Security—at higher amounts reflecting delayed retirement credits—she will need to withdraw less money from her 401(k) than would be the case otherwise.[48]

Inflation Risk

As mentioned earlier, Social Security COLAs are not guaranteed, but it might be politically dangerous for any administration or member of Congress to vote to remove them, especially if such action affects people who are in their 50s today.

Consider how differently a two-percent future COLA impacts the Quicks as opposed to the Delays. Because the Quicks have a lower base amount of Social Security of $30,000, a 2-percent COLA provides an increase of $600. But with a higher base Social Security of $60,000, the same two-percent COLA increases the Delays' income by $1,200:

---

[48] Society of Actuaries. "Deciding When to Claim Social Security" *Managing Retirement Decisions Series* 2012, pg. 7.

> Our Social Security benefits increase each year to keep up
> with the cost of living by a percentage of the current
> payout. If we start collecting a higher amount by delaying
> our start date, the same percentage COLA increase will
> have a higher dollar value than if we started at a lower
> base.[49]

An argument can be made that the Quicks could make up this
difference with the earnings on their larger IRA balance. But this points
to another possible advantage of Social Security.

Investment Risk

Some people would rather trade Social Security dollars for more IRA
dollars. These people typically start their Social Security early. Their
benefit amount is smaller, but they don't need to withdraw as much
from their IRAs. This leaves them bigger IRA balances with a potential
of generating greater investment returns. But people using this strategy
must recognize that they may also be subjecting themselves to a higher
degree of investment risk. They must find investments for their IRAs
that not only provide returns sufficient to allow them to keep pace with
inflation, but even greater returns if they want *real* growth. The higher
the returns they seek, the greater the degree of investment risk that they
will likely have to expose their IRAs to.

And for many people, the returns they earn on their IRAs must also be
high enough to offset any investment fees.

Investment Fees

Management fees, 12B-1 fees, loads and other charges eat away at the
real returns that many people experience from their IRAs:

---

[49] Ning, David. "5 Reasons to Delay Collecting Social Security" *U.S. News and World Report online* 29 August 2012.
<http://money.usnews.com/money/blogs/On-Retirement/2012/08/29/5-reasons-to-delay-collecting-social-security>

And for some investors, the bad news does not stop here. For instance, investors may turn to advisers who, according to a recent study, charge an average of 1.1 percent annually for further disservice. The net can be devastating. A 2.5 percent fee drag over 20 years can mean retiring with as much as 40 percent less compared to an investor who stayed the course with a passive portfolio.[50]

When trading IRA dollars for more Social Security dollars, a person is also trading away investment expenses.

Survivor Risk

The strategy of trading IRA dollars for more Social Security dollars can be a particularly effective way to combat the survivor risk faced by many married spouses.

At the death of the first spouse, the surviving spouse will receive the greater of his or her own Social Security *worker's* benefit or 100 percent of the deceased spouse's *worker's* benefit. Because women live longer and tend to marry men who are older, they are most often the ones who ultimately become the surviving spouse:

> Over 40 percent of elderly women (but only about 30 percent of elderly men) depend on Social Security for more than 90 percent of their income.[51]

And because women tend to be the ones who leave the work force to tend children and aged parents, it is not uncommon for them to earn less income over their lifetimes. As a result, the primary source of

---

[50] Beck, Steve. "Stop Paying Wall Street to Take Your Money" *U.S. News and World Report online 17 November 2011.*
<http://money.usnews.com/money/blogs/the-smarter-mutual-fund-investor/2011/11/17/stop-paying-wall-street-to-take-your-money>
[51] "Women and Social Security" *Issue Brief: American Academy of Actuaries* June 2007, pg. 3. <http://www.actuary.org/pdf/socialsecurity/women_07.pdf>

income for many older women will ultimately be the *worker's* benefit that they "inherited" from their deceased husband. Delaying the start of Social Security to boost the income amount might be one of the best ways to provide longer-term security for surviving spouses:

> If one member of a married couple dies, the surviving spouse can continue to receive her own Social Security benefit, or 100% of the deceased spouse's benefit, whichever is more. If your wife earned less over her lifetime than you did, and she outlives you, she'll start receiving your benefits. If you file at 62, she'll inherit a reduced amount of benefits for the rest of her life, says Ron Gebhardtsbauer, senior pension fellow at the American Academy of Actuaries.[52]

And:

> Rising the age at which married men claim Social Security benefits would significantly improve retirement income security. The improvement is most pronounced in the retirement income security of widows, currently a serious social problem.[53]

Longevity Risk

A good financial professional will help clients manage all forms of risk. One of the biggest risks that people will face in the future is that of living longer than their assets will last.

---

[52] Block, Sandra. "Husbands should consider delaying Social Security benefits" *USA Today online* 15 January 2008.
<http://usatoday30.usatoday.com/money/perfi/columnist/block/2008-01-14-social-security-early-benefits_N.htm?>
[53] Sass, Steven A., Sun, Wei, and Webb, Anthony. "When Should Married Men Claim Social Security Benefits?" *Center for Retirement Research at Boston College* March 2008, pg. 4.

Much of the reasoning behind the position that people should start Social Security as early as possible in spite of the smaller resulting income amounts has to do with the fact that those monthly checks will be received over a longer period of time. So in the long run, starting Social Security at age 62 will net you about the same amount as waiting until age 70 to start larger income checks. This argument is valid, but only when it is assumed that the recipient lives to life expectancy. In fact, the earlier a person dies prior to life expectancy, the greater the advantage to starting Social Security early. However, the longer a person lives beyond life expectancy, the greater the advantage to starting Social Security late.

But there is a more practical side to this argument that often goes unappreciated. It is that for many people, the longer they live the more significant their financial problems can be. This is especially true for married couples, for which the chances are better than 50/50 that one spouse will live beyond age 90.

The decision of whether it is better to trade IRA income for higher Social Security income should be considered from the perspective of which income *source* puts the recipient in a better position to deal with longevity risk.

When viewed from this perspective, some people would argue that there is too much *risk* that Social Security will go broke to depend on it to help provide long-term financial security. While this might prove to be true, it is important to consider that many people might become exposed to even greater risk when they choose to rely less on Social Security and more on other instruments, such as IRAs, for their future long-term security. People who start Social Security early are trading Social Security dollars for more IRA dollars. With the larger IRA balance invested properly, they believe that over time this gives them a better opportunity to more effectively deal with the longevity risk, while reducing their exposure to the risk that Social Security could go broke. The future may show this strategy to be correct, but it will be contingent to some degree on the success of the IRA investments. If the

IRAs don't grow as hoped, or if there are investment losses inside the IRAs, then the longer the people who use this strategy live, the greater the risk might be that one day, their IRA balances will be exhausted, and their only source of income will be their *reduced* monthly income check from Social Security.

The point is not if one risk outweighs the other. Instead, it is simply that there is risk associated with relying on Social Security, and risk associated with choosing to not rely on it.

Reducing Taxation

Advisors need to integrate Social Security claiming strategies into their overall retirement planning recommendations, because the combined synergistic effect will often be to significantly boost the client's net spendable retirement income.

The reason that the opportunity to boost spendable income exists for many clients can be illustrated with the following two equations:

SOCIAL Security Retirement Income
+ The WRONG Sources of Other Income
= LESS After-Tax Income

SOCIAL Security Retirement Income
+ The RIGHT Sources of Other Income
= MORE After-Tax Income

The *wrong* sources of other income might include traditional IRAs, 401(k)s and other tax-deferred retirement plans. The *right* sources of income that might boost the client's spendable income are distributions from Roth IRAs and cash value loans from permanent life insurance contracts.

SOCIAL Security Retirement Income
+ Traditional IRAs and/or 401(k)s
= LESS After-Tax Income

SOCIAL Security Retirement Income
+ Roth IRAs and/or Cash Value Loans
= MORE After-Tax Income

When it comes to possibly paying federal income taxes on your Social Security benefits, withdrawals from Roth IRAs aren't counted, but withdrawals from 401(k), 403(b), regular IRAs, and other tax-deferred accounts are. So there may be a significant advantage in a) withdrawing from your tax-deferred accounts after you retire, but before you start collecting Social Security, b) using up your tax-deferred accounts before you withdraw from your Roth accounts, and c) converting your tax-deferred accounts to Roth IRA holdings after or even before you retire, but before you start collecting Social Security.[54]

Note that the above article refers specifically to the potential advantage of withdrawals from Roth IRAs. It makes no mention of cash value loans, and I have no way of knowing the author's attitude about using permanent life insurance as a retirement-funding vehicle. However, the tax advantage relating to Social Security that the article refers to concerning withdrawals from a Roth IRA are potentially the same for cash value loans from a permanent life insurance policy.

In fact, distributions from Roth IRAs and life insurance cash value loans are just about the only retirement income sources that are not counted in the provisional income calculations used to determine the amount of Social Security retirement income that will be included as

---

[54] Kotlikoff, Laurence. "29 Social Security 'Secrets' All Baby Boomers and Millions of Current Recipients Need to Know – Revised!" *Forbes online* 3 July 2012.

taxable income. This means that a knowledgeable advisor has two financial instruments available, which can be blended with Social Security in a way that can potentially reduce income taxes for many clients. If the advisor also has enough knowledge of claiming strategies, it may be possible to increase the monthly income received from Social Security and at the same time reduce the portion of that income that is taxable.

Increase Social Security Income

Reduce Social Security Taxation

This can have a synergetic effect of significantly boosting spendable retirement income.

Social Security's *provisional income formula* requires that 100 percent of a person's income, from virtually any source, even tax-free bonds, is counted towards calculating the taxable portion of Social Security.

There are three exceptions that are of particular importance:

Only 50 percent of income from Social Security is included.

Zero income from Roth IRAs is included.

And, potentially, zero income from cash value loans from life insurance contracts is included.

In the previous chapter, the example of two hypothetical couples, the Quicks and the Delays, was used to illustrate how taxable income might be significantly reduced by trading IRA dollars for more Social

Security dollars. Here, a new example will be used to show how taxable income might be even further reduced by adding a new source of income that is not required to be included in the provisional income formula for determining the taxable portion of Social Security. For the purpose of this example, it does not matter if this new source of income is a Roth IRA or cash value loans of a properly-used life insurance contract. These sources are similar in that not only are they not included in the provisional income formula, they are also not added to the adjusted gross income of the recipient.

To illustrate this we use a new couple, Mr. and Mrs. Smart. As was the case with the Quicks and the Delays, the Smarts have an identical pre-tax retirement income need of $80,000.

Mr. and Mrs. Smart's Taxable Income

Like the Delays, the Smarts postponed the start of their Social Security, so their annual check is also a much higher $60,000. But unlike the Delays, instead of withdrawing all of the other $20,000 they need from their traditional IRA, they reduce their withdrawal from this source to $10,000, and take the other $10,000 from a source that is both tax-free and not included in the provisional income formula. Their provisional income used in the formula to determine their taxable Social Security would be only $40,000.

Social Security Income at 50 percent = $30,000
+ IRA Income at 100 percent = $10,000
+ Roth IRA Withdrawal or Cash Value Loan at zero percent = 0
Provisional Income = $40,000

Of the three provisional income tests, the following (the third test) results in the least taxable Social Security, so it is the one used:

Provisional Income = $40,000

Minus   <u>$32,000</u> *(first threshold)*
        $ 8,000 *(amount over first threshold)*
        <u>50</u> percent

(A) **$4,000** *(taxable)*

Provisional Income = $40,000
    Minus   <u>$44,000</u> *(second threshold)*

        $0 *(amount over second threshold)*
        <u>35</u> percent

(B)   **$0** *(taxable)*

The total amount of the Smarts' Social Security that will be included as taxable income is **$4,000** (A + B). They must add this to their total traditional IRA income of $10,000. But they don't add the other $10,000 from the source that was tax-free and not included in the Provisional Income formula. Their total taxable income is **$14,000.**

The Smarts' strategy allowed them to reduce their taxable income by more than half compared to the Delays, and their taxable income was almost $60,000 less than what the Quicks must include when they file their tax return.

In fairness, it must be pointed out that the reason for this decrease was that the Smarts might have diverted money from their traditional IRA to either a Roth IRA or to a permanent life insurance contract. And by doing so, they would have likely paid more income taxes at the time this money was diverted.

For example, during their working years, the Smarts may have decided to divert some of the contributions they had been making to their 401(k) or traditional IRA and instead put that money into a Roth IRA, or used it to pay the premiums on a life insurance contract. In either case, they would have lost the tax deduction and likely would have paid higher income taxes at that time in their lives. Or, possibly they decided to convert a portion of the money in their traditional IRA to a Roth IRA, and by doing so, they would have likely paid a conversion tax at the time. Or, possibly they took taxable withdrawals from their IRA, once they reached the age of 59½ (to avoid the 10 percent penalty), and used that money to pay premiums on a life insurance contract, and by doing so they would have likely paid income taxes at that time.

Regardless of how they did it, the fair assumption is that sometime before the Smarts found themselves in the position that allowed them to enjoy the reduced taxable income illustrated by the prior example, they would have likely been required to pay a greater amount of *current* income taxes earlier in their lives.

Whether the Smarts or anyone else would be better off paying higher *current* taxes in an effort to reduce *future* taxes is based entirely on their specific circumstances, and if they expect that their tax rates might be higher in the future.

Find tools, articles, webinars, live training,
case studies and more resources devoted
to *the Synergy Effect*™
at ***Doug-Warren.com***

Chapter 5

Life Insurance: Protection With Tax Advantages

Permanent life insurance is a key component in *the Synergy Effect*™ strategy for several reasons. The right product can provide great upside potential to grow wealth for the risk-averse individual. If the insured becomes disabled or dies prematurely, its wealth-growing potential becomes self-completing. At retirement, the accumulated cash value can be accessed using policy loans without the taxation that reduces spendable income from just about every other alternative investment or financial instrument. And, policy loans are not included in the provisional income calculations to determine the taxable portion of Social Security. And, last but not least, there is a good chance that cash value loans will not be included in any future means-testing calculations to determine a senior's eligibility to receive any government-provided health care or other benefits.

If a person's sole source of income is a Social Security retirement income boosted by using the right claiming strategy and cash value loans from a life insurance contract, under current law, some recipients would be able spend 100 percent of the total on their retirement because there would be no income tax due on this combined income. This is synergy in action.

The purpose of this and the following chapters is not to make a case for using permanent life insurance as a person's only savings and wealth-accumulation vehicle. That would not be prudent planning.

But, before going further, one very important question needs to be answered: Should permanent life insurance even be considered as a legitimate wealth-accumulation vehicle at all?

Listen to most financial commentators in the media and the answer is a clear NO! Go to your local bookstore, and you will be lucky to find a single book that offers any other conclusion.

Look deep into the reasons why so many so-called experts believe that permanent life insurance is such a poor wealth-accumulation vehicle, and at the heart of it all will be the high loads, fees and charges associated with these policies.

Permanent Life Insurance

Permanent is expensive. In fact, it is very expensive. But so are taxes. And the one advantage seldom mentioned in the negative commentaries targeting permanent life insurance is its significant tax advantages.

Consider a male age 50 who only wants to pay a premium of $12,000 per year for ten years. Run an illustration, assuming standard non-tobacco, an increasing death benefit year one through ten, and then change to level death benefit from year 11 to maturity. Below you will see all of the projected non-guaranteed loads, fees and charges included in one highly-rated carrier's IUL policy over the next 15 years.

Life Insurance: Protection With Tax Advantages

Yr	Planned Premium	Premium Charge	Policy Fee	Per Unit Charge	Cost of Ins.	Total
1	$12,000	$600	$90	$1,310	$442	$2,442
2	$12,000	$600	$90	$1,310	$483	$2,483
3	$12,000	$600	$90	$1,310	$533	$2,533
4	$12,000	$600	$90	$1,310	$591	$2,590
5	$12,000	$600	$90	$1,310	$664	$2,664
6	$12,000	$600	$90	$1,310	$694	$2,693
7	$12,000	$600	$90	$1,310	$710	$2,710
8	$12,000	$600	$90	$1,310	$715	$2,714
9	$12,000	$600	$90	$1,310	$711	$2,711
10	$12,000	$600	$90	$1,310	$709	$2,708
11			$90		$257	$347
12			$90		$244	$334
13			$90		$222	$312
14			$90		$222	$312
15			$90		$245	$335
16			$90		$267	$357
17			$90		$297	$387
18			$90		$329	$419
19			$90		$364	$454
20			$90		$402	$492

The total annual costs from year 11 on are made up of the $90 policy fee and the cost of insurance (COI), which is small. In fact, these costs are well under one percent of the accumulated cash value (not considering surrender charges). For example, the non-guaranteed accumulated value, assuming a 7.5 percent index rate at the end of year 11, is projected to be $154,281. The total charges that same year are projected to be $347. As a percentage of accumulated value, the total charges are less than one quarter of one percent.

This is far less than what a person would expect to pay in fees with most other financial instruments or investments. Plus, the insured receives a death benefit in return for the fees paid. So when financial commentators in the media criticize permanent life insurance as being too expensive, they must be looking at something other than the fees charged after the first ten years using the above example.

We can assume that these experts would instead be referring to the loads, fees and charges that occur in the first ten years in the above example. And if you total them up, it comes to $26,248. That is indeed a fairly large amount of money. In fact, it represents almost 22 percent of the total premiums paid ($26,248 / $120,000 = 21.87%). Is that expensive? Absolutely! There is no getting around the fact that the loads, fees and charges associated with permanent life insurance are very expensive.

But so are taxes! And the one expense that we can potentially avoid with a properly-used life insurance contract is income taxes.

When you factor in the income taxes along with the typical fees that a person must pay when using just about any other financial instrument, a properly-structured life insurance policy can be a bargain in comparison.

Unfortunately, when you read the criticism levied against permanent life insurance by those in the media, you rarely hear a discussion of the potential tax advantages of a life insurance contract. This is a glaring omission that is hard to explain. It would be similar to comparing the relative merits of traditional IRAs to Roth IRAs, forgetting to mention that distributions from Roth IRAs are tax-free, and then concluding that traditional IRAs are superior.

The focus of *the Synergy Effect*™ strategy is to use and combine financial instruments in a way that boosts *spendable* retirement income. For many people, the income taxes they pay on their retirement income, including the extra taxes many are forced to pay on their Social Security, will greatly reduce their spendable income. For this reason and many others, permanent life insurance is a product definitely worth considering as a wealth-accumulation vehicle.

Some critics of this product will no doubt say that if it is a tax advantage that a person is after, they would be better-served purchasing term insurance and investing the rest in a Roth IRA. The argument would be that Roth IRAs provide many of the tax advantages of permanent life insurance, but without all of the loads, fees and charges. And while this strategy has its merits, there are restrictions on how much money can be contributed to a Roth IRA.

But before going too far into a discussion of which is better, a more important point is that *the Synergy Effect*™ strategy advances the use of both Roth IRAs and permanent life insurance. These financial instruments, when precisely combined with annuities and Social Security claiming strategies, can greatly increase spendable income.

Life Insurance Tax Advantages

Permanent life insurance is expensive. If 22 percent or more of what a person pays in disappears to cover the loads, fees and charges, then we wouldn't expect that it could provide the same level of distributions at retirement as some other financial instrument that does not have those same loads, fees and charges.

For some people, a dollar coming out of a 401(k) might only provide 65 cents or less of spendable money after they pay federal taxes, state taxes and the extra tax that dollar might create on their Social Security income. Because of the tax advantages of life insurance, it is possible to escape or greatly reduce all of those taxes. With this advantage, a life insurance policy might only need to provide tax-free retirement distributions greater than the 65 cents (assuming that is what remains after tax from an IRA) in order for it to be worthy of being considered a viable wealth-accumulation vehicle. Add the death benefit and its ability to secure a surviving spouse's financial future, and an argument can be made that permanent life insurance is absolutely essential in retirement planning.

Interestingly, research from the Life Insurance and Market Research Association, LIMRA, shows that while the average person may see little benefit in owning permanent life insurance, the opposite can be said of wealthy people. It turns out that people with wealth have caused the sales of larger permanent policies to explode:

> High-end policies for $2 million and up, which can carry annual premiums of $20,000 or more, made up nearly 40% of the face value of new whole-life and universal-life policies sold in 2007, according to an analysis done for The Wall Street Journal by LIMRA, an industry-funded research group. Such large policies accounted for just 10% a decade earlier, and 1% two decades ago.[55]

Is the reason that wealthy people having been "investing" large amounts of premium dollars into permanent life insurance that they care more about the well-being of their families than average people do? Or might there be other reasons for the popularity of permanent life insurance among the rich?

Charlie Smith, a former head of an international association of insurance managers, says that permanent life insurance has "become a

---

[55] Maremont, Mark, and Scism, Leslie. "Shift to Wealthier Clientele Puts Life Insurers in a Bind" *Wall Street Journal Online* 3 October 2010. <http://online.wsj.com/article/SB10001424052748703435104575421411449955240.html>

tax shelter for the rich." As politicians call for higher tax rates, we can expect even more people to recognize and appreciate the tax advantages of life insurance:

> Whole and universal life's tax benefit could become still more important to affluent families if their income-tax rates rise, as they would under Obama administration plans to restrict the extension of the Bush-era tax cuts.[56]

People who understand these tax advantages already know that life insurance can be a superior wealth-accumulation vehicle.

> Some tax-policy specialists contend the provision artificially favors income in insurance policies over things like interest on bank certificates of deposit. Some also say that because the break enables people who can afford large life policies to accumulate earnings free of taxes, it gives the affluent tax advantages far beyond those available to middle-income people through a 401(k) or IRA.[57]

What does this mean for the average person who follows the "buy term and invest the difference" advice advocated by so many financial commentators in the media?

> Meanwhile, middle-class families have been getting a smaller portion of the overall tax benefits, in part because they tend to hold less-costly "term" insurance, which provides coverage just for a designated period and doesn't involve a tax-advantaged investment account.

---

[56] Maremont, Mark, and Scism, Leslie. "Shift to Wealthier Clientele Puts Life Insurers in a Bind" *Wall Street Journal Online* 3 October 2010. <http://online.wsj.com/article/SB100014240527487034351045754214114495 55240.html>

[57] Lowrey, Annie. "Tax Preferences of the Rich" *The Washington Independent* 5 October 2010.

> With term insurance, the only tax break is an untaxed
> death benefit, and this break comes into play infrequently.
> That's because most buyers are in their 30s or 40s and
> remain alive at the end of the policy's term.[58]

Apparently, there are many wealthy people who chose to ignore the *buy term and invest the difference* advice, because according to data from the Federal Reserve in 2007, a striking 55 percent of tax-free investment gains inside universal life and whole life policies belonged to the wealthiest 10 percent of U.S. families. In fact, 22 percent of these assets belonged to the richest one percent of American families.

The History of Life Insurance and Taxation

Because tax advantages are often one reason that many agents advocate the purchase of permanent life insurance, it can be of benefit to become familiar with the history of permanent life insurance's tax treatment.

For the purpose of federal income taxation, an insurance policy will not be considered a *life insurance contract* unless it satisfies the statutory definition of what is or is not considered a life insurance policy. If a policy fails to meet the IRS definition, it will not qualify for the favorable tax treatment given to true life insurance contracts. These IRS definitions are really nothing more than tests that the policy must pass. If a policy fails to pass these tests, it is considered to be more like an *investment* vehicle and not a life insurance contract, so the tax treatment is different.

Life insurance as a commercial product actually predates income taxes in the United States. Companies were selling life insurance long before the American Civil War. It was at this time that our country first started taxing income. This tax on income was initially proposed as a temporary measure to help pay the cost of that war.

---

[58] Maremont, Mark, and Scism, Leslie. "Shift to Wealthier Clientele Puts Life Insurers in a Bind" *Wall Street Journal Online* 3 October 2010. <http://online.wsj.com/article/SB100014240527487034351045754214114495 55240.html>

It is interesting to note that while most forms of income or increases in wealth were subject to tax, the death proceeds of life insurance were specifically exempt from such tax. The reason was that life insurance was deemed to serve a social good in that it could prevent widows and orphans from becoming financially destitute. Besides, it is likely that no politician wanted to run the risk of being criticized for supporting a tax on benefits received by virtue of the death of a soldier serving his country.

In 1913, the income tax came back to the USA, and this time it was made permanent. This was the start of what has evolved into our current federal income tax code. But again, throughout this period, the preferable tax treatment of life insurance death benefits has remained essentially the same.

As permanent life insurance products evolved, the inside buildup of cash values was identified as a form of savings that policy owners could access through the cash surrender values.

Through periods during which interest rates and inflation rates were low, many consumers were attracted to permanent life insurance for both the protection provided by the death benefit, and the systematic savings provided by the growth of the policy's cash value. But in the late 1960s and early 1970s, both interest rates and the rate of inflation rose dramatically. As these rates climbed, the benefits of using *traditional* permanent life insurance as a savings vehicle decreased in the view of many consumers.

The Emergence of Investment-Grade Life Insurance

The insurance industry responded by developing a new generation of products. These products were designed to provide greater flexibility and more attractive opportunities to accumulate and grow the policy's cash values.

The term "investment-grade life insurance" was first used to describe this new generation of products.

One new form of investment grade life insurance was the universal life contract introduced by the company that is now known as E.F. Hutton Life in December of 1978.

With this revolutionary product, for the first time consumers could purchase a policy with flexible premiums and flexible death benefits. This was the primary reason that this new form of life insurance received a great amount of attention. Best's Life and Health Review called it *"the most successful new product the industry has seen in decades."*

With universal life insurance's flexibility, policies could be designed in a multitude of different ways. With each small change in design, a universal life policy would change position on the cash value/death benefit spectrum.

Now agents could structure the life insurance policies they sold to build more cash value by including less death benefit.

But because universal life and the other policies in this new generation of insurance could be structured with greater emphasis on the inside build up of cash value, potential purchasers and life insurance companies wanted clarification from the IRS regarding its position on the tax treatment of these policies.

The IRS' Reaction

In early 1981, the IRS provided E.F Hutton Life with a favorable private letter ruling that held that the tax treatment of universal life insurance would be the same as traditional life insurance. This IRS position was confirmed in a series of additional public and private rulings.

The more that it appeared that the IRS position on the tax treatment of universal would remain favorable, the more popular the product became as a wealth-accumulation vehicle. In the July 1981 issue of Money magazine, an article on universal life appeared titled, "Life Insurance – At Last An Almost Ideal Policy." The May 10,1981 *Wall Street Journal*, the May 25, 1981 *New York Times*, and the May 25, 1981 *Time* magazine, along with a host of other publications, all ran favorable stories on universal life as well.

But as the popularity and visibility of these new forms of insurance grew, so did the attacks on their favorable tax treatment:

> By the spring of 1981, however, the ruling position of the IRS on universal life came under attack, with critics focusing on the degree of risk required under universal life and similar plans. Under the products then available in the marketplace, a large amount of cash value could accumulate with a relatively small amount of risk. If the Hutton Life rulings were followed, it was argued, these plans would qualify for favorable treatment under sections 101(a) and 72(e) with only minimal required risk amounts.[59]

Who were the parties behind these attacks? Who would be dissatisfied with the favorable tax treatment that the IRS was willing to bestow on a life insurance policy that could be structured so that it functioned more as a superior wealth-accumulation vehicle, and less as a life insurance contract? As might be expected, these parties included some people in government who argued against the ultimate loss of tax revenue. There

---

[59] DesRochers, Christian J. *Life Insurance Modified Endowments: Under Internal Revenue Code Sections 7702 and 7702a* Society of Actuaries, 2004. p. 194.

were other less visible critics as well. These were people in the banking and investment industries who feared that consumers might choose a tax-advantaged universal life policy over the more traditional investments that did not enjoy the tax advantages of life insurance. The fear was that it would be more difficult to convince consumers to purchase stocks, mutual funds, bank CDs and other financial instruments if the net after-tax returns of these vehicles were less than the tax-favored returns of a life insurance policy. This concern not only existed outside the insurance industry, it was also voiced by competing insurance companies that were slow to adopt these new forms of life insurance.

In the face of these attacks, the IRS decided to review its position in 1982. This caused concern among those life insurance companies that were then issuing universal life policies. They feared that the IRS would reverse its earlier position and decide to tax universal life less favorably. A group of insurance companies marketing universal life came together and lobbied members of Congress, encouraging them to pass laws that would ensure the continuation of the favorable tax treatment of their policies.

TEFRA Legislation

A compromise of sorts was reached when Congress added section 101(f) to the Tax and Fiscal Responsibility Act of 1982 (TEFRA). With the passage of this legislation, for the first time, a formal and specific definition of a life insurance contract was added to the Internal Revenue Code. More importantly, now there was legal clarification regarding the rules for taxing contracts that did not meet the definition of a life insurance contract.

The way that the definition in section 101(f) determines what is and what is not a life insurance contract centers around the net amount at risk (the difference between the contract's death benefit and its cash value):

> In return for clarifying that flexible premium contracts
> would be treated as life insurance contracts, section 101(f)
> required that a minimum amount of insurance risk be
> present in each contracts death benefit.[60]

Unfortunately, the enactment of TEFRA did not end the debate over the taxation of life insurance. The Treasury Department, IRS and some members of Congress continued to question the appropriateness of the favorable tax treatment of insurance contracts that seemingly met the definitions prescribed by section 101(f).

DEFRA Legislation

In 1984 the Deficit Reduction Act (DEFRA) was passed, and with it a new section, 7702, was added to the tax code.

The hope of TEFRA and DEFRA was to clarify and more permanently define what constitutes a life insurance contract and the tax treatment of contracts that either meet or do not meet this definition.

This was done by essentially dictating the minimum death benefit that must be present to accommodate the ultimate total premium paid for an insured of a given age and sex. This meant that a person motivated to use a life insurance policy as a vehicle to accumulate cash value on a tax-favored basis could do so, but only if that policy maintained a certain minimum death benefit.

Generally speaking, there are two different ways to see the TEFRA and DEFRA limitations at work in a policy in which the objective is to meet the definition of a life insurance contract. If an insured wants a life insurance contract with a death benefit in a specific amount, say $500,000, TEFRA and DEFRA will place a limit on the total premiums that can be paid into the policy to fund that death benefit. Or, if an insured wants to "invest" a specific total amount of premiums into a

---

[60] Harman, Jr., William B. "Two Decades of Insurance Tax Reform." *Insurance Tax Review* (Oct. 1992).

life insurance contract, TEFRA and DEFRA will require the existence of a minimum death benefit based on those premiums.

Regardless of which view is taken, both serve to require the existence of a corridor between the accumulations of cash values created as the premiums are paid, and the death benefit provided by the life insurance contract. Instead of taking the tax advantages away from life insurance contracts, TEFRA and DEFRA inhibited the ability of the contract's cash value to grow as a non-insurance investment might, by requiring the existence of a minimum corridor of pure insurance.

Another name for this corridor is the *net amount at risk* that the insurance company has in the contract. Because the cost of insurance (COI) to maintain this corridor will be charged against the accumulated cash values, life insurance contracts should not be able to experience the same rate of growth as could a non-insurance investment that doesn't have those same costs. So in theory, a policy meeting the TEFRA and DEFRA definition of a life insurance contract would not be able to perform as well as a non-insurance investment might because of the "drag" on its performance created by the cost of insurance to maintain the required corridor.

In reality, conditions can exist in which we might expect that the growth of the cash value inside a well-structured IUL might actually outperform some non-insurance investments, even after considering the cost of insurance. The actual historical returns experienced by some IULs during periods in which the stock market has been particularly volatile can compare favorably to direct investments in the stock market. This is possible because of the structure of the indexed crediting method that can provide protection from the downward movement of the market index, the ability to lock in previously credited gains, and the reset feature. However, over a long period of time, the expectation is that an IUL will not provide the same returns as a direct investment in the stock market. And part of the reason for this expectation is that a portion of the growth in the IUL will be offset because of the cost of insurance within the contract.

After TEFRA and DEFRA, the potential returns from a life insurance contract structured as a wealth-accumulation vehicle were decreased relative to the returns from non-insurance investments. But life insurance contracts retained the ability to effectively shelter those returns from income taxes. So while the cost of insurance places the IUL at a disadvantage when it is viewed as a wealth-accumulation vehicle and compared to non-insurance investments, its tax treatment gives it an advantage that few non-insurance investments can match.

The Tax Reform Act of 1986

President Ronald Reagan and the U.S. Congress made major changes in the tax code with the Tax Reform Act of 1986.

People typically remember this legislation as being responsible for a major reduction in tax rates. This is certainly true, considering that the top rate was lowered from 50 percent to 28 percent. What people often forget is that this legislation was designed to be *tax revenue neutral*, which meant that other parts of the legislation would raise revenue to pay for these lower tax rates. This was accomplished in part by removing most of the tax shelters that had been used by many investors to reduce their taxes.

The tax advantages of participating in gas, oil and real estate syndications, and just about every other method of sheltering income were effectively eliminated. Deductions for depreciation of equipment and real property were curtailed. And restrictions were placed on the deductibility of IRA contributions.

A striking exception was that the shelter protecting life insurance contracts from taxation remained unchanged.

While the earlier TEFRA and DEFRA legislation may have taken away some of the attraction of using a life insurance contract as an a wealth-accumulation vehicle, the gutting of tax shelters by the Tax Reform Act of 1986 unintentionally elevated the appeal of life insurance by narrowing the availability of tax-favored financial instruments.

Before 1986, a wealthy person might scoff at the suggestion of putting large amounts of money in a life insurance contract when he could put the same money in a real estate syndication that had the potential for much higher returns and allowed him to deduct any passive investment losses. But after these deductions were eliminated in 1986, the *tax-sheltered* potential gains of a life insurance contract made that option appear even more attractive.

Single Premium Life Insurance

One change that neither TEFRA nor DEFRA made was to disqualify a single premium contract from meeting the definition of a life insurance contract. As long as the other guidelines and the corridor requirements were met, the single premium life insurance policy could still be defined as a life insurance contract and receive all of the tax advantages of traditional life insurance, even though it was funded with one initial premium payment.

Funding a life insurance contract with a large initial single premium payment will immediately reduce the net amount at risk in the policy. This means that the net amount of risk starts out much lower, and will reduce more rapidly than if the same policy was funded over a period of ten years, 20 years, or longer. Because single premium life insurance policies accelerate the reduction in the net amount at risk, the deductions to cover the COIs (cost of insurance) are reduced and as a result the policy's cash value growth rate is accelerated.

Combine this with the tax advantages that these contracts once enjoyed, and it is not a surprise that some insurance companies ramped up their marketing of single premium life insurance policies at precisely the same time that the Tax Reform Act of 1986 eliminated the other tax shelters. Take, for example, the advertisement which appeared in *Fortune* magazine just two months after the passage of this tax legislation.

All Life Insurance Lets You Provide For Your Children. Ours Lets You Buy Toys Of Your Own.

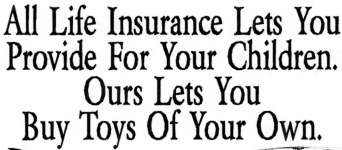

Regular pianos are fine for three-year-olds. But we can help you get one that is really grand.

Why settle for being the first kid on the block when you can be the first one ever?

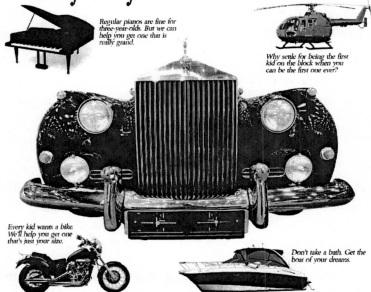

Every kid wants a bike. We'll help you get one that's just your size.

Don't take a bath. Get the boat of your dreams.

Of course, it's very commendable to provide for your children. But with an Integrity Single Premium Life Insurance policy you can provide for yourself.

How is it all possible?

It's not only possible, it's simple. All you do is pay your premium in one single payment. At that instant, your money begins to grow substantially. And what's even more rewarding is that as long as your policy is in force, all of your gains are completely tax-deferred.

A loan with real interest—it's free.

Should you wish to borrow against your policy you can to it at a cost that nets out to zero. You suffer no adverse tax consequences. What's more, you never have to pay back any of the money (although your loan does affect the amount of death benefit or cash surrender value).

And all while you are enjoying free loans and accumulating cash, your death benefit is guaranteed.

Here's even more insurance.

It's risk free! Your principal and interest are guaranteed against loss by contract with Integrity Life. And they're always available to you (less, of course, any surrender charges where applicable).

So why toy around with ordinary life insurance? With ours, you could end up playing with your own 90 foot boat.

For more information on Single Premium Life and other Integrity products Send us the coupon or call 1-800-241-0025, 9 AM – 9 PM. Seven days a week. Integrity Life Insurance Company, Phoenix, Arizona.

This ad and similar ones touting single premium life insurance as the "last remaining tax shelter" not only attracted interest from investors, they ultimately caught the attention of those members of Congress who believed that the tax advantages of life insurance were still too rich, even after the limits of TEFRA and DEFRA.

TAMRA Legislation

In 1988 Congress passed the Technical and Miscellaneous Revenue Act (TAMRA), which further modified the tax rules in a way that dramatically affected single premium insurance policies.

TAMRA created a new special category of life insurance referred to as a modified endowment contract (MEC). A MEC is a life insurance contract that fails to meet TAMRA's "seven-pay rule." This rule specifies that if you fund a whole life insurance policy faster than in seven level annual installments, it will be classified as a MEC.

Under TAMRA, if a contract meets the definition of a MEC, any pre-death distributions, including policy loans, are taxed like annuities, and subject to the same 10 percent penalty as withdrawals from an annuity, an IRA or any other tax-deferred vehicle when the participant is under the age of 59½.

Note that the "seven-pay rule" described above specifically relates to a *whole life* insurance policy. To name the rule "seven-pay" adds confusion as it is applied to a universal life insurance policy. Because of the corroder limits imposed on universal life insurance contracts under TEFRA and DEFRA, they can be funded in as little as three years and one day when the client is approximately under the age of 50, or as little as four years and one day when the client is older.

It is accurate to say that the combined impact of TEFRA, DEFRA and TAMRA was to water down the effectiveness of the life insurance contract when the desire was to use it primarily as an alternative wealth-accumulation vehicle. If we could construct an insurance contract using the rules prior to TEFRA, DEFRA and TAMRA, and compare it to one that was constructed after and in compliance with those rules, we would expect that the pre-TEFRA, DEFRA and TAMRA policy would be a superior wealth accumulation vehicle.

But the investment landscape since 1982 has changed in many ways, not just in terms of life insurance. As was previously pointed out, the elimination of tax shelters with the 1986 Tax Reform Act increased the value of life insurance's tax advantages. So even though TEFRA, DEFRA and TAMRA took away **some** of the tax advantages of life insurance, tax laws also took away most, if not all of the tax advantages of non-insurance investments as well.

The "Clinton" Tax Increase

In 1993, President Bill Clinton pushed a major tax increase through Congress named the Omnibus Budget Reconciliation Act of 1993. While it impacted taxpayers in a number of ways, there were two changes that are important to note. First, it added two tax rates, a 36 percent and 39.6 percent rate to be applied to top wage-earners. Second, it increased the maximum amount of Social Security income that was taxable from 50 percent to 85 percent.

Remember that the significant reductions in tax rates under the earlier Tax Reform Act of 1986 were revenue-neutral. They were paid for in part by the elimination of tax shelters (other than life insurance). You can argue that the tax rate increases under president Clinton were harsher than might appear, because not only did the tax rates increase, but now there were far fewer ways to shelter investments from taxes. These tax rate increases automatically made any wealth-accumulation vehicle that provides tax advantages potentially more attractive. And just about the only remaining tax-advantaged vehicle was a properly-structured life insurance contract. Because of this, you could argue that the Omnibus Budget Reconciliation Act of 1993 increased the value of life insurance when used as a tax-advantaged, wealth-accumulation vehicle.

For example, consider the impact of increasing the taxable portion of Social Security income. Virtually all forms of income that a client might receive are included in the Social Security provisional income calculations to determine if those benefits will be taxed at the new, higher 85 percent rate specified in the 1993 tax law. One of the few exceptions is a cash value loan from a life insurance contract. An owner of a life insurance contract can borrow as much money as the policy will provide, and none of the proceeds will be included in the Social Security provisional income calculations, assuming that the loan is ultimately repaid from the life insurance death benefit.

The increase in individual tax rates and the increased Social Security tax rate from the Omnibus Budget Reconciliation Act of 1993, and the lack of alternative tax shelters since the Tax Reform Act of 1986 have combined to increase the value of a life insurance contract used as a wealth-accumulation vehicle. You could argue that other tax legislation has offset or neutralized some of the adverse effects that TEFRA, DEFRA and TAMRA legislation imposed on life insurance contracts.

The "Bush" Tax Cuts

In 2001, Congress passed the Economic Growth and Tax Relief Reconciliation Act, and in 2003, it passed the Jobs and Growth Tax Relief Reconciliation Act. The combination of these two acts is typically referred to as the "Bush Tax Cuts."

Generally speaking, neither of these laws directly changed the tax treatment of life insurance, but it can be argued that the indirect effect of the tax cuts provided were not favorable to life insurance as a wealth-accumulation vehicle.

The tax rates for both long-term capital gains and dividends were cut to historic lows. Taxpayers who found themselves in a 15 percent or lower income tax bracket would pay zero tax on long-term capital gains and dividends. Those in the 25 percent or higher brackets would only pay 15 percent on these capital gains and dividends.

By lowering these tax rates, stocks and other investments became more attractive relative to the value of life insurance used as a wealth-accumulation vehicle, even after factoring in the tax advantages of life insurance.

On January 1, 2013 a total of seven tax increases kicked in as a result of a deal that Congress and President Obama struck that only *partially* avoided the fiscal cliff. Those increases are in addition to the six tax increases from Obamacare that also began on that same day. What is worse is that all 13 tax increases combined fail to provide any permanent solution to projected future revenue shortfalls.

Today we live in an environment in which many people expect that tax rates will increase even more over future years. If this proves to be true, the relative value of the tax advantages of life insurance will receive even more interest by people searching for ways to escape the higher taxes associated with both investment gains and the transfer of their estates to their heirs.

Might Future Tax Legislation Harm or Benefit Life Insurance?

The one thing we can be absolutely certain of when it comes to tax law is that it will change in the future. Whether those changes will harm or benefit life insurance is impossible to know.

Throughout history, tax legislation has either increased or decreased the value of life insurance as a wealth-accumulation vehicle, relative to non-insurance investments. The combined impact of TEFRA, DEFRA and TAMRA served to reduce the value of life insurance. The elimination of non-insurance tax shelters increased its value. Legislation that reduced tax rates reduced its value, while legislation that increased tax rates and the taxation of Social Security increased its value.

Understanding how these changes have influenced the relative value of life insurance in the past can be helpful in predicting how different types of changes might influence its value in the future, relative to other non-insurance investments.

We might surmise that if tax rates are reduced in the future, or if Congress creates new tax shelters, or reduces taxation of Social Security, that life insurance as a wealth-accumulation vehicle will have less value when compared to non-insurance investments. On the other hand, if tax rates increase, other tax shelters disappear, or the taxation of Social Security reaches 100 percent, then the relative value of life insurance might increase.

Is it More Reasonable to Assume that Taxes Will Increase Or Decrease in the Future?

If the value of life insurance relative to other non-insurance investments is linked to the county's future tax policy, then a sensible question to ask is whether it is more reasonable to assume that taxes will go up or go down in the future.

Since it is Congress that will ultimately make that decision, it may be valuable to consider the fiscal information that the Congressional Budget Office (CBO) presents to Congress. According to the CBO, unless dramatic changes are made, our country's deficits will total $7 trillion over the next 10 years. This, combined with the seemingly unstoppable exponential growth of Social Security, Medicare and other entitlement programs, will make any sane person realize that our country is on the verge of a major fiscal crisis.

If we put politics aside and simply view our country's present circumstances the way a calculating gambler might, then which is the wisest bet: that taxes will decrease in the future, or that they will increase?

In the same report, the CBO makes it clear what Congress must do to avoid disaster:

>An immediate and permanent cut in spending or increase
>in revenues equal to 4.8 percent of GDP—equivalent to
>almost $700 billion today—would be needed to create a
>sustainable fiscal path for the next quarter century.

Does Congress have the courage to take this action? Remember that
the 112th Congress "kicked the can down the road" when it created the
so-called "Supercommittee" and asked the members of this committee
to come up with a way to reduce the deficit. There are two points to
consider regarding this action. First, Congress charged this committee
with shaving at least $1.2 trillion from the deficit…but over the next
ten years. That is "only" $120 billion a year, $580 billion short of the
$700 billion that the CBO said was needed annually. The second point
is that the Supercommittee could not even get this done. On November
21, it dissolved, and issued a statement that began with:

>After months of hard work and intense deliberations, we
>have come to the conclusion today that it will not be
>possible to make any bipartisan agreement available to the
>public before the committee's deadline.[61]

Congress can kick this can as far down the road as it wants to, but
ultimately, Americans will have to pay the price for all of this
foolishness. The likelihood is that tax rates will climb significantly, and
as they do, it is *possible* that the relative value of life insurance as a tax
advantaged wealth-accumulation vehicle will increase.

Will Congress Eliminate the Tax Advantage of Life Insurance?

The fiscal problems facing this country are so severe that it is likely
that future Congresses will be willing to look at any and all options for
changing tax laws in order to increase revenues. If Congress is willing

---

[61] ("Statement from Co-Chairs of the Joint Select Committee on Deficit
Reduction",<http://www.murray.senate.gov/public/index.cfm/2011/11/statement-
from-co-chairs-of-the-joint-select-committee-on-deficit-reduction)>

to consider eliminating the mortgage interest deduction, raise the age of eligibility for Medicare and Social Security, reduce spending on defense, and many of the other things that are discussed today, then it is reasonable to assume that the current tax advantages of life insurance contracts might also be in jeopardy.

No one can predict what might happen in the future, but it's only prudent to at least consider that one way or another, Congress might diminish or completely remove the tax advantages currently enjoyed by life insurance.

In the past, when Congress has made major changes to the tax code relating to life insurance, it has "grandfathered" policies that were in existence at the time. This was true for TEFRA, DEFRA and TAMRA. Generally speaking, these laws had no effect on existing insurance contracts; they only impacted policies purchase after those laws were enacted.

As previously discussed, it can be argued that the insurance contracts issued after TEFRA, DEFRA and TAMRA were not as good as contracts issued before TEFRA, DEFRA and TAMRA with regards to their ability to perform as wealth-accumulation vehicles. This then means that all of those grandfathered, pre-TEFRA, DEFRA and TAMRA contracts became even *more* valuable after these laws were passed.

Before TEFRA, DEFRA and TAMRA, a person owning a life insurance policy purchased as a wealth-accumulation vehicle might say, "I am going to cancel this policy today and later if I decide I want another one I can always purchase it then." After TEFRA, DEFRA and TAMRA, he would likely think twice before cancelling, because he could never again purchase a duplicate of the original policy with all of the same advantages.

If a future Congress decides to reduce or remove the tax advantages enjoyed by policies issued today, the likelihood is that the people who purchased today's policies for their current tax advantages will come to value them even more, and those who had delayed in purchasing policies might come to regret that decision.

Can We Depend on Grandfathering of Tax Laws?

Past Congresses have set a precedent of applying the principals of "grandfathering" whenever comprehensive changes are made to not only life insurance, but to tax law in general.

While this may be comforting, it is important to consider that past Congresses have not had to deal with the fiscal crisis storm that is gathering and that future Congresses are certain to face.

Some agents who advocate using life insurance as a wealth-accumulation vehicle largely due to its current tax advantages mistakenly go so far as to suggest that if Congress were to change tax law relating to life insurance, it would be *forced* to grandfather the favorable tax treatment of any existing policies due to a constitutional prohibition on ex post facto legislation. This is a dangerous position to take, because it could prove to be wrong.

> One question often asked is whether legislation that amends the federal tax laws in a way that retroactively increases a taxpayer's tax liability is constitutional.

> The short answer is that retroactive tax legislation is not absolutely barred by the U.S. Constitution. In fact, the Supreme Court, recognizing that retroactive application of tax laws is sometimes required by "the practicalities of producing national legislation," has deemed it a "customary congressional practice." As such, there are few examples of retroactive tax legislation being struck down as unconstitutional.[62]

---

[62] "Constitutionality of Retroactive Tax Legislation" *Congressional Research Service* 25 October 2012. < http://www.fas.org/sgp/crs/misc/R42791.pdf>

The point here is not to attempt to make a legal argument for or against whether tax treatment of existing policies can be changed in the future. Instead, it is to suggest that insurance agents might want to think twice before providing assurances to their clients as to how future tax law might impact their current life insurance contracts.

Congress could change mortgage interest deductibility, the tax treatment of 401(k)s and other qualified retirement plans, or who knows, maybe one day it will replace our current income tax system with a consumption tax. In spite of the fact that tax law can change in the future, people don't stop purchasing homes, making contributions to 401(k)s or other actions that could be greatly impacted if certain changes were made.

What we do know is that under current law, life insurance enjoys some pretty significant tax advantages. And, we know that in the past when Congress did change the rules concerning life insurance, those changes did not negatively impact existing owners of life insurance.

Those two things are significant, especially in a world where we face so much uncertainty.

Find tools, articles, webinars, live training,
case studies and more resources devoted
to *the Synergy Effect*™
at ***Doug-Warren.com***

Chapter 6

Why Indexed Universal Life?

This book focuses primarily on using indexed universal life for wealth accumulation. This should not necessarily be interpreted to mean that this is the best form of permanent life insurance. There are many great forms of life insurance that can efficiently accumulate cash values, and distribute those values during the insured's lifetime.

Traditional whole life insurance has guarantees that you won't find in indexed universal life.

IULs provide an upside potential and other features that do not exist in most forms of whole life insurance. It's not a question of which is the superior form of life insurance; instead it is which is better suited to the specific needs of a client.

Indexed universal life has some unique features that make it a very attractive option for wealth accumulation and cash value loans. Here is a short list of a few of those features:

- Because it is built on the universal life "chassis," agents can lift the hood and not only see exactly what is going on inside the policy, but also make some fairly significant changes in the design of the engine.
- The loads, fees and charges are totally transparent to both the agent and the client. The agent can and should always print out and review a copy of the policy cost breakdown, which every life insurance company's illustration software will allow.
- There is upside potential for growth, with protection from stock market volatility. The use of indexed crediting provides the powerful features of *locking in gains* and the *annual reset*, which have proven to be attractive to risk-averse clients.
- Most IULs offer the choice of a fixed or participating loan option that provide access to cash values before and after retirement.

Of the many features of indexed universal life, the best may be the flexibility that the agent has with regards to designing the product to meet the specific needs and objectives of the client.

Design Flexibility

Due to the flexibility of indexed universal life, knowledgeable agents who are skilled in the use of their life insurance company illustration software can tailor a policy to better meet the specific needs of their clients.

Flexibility of Design

They can in effect "lift the hood," looking inside the policy and making adjustments. One set of adjustments will effectively boost the policy's death benefit. Another set will supercharge the growth of cash values. There are a multitude of possible tweaks and calibrations that can be used to obtain a precise mixture of death benefit and cash value growth.

It is important to understand that an indexed universal life policy is not an "off-the-shelf" product. When you create an IUL illustration, you are effectively building products for individual clients. Within broad limits, you are dictating the amount of the death benefit both today and in the future, and your choices will not only impact the level of earnings credited to the policy's cash values, but also the degree to which deductions for mortality charges and other expenses will be made from these cash values each month to cover the cost of the death benefit, as well as other expenses.

The Upside Potential of IULs

One of the first questions agents new to IULs ask, especially those with experience in marketing fixed-rate indexed annuities, is how can the caps be so high? It can be baffling to see the same insurance company offer 14 percent cap on their IUL product, but only a four percent cap on their indexed annuity. This invites the question of: Are these higher caps sustainable, or are the current caps some form of "bait and switch"?

While it is impossible to predict if caps rates will be higher or lower in the future, it is important to understand that there are sound reasons for higher IUL cap rates.

Most agents understand that the insurance companies are able to offer the upside potential provided by both IULs and indexed annuities by purchasing derivatives (more commonly referred to as call options) linked to the stock market index. Insurance companies will not make a bet on whether the stock market will go up or down in order to profit if they are right. Instead, they structure both their indexed annuity and IUL products so they will profit no matter what happens, and they transfer or hedge the risk of raising or falling indexes to someone else. Generally speaking, the "someone else" is an investment banker. The way the insurance company transfers this risk is by purchasing a derivative from the investment banker.

Indexed annuities are "spread products," meaning that normally there are no annual fees or sales charges. This can prove to be a disadvantage as it relates to the cap rates they are able to offer, especially during periods when interest rates are low, as in the current environment.

When insurance companies can't generate revenue by charging the contract owner fees or other expenses, their only source of revenue comes from any "spread" between the interest they are able to earn through their investment activity in their general account, and what they are obligated to provide the contract owner. One of the primary reasons that indexed annuity cap rates have declined is that the insurance company general account yields have reduced significantly during the extended low interest rate environment that we have been experiencing.

Insurance companies really only have only two options when interest rates decline: they can lower the cap, or they can subsidize the cost of the options through other revenue generated by the contract. Here's the problem: generally speaking, with regards to fixed indexed annuities, there is no other revenue generated beyond the spread.

So really, insurance companies have only one option when the yields from the general account fall below the cost of the options: they must reduce the cap rate.

Reducing the cap is effective because the investment bankers charge the insurance companies less for options that cap the index returns at say, five percent, than for options that cap the returns at a higher level, such as seven percent.

The reason that IULs are able to offer much higher cap rates is simple: In addition to the interest earned on the company's general account; additional revenue is generated by the loads and fees typically associated with indexed universal life policies.

What we can expect is that cap rates on both indexed annuities and IULs will fluctuate in the future, because yields from insurance companies' general accounts will fluctuate and the cost of the options they must purchase will fluctuate. It's also reasonable to expect that cap rates offered by IULs will always be higher than indexed annuities, because they provide more revenue that can be used to purchase the options.

Cap Rates Are Only One Side of a Two-Sided Coin

A common mistake agents make when searching for the "best" IUL policy is to pay too much attention to the current caps or indexing crediting method structure used by the policy.

Caps and other details of indexing are certainly important, but they are only one side of the IUL coin. The other side of this coin represents the loads, fees and charges that will either directly or indirectly reduce the potential growth of the policy's cash value.

These charges are every bit as important as the cap rate when it comes to the policy's potential to perform as a wealth-accumulation vehicle. A policy with a very high cap definitely increases the potential for greater interest credited to the policy's cash value in years when the underlying index performs well. But if that same policy has higher annual charges, its cash value will be drained to a larger degree than if those annual charges were less.

It can be argued that there is a direct relationship between IUL cap rates and annual policy charges. In other words, it is reasonable to assume that IULs with higher cap rates could also have higher cost structures. Take a close look at an IUL contract with lower cap rates, and you will likely also find lower annual policy charges.

Certainly there will be exceptions, but generally speaking, a relationship exists between the cap rates provided and the expenses charged to IUL policies.

Assume we have two insurance companies offering IULs. Both use an annual point-to-point design in their crediting method structure with a 100 percent participation rate, linked to the same index. The floor for both companies is an identical zero percent. The only difference is that company A caps the rate credited at 12 percent, while company B's cap is 15 percent. How can company B offer a higher cap? The answer is that company B is spending more money on the derivatives used to provide a greater upside potential. The more important question is: Where does this extra money come from?

If the two primary sources of revenue available to the insurance companies are the yield from their general accounts and the annual policy charges, then the extra money needed to purchase the options to provide a higher cap rate must come from one or both of these two sources.

For company B to be able to offer a higher cap rate, it must figure out a way to generate more revenue than company A. This will require either increasing the yield from its general account, or increasing its IUL's annual policy charges.

Consider the difficulty of attempting to increase the yield a company generates from its general account. Generally speaking, the primary investment in all insurance companies' general accounts are bonds. The investment departments of the various insurance companies are all purchasing from the same pool of available bonds. Certainly the potential exists that one company's investment department will outperform another's, but any difference will likely be relatively small and rather inconsistent. A more reasonable assumption is that they will all obtain fairly similar yields on their general accounts over time.

Assume that the yield from the general accounts of both company A and company B is an identical six percent in a given year. Company A goes to an investment banker to see how much the options will cost in order to provide an upside potential capped at a 12 percent rate. It finds that the price for the options necessary to provide this cap will represent five of the six percent general account annual yield. In other words, company A will use the majority of the earnings from the investments in their general account to purchase the options. After this purchase, the company still has a net one percent return from its general account.

Company B wants to offer an even greater upside potential. It believes that more agents will want to sell their product if that product offers a higher cap rate. So it wants to purchase options that can provide a 15 percent cap. Company B's investment banker tells it that the amount of money required to purchase these options would require seven of the six percent yield on the general account (an amount greater than the actual yield). Its six percent general account yield is not enough to cover this cost. Company B must find additional revenue in order to offer the higher cap rate. In order to do this, company B would need to structure higher expenses in its IUL policy, and use some of that money to make up the difference in the cost of the options.

Generally speaking, any time you find two companies that appear to be identical is every way, with the same crediting method structure and earning the same yields on general accounts, but one company caps the upside potential at a higher level than the other company, the chances are that the company with the higher cap will also have higher fees built into its IUL.

One way to look at paying higher fees in a IUL that provides a higher cap rate is that you are paying for performance.

However, the primary point is that an IUL with a higher cap but with higher fees is not necessarily better or worse than an IUL with lower fees and a lower cap. The actual *net* growth rate of cash values in a policy with a 15 percent cap and higher fees could be identical to the *net* growth rate of cash values in a policy with a 12 percent cap and lower policy charges.

Because of this, you can't always assume that your client will benefit more from an IUL with a higher cap rate. But you also can't automatically assume that your client will benefit more from an IUL with lower cost structure charges.

This is why it is so important to consider both the interest earning potential provided by cap rate and the loads, fees and charges of the IUL that you will be offering to your clients.

Three Expenses Built Into IULs

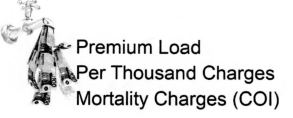

Premium Load
Per Thousand Charges
Mortality Charges (COI)

In addition to an annual policy fee and charges for any riders that might be added, the three categories of charges that you will find in all IUL products are the *premium load*, the *per thousand charges* and *mortality charges* (COI). All will impact the net potential cash value growth, but in different ways and at different times over the life of the contract.

The insurance company-provided illustration software will allow the agent to print a report that will be titled something like the *Annual Cost Summary* report. A detailed breakdown of the IUL expenses specific to the policy will be shown on this report.

Premium Charge

A premium charge (often referred to as a premium load) is a percentage amount charged against all premiums paid into a policy. Premium charges will typically range from five percent to 10 percent, and will be deducted at the time that a premium payment is made.

If a policy is designed to be totally funded over a five-year period with annual premiums of $20,000 and a premium charge of six percent, the *Annual Cost Summary* report would show the following:

Year	Premium Outlay	Premium Charge
1	20,000	1,200
2	20,000	1,200
3	20,000	1,200
4	20,000	1,200
5	20,000	1,200
6	0	0
7	0	0
8	0	0
9	0	0
10	0	0
Total	$100,000	$6,000

If a policy is designed to be totally funded over a ten-year period, with annual premiums of $5,000 and a premium charge of six percent, the *Annual Cost Summary* report would show the following:

Year	Premium Outlay	Premium Charge
1	5,000	300
2	5,000	300
3	5,000	300
4	5,000	300
5	5,000	300
6	5,000	300
7	5,000	300
8	5,000	300
9	5,000	300
10	5,000	300
Total	$50,000	$3,000

Generally speaking, the premium charge will not directly increase or decrease based on the policy's death benefit. The only factor in determining the premium charge is the amount of premiums paid.

Per Thousand Charges

This charge will typically be deducted each month during the first ten years or longer, regardless of the number of years that premiums are paid.

If a policy is designed to be totally funded over a ten-year period with a per thousand charge assessed for a period of 12 years, the *Annual Cost Summary* report would look something like this:

Year	Premium Outlay	Premium Charge	Per $1000
1	5,000	300	700
2	5,000	300	700
3	5,000	300	700
4	5,000	300	700
5	5,000	300	700

6	5,000	300	700
7	5,000	300	700
8	5,000	300	700
9	5,000	300	700
10	5,000	300	700
11	0	0	700
12	0	0	700
13	0	0	0
14	0	0	0
15	0	0	0
Total	$50,000	$3,000	$8,400

Mortality Charges (COI)

Mortality charges, also referred to as the Cost of Insurance or the COIs, will be deducted each month over the life of the policy. The amount charged will typically be different each year.

When people criticize using life insurance as a wealth-accumulation vehicle, one of their primary reasons is that the cost of insurance increases as the insured ages. And while it is true that the cost of insurance does increase with age, it is important to understand that it is only charged against the net amount at risk in the policy.

When a level death benefit is selected, the amount that the beneficiary receives is made up of both the cash value and the insurance element. The net amount at risk is this insurance element.

Because of the flexible design of a universal life insurance contract it is possible to manage the total death benefit (to a degree) which will help to limit the net amount of risk. This will in turn limit the COIs that are deducted from the policy's cash value.

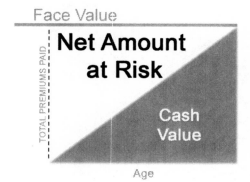

As the cash value grows within the policy, it will represent a larger portion of the death benefit, and the net amount at risk will decrease. So while it is true that the mortality charges (COIs) increase with age, the policy can be designed so that the net amount at risk reduces (to a point) as the insured ages. A lower net amount at risk will offset a higher per-thousand charge for the cost of insurance. With a proper design, it is possible for the agent to control, to a certain extent, the total amount that is deducted each year from the policy's cash values to pay the mortality charges.

The table below might be similar to what you would see in an *Annual Cost Summary* report for a client who wanted to put $100,000 into a non-MEC contract as quickly as possible, assuming a 5.5 percent premium charge, and for which the per-thousand charges were limited to ten years.

Year	Premium Outlay	Premium Charge	Per $1000	Cost of Ins.
1	20,723	1,140	1,650	695
2	20,723	1,140	1,650	715
3	20,723	1,140	1,650	744
4	20,723	1,140	1,650	768
5	17,108	941	1,650	804
6	0	0	1,650	895
7	0	0	1,650	981

8	0	0	1,650	1068
9	0	0	1,650	1128
10	0	0	1,650	1194
11	0	0	0	1266
12	0	0	0	1344
13	0	0	0	1433
14	0	0	0	1515
15	0	0	0	1570
Total		$5,501	$16,500	

In this example, after ten years, the only ongoing annual charges would be for the cost of insurance and the policy fee.

As mentioned earlier, whenever criticism is aimed at using permanent life insurance as a wealth-accumulation vehicle, it is usually because of the loads, fees and charges. In the case of indexed universal life insurance, is this criticism warranted? Are IULs expensive to own?

Front-End Loads of IULs

Assuming that the policy is designed to be completely funded in five to ten years, both the *premium charges* and the *per-thousand charges* occur more towards the "front-end" of the contract. In the above example, these two charges amount to a total of $22,001 paid over the first ten years of the contract.

No doubt this is a steep price to pay when compared to non-insurance vehicles. But aside from the death benefit, a life insurance contract, when used properly, has tax advantages that most other vehicles do not.

Owners of vehicles that are taxed currently could see 15 percent, 25 percent or more of their earnings disappear each year in the form of federal and state income taxes. Owners of vehicles that grow tax-deferred could see the same percentages or more of the distributions taken in the future vanish. These taxes represent a load or fee that governments take over and above in charges levied by the sponsors of the financial instrument.

Any time the front-end loads of life insurance are examined and compared to non-insurance financial instruments, it is only fair and reasonable to do so from the perspective of what each can provide the owner *after* income taxes are taken into consideration.

The Ongoing Mortality Expense (COIs) of IULs

Depending on how the product is designed, the premium charge and the per-thousand charge can ultimately disappear, but from a practical standpoint, the life insurance contract will never be without the mortality expense or cost of insurance (COI).

In the above example, the only charge (other than the policy fee and the charge for any added riders) in year 11 would be the $1,266 cost of insurance (mortality charge).

Some would argue that this charge erodes the rate of growth of the cash value of the IUL to such a degree that it supports the argument that an IUL is a poor wealth-accumulation vehicle. And while it is true that non-insurance financial vehicles do not have a charge for a cost of insurance, they often have other charges that you don't find in IULs. Many mutual funds and brokerage accounts assess fees for administration, management and other charges. The same is true of 401(k)s and other retirement plans. Often, these fees can amount to one percent or more of the account value each year.

Assume that the projected accumulated cash value in the 11th year of the IUL used in the above example (the one funded over five years) was $150,000. Apply a one percent charge against this amount and the total would be $1,500. Now compare that one percent charge to the mortality fee that year of $1,266.

What would a person rather pay, a $1,266 charge for the cost of insurance and in exchange enjoy the protection of the death benefit, or a $1,500 charge for administrative and investment management fees? What does the client receive in exchange for whatever his mutual fund, brokerage account or 401(k) charges each year?

"Fortunately, we were able to pick up on the negative indicators early and extract our brokerage fees before your share portfolio hit the fan"

The more the agent positions the IUL as a wealth-accumulation vehicle, the greater his responsibility to discloses all of the loads, fees and charges that will inevitably dictate how well the policy performs to that end. Some may initially view these charges as excessive, but if viewed in contrast to the typical loads and fees that must be paid with non-insurance accumulation vehicles, and especially considering its potential tax advantages and death benefit, a well-constructed IUL should look attractive by comparison.

The Indexing Advantage for Risk-Averse Investors

Generally speaking, investors wanting to participate directly in the potential gains of the stock markets can be placed in one of two categories. They are either "buy-and-hold" investors or "market-timing" investors.

The overwhelming advice provided by almost every how-to investment book and articles online or in financial publications, including the recommendations given by many brokers and financial advisors, is that it's next-to-impossible for investors to successfully time when to jump in and jump out of the market. Instead, the recommendation, especially for the average individual, is to be a buy-and-hold investor.

This was great advice in the early 1980s and right up to March 2000, because that period was one of the greatest bull markets for stocks that had ever occurred or may every occur again.

We see that the market had generally headed up ever since it had bottomed out in July 1982, until March 2000. The spiking of prices in the years 1995 through 2000 has been most remarkable: the price indexed looks like a rocket taking off through the top of the chart, only to sputter and crash. This largest stock market boom ever may be referred to as the millennium boom.[63]

When you are in the midst of a bull market, buy-and-hold can work like a charm. What is the point of timing the markets when the S&P 500 index went up 34 percent in 1995, 20 percent in 1996, 31 percent in 1997, 26 percent in 1998, and jumped again by 20 percent in 1999?

Unfortunately, March 2000 signaled the peak of this super-charged bull market. By March of 2003, the S&P 500 index had fallen by half on a real inflation-adjusted basis.

Instead of this being the end of the problem for investors, it was the beginning of a global financial crisis that played out in 2007 and 2008. Stock markets plummeted around the world; large financial institutions collapsed or were bailed out by governments. And the psychology of investors changed in ways that might prove to last for the rest of their lives.

Google the phrase "buy and hold is dead" and you'll find around 1.5 million links.

If the turmoil of the recent decade has caused risk-averse investors to abandon the buy-and-hold approach, what is left for them? Will they try their hand at timing the market even when all of the experts say it's a mistake?

"My favorite time frame is forever." - **Warren Buffett**

---

[63] Shiller, Robert J. *Irrational Exuberance*. Crown Business, 2006. p. 4

"I can't recall ever once having seen the name of a market timer on Forbes' annual list of the richest people in the world. If it were truly possible to predict corrections, you'd think somebody would have made billions by doing it." - **Peter Lynch**

"Only liars manage to always be out during bad times and in during good times." - **Bernard Baruch**

It's unlikely that risk-averse investors will switch from a buy-and-hold approach to an even riskier market-timing approach. Instead, what many will do is to either stay out of the stock market altogether, or continue with their buy-and-hold approach. The problem for those that stay in the market might be that the past crises may have damaged their psychology to such a degree that any future plunge in the markets could spook them out of stocks any time that markets drop in the future.

An even more ominous problem could await those who decide to abandon stocks altogether. This problem could come in the form of the inflation that many experts predict will be the result of the Federal Reserve dumping trillions of dollars into the economy in recent years.

How high might inflation climb? If we saw a return to the "stagflation" period of the 70s, it could be very bad.

Year	Inflation
1971	4.3%
1972	3.3%
1973	6.2%
1974	11.0%
1975	9.2%
1976	5.8%
1977	6.5%
1978	7.6%

1979	11.2%
1980	13.6%

Source: Bureau of Labor Statistics.

The average inflation rate over this ten-year period from 1971 to 1980 was 7.87 percent.

If the future inflation rate averages even six percent over the first 20 years of a person's retirement, a $100,000 nest egg at the start would only purchase about $33,000 of goods and services by the end of this period. That means that the nest egg would need to grow by at least six percent just to keep its purchasing power up with inflation.

Even if interest rates on bank CDs, T-Bills and other safe-money instruments increase as the rate of inflation climbs, most retirees will still need to find a way to earn greater returns if they are to meet their income needs throughout retirement.

Fixed indexed annuities might be an option for risk-adverse individuals, but probably not, unless we see an increase in cap rates from their present low levels. Until then, the role of annuities in helping clients will be limited to that of providing income. In addition to income, many people will want and need vehicles that allow them to accumulate and preserve true wealth.

A good long term wealth-building option today for many risk-averse individuals is an indexed universal life policy specifically structured as a wealth-accumulation vehicle. If the agent starts with a good product and designs it well, it is reasonable to expect that over time, the cash values inside an IUL could grow at an average rate of between four to six percent, net of the cost of insurance. Combine this with the current tax advantages, and the value of that four to six percent is actually much greater when compared to the after-tax distributions from other alternatives.

Why Indexed Universal Life?

The question most clients and many agents will ask is: Is it still reasonable to expect a net growth rate of four to six percent if the stock market performs poorly in the future?

One way to answer this question is to see what might have been the gross amounts credited (before the cost of insurance or other loads or fees were deducted) if we had an IUL indexed to the S&P 500. Assuming a consistent cap rate of 13 percent and a floor of zero percent over the past 20 years, the gross amounts would have looked like this *(note that the S&P price change figures do not include dividends.):*

Year	1992	S&P Price Change	Indexed Product
1	1993	7.06	7.06
2	1994	-1.54	0.00
3	1995	34.11	13.00
4	1996	20.26	13.00
5	1997	31.01	13.00
6	1998	26.69	13.00
7	1999	19.51	13.00
8	2000	-10.14	0.00
9	2001	-13.04	0.00
10	2002	-23.37	0.00
11	2003	26.38	13.00
12	2004	8.99	8.99
13	2005	3.00	3.00
14	2006	13.62	13.00
15	2007	3.53	3.53
16	2008	-38.49	0.00
17	2009	23.45	13.00
18	2010	12.78	12.78
19	2011	0.00	0.00
20	2012	13.41	13.41
20 Year Totals		6.10%	7.47%

Assuming the cap rate did not change, the hypothetical indexed product would have experienced a growth rate of 7.46 percent over this period. But at best, this is only a reflection of the potential gross rate that might be credited. This rate does not take into consideration that expenses associated with the insurance policy would need to be deducted. Net of these expenses, the actual growth rate would be lower.

IULs, as with most forms of permanent life insurance, are front-end loaded contracts, so a much greater amount will be deducted in the early years of the contract. The longer the contract is in force, the more the front-end loads and fees can be offset with credited interest. But time is needed for this to occur.

So the real question is, if after considering all of these expenses, it is still reasonable to assume that the money paid into an IUL will grow at a rate of between four and six percent?

A good way to answer this question is to look at the internal rate of return (IRR) of the net projected cash values. An IRR calculation shows the return after all loads, fees and charges have been considered. Most, insurance company software will allow you to print a supplemental IRR report along will the regular illustration you have prepared.

The following table contains the results of the IRR report for an IUL funded over a ten year period.

Policy Year	Planned Premium	Non Guaranteed Net Cash Value	Cash Value IRR
1	$12,000	$3,162	-73.65%
2	$12,000	$14,711	-28.51%
3	$12,000	$27,039	-13.65%
4	$12,000	$40,197	-6.97%
5	$12,000	$54,228	-3.35%
6	$12,000	$69,245	-1.11%

7	$12,000	$85,335	0.39%
8	$12,000	$102,591	1.47%
9	$12,000	$121,108	2.28%
10	$12,000	$140,984	2.91%
11		$151,890	3.61%
12		$163,591	4.12%
13		$176,158	4.52%
14		$189,631	4.83%
15		$204,055	5.08%
16		$219,502	5.29%
17		$235,562	5.45%
18		$252,793	5.58%
19		$271,280	5.69%
20		$291,114	5.80%
21		$312,391	5.88%
22		$335,253	5.96%
23		$359,833	6.03%

This particular IUL product had a higher cap rate then the 13 percent used to cap the S&P in the above illustration. While the product would have allowed for a greater assumed annual index interest, the actual rate used to prepare the illustration was 7.5 percent.

As the table shows, the internal rate of return by year 23 has climbed to 6.03 percent. The difference between the 7.5 percent assumed annual index interest and the 6.03 percent IRR is due to the loads, fees and charges that will be deducted.

The question we are trying to answer is if it is reasonable to assume a net growth rate of between four and six percent. As the table above shows, we can expect that this range will be met anywhere between the 12th and 23rd years assuming current non-guaranteed interest crediting and cost assumptions.

If the client has a shorter time horizon, then perhaps the IUL should not be considered. Again, these are front-end loaded contracts. Because of these expenses, the internal rates of return register as negative numbers in the early years.

With a long enough time horizon, the IUL is an excellent vehicle for wealth accumulation. After 23 years, the projected, non-guaranteed internal rate of return is 6.03 percent. And, because of the tax advantages of life insurance, an argument can be made that a person taxed at an average rate of 25 percent would need a vehicle providing an internal rate of return of approximately 7.5 percent to match the IUL.

The purpose of the example is not to suggest actual performance, but instead to highlight features of the IUL's crediting method structure that might prove to be valuable to individuals who are trying to cope with future volatility of the financial markets.

This may be especially relevant considering the volatile period starting in 2000 with the bursting of the tech bubble, and the market melt-down in 2008.

Why Indexed Universal Life?

Year	1998	S&P Price Change	Indexed Product
1	1999	19.51	13.00
2	2000	-10.14	0.00
3	2001	-13.04	0.00
4	2002	-23.37	0.00
5	2003	26.38	13.00
6	2004	8.99	8.99
7	2005	3.00	3.00
8	2006	13.62	13.00
9	2007	3.53	3.53
10	2008	-38.49	0.00
11	2009	23.45	13.00
12	2010	12.78	12.78
13	2011	0.00	0.00
14	2012	13.41	13.41
14 Year Totals		1.07%	6.50%

As the table above shows, the price change (not including dividends) in the S&P over this 14-year period was a fraction over one percent. And, with the application of a cap rate of 13 percent and a floor of zero percent, the hypothetical indexed product registers 6.5 percent.

Prospective purchasers of IULs might wonder how it is possible to achieve growth rates six times greater than the underlying stock market index that the IUL is linked to.

Of course it is possible, and the reason is the valuable features that allow the *locking in gains* and the *reset*.

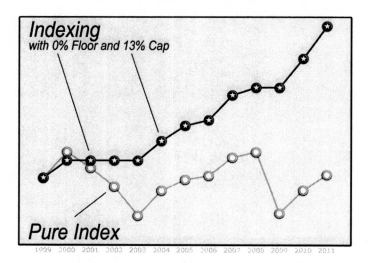

THE POWER OF INDEXING

During the periods when the underlying index declines, prior gains credited to the IUL cash value would be *locked in*, and are never subject to future stock market losses.

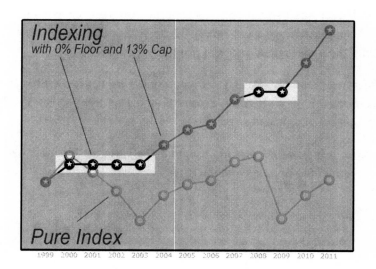

THE IMPACT OF LOCKING IN GAINS

However, it is important for the agent to remember and client to understand that unlike an indexed annuity that has no loads or fees, the cash values in an IUL could decline because deductions would continue to be taken from the cash value to cover the costs of insurance, policy fees and other expenses. The chart below more accurately reflects this possibility, because it shows a slight decline (as a result of the ongoing costs of insurance and fees) even though the cash value was protected from market losses. This decline could be even greater in the early years of the IUL because of the previously discussed front-end loads.

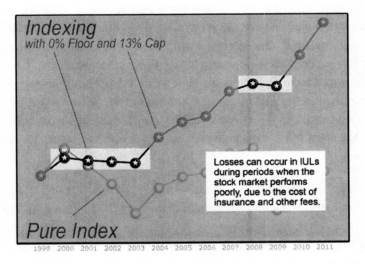

Indexing
with 0% Floor and 13% Cap

Losses can occur in IULs during periods when the stock market performs poorly, due to the cost of insurance and other fees.

Pure Index

1999 2000 2001 2002 2003 2004 2005 2006 2007 2008 2009 2010 2011

THE IMPACT OF LOSSES DUE TO COIs AND FEEs

Some IULs offer a floor that is greater than zero. In that case, the policy owner *could* be guaranteed to have a minimum amount of interest credited to the cash value *each year,* regardless of how the stock market index performs. If the index experienced a loss in a given year, but the IUL provided a contractually-guaranteed *floor* of one percent, the client would be assured that every year, the IUL cash value would be credited with at least one percent. This would provide a minimum growth rate of cash values that would then be available to offset a portion — or perhaps all — of the cost of insurance and other fees that would be deducted from the cash value in any given year.

Some IULs guarantee that the cash values will be credited with a minimum interest rate over a period of time. This type of guarantee can have a much different impact than does an IUL that provides an annual *floor* of say one percent. For example, if an IUL contractually guarantees that over a ten-year period, the minimum interest rate that will be credited on average will be one percent annually, theoretically the stock market index could have no gains in the first nine years, but could still achieve the minimum growth rate as long as the index had a large enough gain in year ten. The guaranteed minimum might have been achieved, but zero interest would have been credited to the cash value during the first nine years. Under these circumstances, the policy owner would have had to endure nine years of receiving annual statements that showed no interest credited to the policy's cash value, and to add insult to injury each year, money would still have been deducted from those cash values to cover the costs of insurance and any other fees.

An owner of a policy that guarantees that minimum interest rate *floor* of one percent will see at least that amount credited to the cash values every year, no matter how the index performs. Some clients might prefer knowing that each year, there will be some minimum amount of interest credited to cover some of the annual expenses. For other clients, this may not be so important. It isn't necessarily that one IUL is better than another. Instead, it is that the structure of one policy might better fit the specific needs or desires of a particular client.

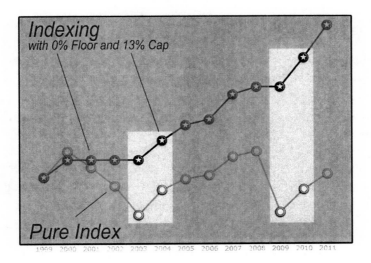

THE IMPACT OF THE RESET

The value of the *reset* becomes apparent during periods when the stock market rebounds after earlier losses. When the crediting method used by the IUL is based on an annual reset design, the measuring point to determine future gains is adjusted each year in which the index declines. This has the effect of allowing the IUL to be credited with additional interest, even before the index fully recovers from any prior low point.

Clients will likely not appreciate the power of indexing until they understand the impact of *locking in gains* and the *reset*.

The IUL's Cash Value Loan Provisions

With most IUL policies, the owner has the option to choose between at least two policy loan provisions. The owner will not need to make this decision until he or she is ready to borrow cash values from the policy. But prior to the client purchasing the policy, an illustration will be created showing the amount of the distributions that the policy is projected to provide in the future. The choice of the loan provision used in that illustration can have a significant impact on the amount of those distributions.

153

The Fixed Loan Provision

One loan provision offered by many insurance companies is commonly referred to as a "fixed loan," or it may also be referred to as a "wash loan." Under the terms of this loan option, the amount borrowed must come from the cash value that has been allocated to the fixed interest account.

IULs allow the policy owner to allocate cash value between either the indexed account, in which the cash value is credited with interest based on the performance of the indexed crediting method used, or a fixed interest account, in which the interest credited each year is a stated rate.

Again, to use the fixed loan provision, the portion of the cash value that will be used as collateral for the loan must reside in the fixed account.

With this loan, the cash value is credited with a specified fixed rate of interest and the policy owner is charged a specified fixed rate of interest on the amount borrowed. The rate *charged* and the rate *crediting* would be equal (or very close to equal), so the net effect is a "wash." In other words, they cancel each other out so that there is no cost (or very little cost) to borrowing the cash values when using the fixed loan provision.

Often, the insurance company will require that the policy must be in force for a certain minimum number of years before the "wash loan" is available. For example, the loan provision might state that it is only after the policy has been in force for a minimum of 10 years that a loan can be taken with a net zero percent cost. Loans taken prior to that minimum period will often have a higher net cost, which might be two percent, three percent, or more.

Many agents prefer to design their illustrations using the fixed or wash loan profession, because they believe that their clients will place greater value on the IUL if its cash value can be accessed in the future without any, or with very little, net interest charged to the client.

This may be a valid point of view, but it is important to understand that by using the *wash loan* provision in the policy illustration, one result will generally be that a lower future amount of distributions might be received during retirement than if the *participating loan* provision was used.

The Participating Loan Provision

This second loan provision is often referred to as a "participating loan," but is also known as an "indexed loan" option.

This loan allows the cash value to continue to receive indexed interest on the amount borrowed. This means that the interest charged can be reduced by the potential credited indexed interest.

With some IULs, the amount of interest that is charged on the loan is a variable rate that is often tied to some index like the Moody's Corporate Bond Index. In this case, the future amount of interest charged will be unknown. It can be said that participating loans that have a variable loan rate have two *moving parts*, meaning that the indexed interest that is credited can *move* up or down each year, and that the interest charged on the loan can also *move* up or down each year.

Some IULs will charge a variable loan rate that can change, but will cap that rate at some fixed maximum rate in order to guarantee that it can never be above a certain percentage.

Some IULs offer a participating loan in which the interest rate that is charged is a contractually-guaranteed fixed rate. In this case, it can be said that the loan has one *moving part*. The indexed interest that is credited can *move* up or down each year depending on the performance of the crediting method used. But the amount of interest charged on the loan is a fixed rate, and cannot ever *move* (assuming that the rate is guaranteed in the contract).

As stated earlier, when a policy illustration is prepared in which future distributions will be shown, the preparer will be asked to select whether the loan option will be a fixed loan or a participating loan. The selection of the *participating loan option* will most often result in a larger amount of illustrated non-guaranteed projected retirement income. This will be true as long as the illustration is assuming that the interest rate credited annually to the cash value is greater than the interest rate charged on the amount borrowed.

For example, if the illustration is projecting future values based on the assumption that the indexed interest that is credited each year equals 7.5 percent, and that the interest rate charged for any outstanding cash value loan is six percent, then the assumption that is reflected in the illustration is that the portion of the cash value that is used as collateral for the loan will continue to be credited with a net positive interest rate of 1.5 percent. If instead, a fixed loan provision was used where the rate charged on the loan amount was identical to the rate credited, the illustration would be reflecting less total interest credited, which would lower the projected future retirement income.

By using the participating loan, the *potential* exists that the policy owner will be borrowing at an interest rate that is lower than is being credited to the cash value. The illustration will always reflect this potential, and can give the appearance that it is a *reality* when the illustration assumes a credited interest rate that is higher than the policy loan rate.

The participating loan can be a great option because it does have the potential to increase retirement income, but it is not without risk. If the stock market performs poorly for an extended period of time while there is an outstanding cash value loan, a situation can occur in which the amount of the indexed interest credited is less than the loan interest rate charged. During periods when this might happen, the cash values will be drained by more than just the amounts borrowed. They will also be reduced because of the negative net interest that will need to be absorbed.

Why Indexed Universal Life?

The wrong question here is which loan provision is better. Each is really nothing more than a tool that the agent has available to do the job that needs to be done with a particular client. Fortunately, most insurance companies do offer both a fixed and a participating loan option, and generally, the policy owner does not select the one to be used until the time of the loan. In addition, many insurance companies will allow the policy owner to change between loan options periodically. This can provide the client with the flexibility of starting with one loan option, and then perhaps in the next year, changing to the other loan option.

However, most illustrations that are prepared only show the impact of using one loan option. As stated before, when that option is the participating loan, the distributions will typically be greater than if a fixed loan was illustrated.

Age	Year	Premium Paid	Surrenders or Loans Received or Repaid	Accumulation Value	Net Cash Value	Net Death Benefit
51	1	$20,000	$0	$15,264	$0	$736,120
52	2	$20,000	$0	$31,564	$8,464	$736,120
53	3	$20,000	$0	$48,957	$27,506	$736,120
54	4	$20,000	$0	$67,511	$47,717	$736,120
55	5	$20,000	$0	$87,277	$69,131	$736,120
56	6	$20,000	$0	$108,569	$92,073	$736,120
57	7	$20,000	$0	$131,562	$116,714	$736,120
58	8	$20,000	$0	$156,436	$143,237	$736,120
59	9	$20,000	$0	$183,361	$171,811	$736,120
60	10	$20,000	$0	$212,501	$202,607	$736,120
		$200,000				
61	11	$0	$0	$226,780	$218,536	$736,120
62	12	$0	$0	$241,981	$235,385	$736,120
63	13	$0	$0	$258,157	$253,210	$736,120
64	14	$0	$0	$275,370	$272,072	$736,120
65	15	$0	$0	$293,700	$292,051	$736,120
66	16	$0	$0	$313,210	$313,210	$736,120
67	17	$0	$0	$333,985	$333,985	$736,120
68	18	$0	$0	$356,118	$356,118	$736,120
69	19	$0	$0	$379,715	$379,715	$736,120
70	20	$0	$24,379	$378,684	$378,684	$711,741

TP: $15,893

$24,379

Illustration A

157

Illustration A, above, was prepared for a male age 50. The annual premium is $20,000 paid for ten years. It provides a level death benefit of $736,120. The assumed interest rate credited was set at 7.5 percent annually. Regarding distributions, the assumptions in this illustration are that they would start at age 70 and those withdrawals would be made until the basis in the contract (total premiums paid) has been recovered, and that a fixed "wash" loan would be used from that point on. The illustration was prepared so that it "solved for" providing the highest amount of retirement income possible. And as the illustration shows, that projected non-guaranteed annual amount, based on current assumptions was $24,379.

A second illustration (B), shown below, uses exactly the same assumptions, with the exception that a participating loan was used with a fixed interest rate charged on the amounts borrowed of 5.3 percent.

TP: $15,893			Surrenders or			
Age	Year	Premium Paid	Loans[2] Received or Repaid[3]	Accumulation Value	Net Cash Value	Net Death Benefit
51	1	$20,000	$0	$15,264	$0	$736,120
52	2	$20,000	$0	$31,564	$8,464	$736,120
53	3	$20,000	$0	$48,957	$27,506	$736,120
54	4	$20,000	$0	$67,511	$47,717	$736,120
55	5	$20,000	$0	$87,277	$69,131	$736,120
56	6	$20,000	$0	$108,569	$92,073	$736,120
57	7	$20,000	$0	$131,562	$116,714	$736,120
58	8	$20,000	$0	$156,436	$143,237	$736,120
59	9	$20,000	$0	$183,361	$171,811	$736,120
60	10	$20,000	$0	$212,501	$202,607	$736,120
		$200,000				
61	11	$0	$0	$226,780	$218,536	$736,120
62	12	$0	$0	$241,981	$235,385	$736,120
63	13	$0	$0	$258,157	$253,210	$736,120
64	14	$0	$0	$275,370	$272,072	$736,120
65	15	$0	$0	$293,700	$292,051	$736,120
66	16	$0	$0	$313,210	$313,210	$736,120
67	17	$0	$0	$333,985	$333,985	$736,120
68	18	$0	$0	$356,118	$356,118	$736,120
69	19	$0	$0	$379,715	$379,715	$736,120
70	20	$0	$30,063	$372,573	$372,573	$706,057

$30,063

Illustration B

This second illustration (B) shows that the amount of projected non-guaranteed retirement income generated when using the participating loan which would be $30,063 annually. That is an increase of almost $500 each month from the fixed loan option used in illustration A.

Again, the reason for the increase in retirement income when the participating loan is used is that the assumption is that all cash values, including any amount used as collateral for the loan, will be credited each year with 7.5 percent interest, and that the amount of interest charged on the cash value loans is limited to 5.3 percent. In this case the amount of the cash value used as collateral for the loan is assumed to still benefit from a net positive interest rate of 2.2 percent being credited to the cash value account.

By understanding this, it is easy to see why the retirement income provided by illustration A that uses the fixed loan is less. It assumes that only the amount of the cash value that is greater than the amount borrowed is being credited with the 7.5 percent interest. In illustration A, the amount borrowed is credited with a net of zero percent, and in illustration B, it is assumed that the amount used as collateral for the loan is credited with a net rate of 2.2 percent.

Again, the purpose of showing the difference in retirement income when each of the two loan options used is not to suggest that one option is better than the other, or that the assumptions used in the comparisons are more or less valid depending on the option used. Instead, it is simply to point out how the loan option used can impact the retirement income that is illustrated.

The participating loan can be used to optimize the distributions, as long as the interest credited is greater than the interest rate charged on the loan.

While discussing the use of loan provisions to optimize retirement income, it is important to know that when the participating loan option is to be used, there will be an additional opportunity to increase retirement income even more. This will be possible by deciding if the illustration will reflect the withdrawal of basis (total premiums paid) before starting loans.

Most illustration software will allow the preparer to determine if the distributions will be made by *loans only,* or by *withdrawing basis first* and then loans. The choice of *loans only* will generally result in a larger retirement income than will *withdrawing basis first,* when the loan option to be used is the participating loan.

Illustration B, shown above, used a participating loan in which basis was withdrawn first, and then loans began. Again, the projected non-guaranteed retirement income generated was $30,063 annually.

Age	Year	Premium Paid	Surrenders or Loans² Received or Repaid³	Accumulation Value	Net Cash Value	Net Death Benefit
51	1	$20,000	$0	$15,264	$0	$736,120
52	2	$20,000	$0	$31,564	$8,464	$736,120
53	3	$20,000	$0	$48,957	$27,506	$736,120
54	4	$20,000	$0	$67,511	$47,717	$736,120
55	5	$20,000	$0	$87,277	$69,131	$736,120
56	6	$20,000	$0	$108,569	$92,073	$736,120
57	7	$20,000	$0	$131,562	$116,714	$736,120
58	8	$20,000	$0	$156,436	$143,237	$736,120
59	9	$20,000	$0	$183,361	$171,811	$736,120
60	10	$20,000	$0	$212,501	$202,607	$736,120
		$200,000				
61	11	$0	$0	$226,780	$218,536	$736,120
62	12	$0	$0	$241,981	$235,385	$736,120
63	13	$0	$0	$258,157	$253,210	$736,120
64	14	$0	$0	$275,370	$272,072	$736,120
65	15	$0	$0	$293,700	$292,051	$736,120
66	16	$0	$0	$313,210	$313,210	$736,120
67	17	$0	$0	$333,985	$333,985	$736,120
68	18	$0	$0	$356,118	$356,118	$736,120
69	19	$0	$0	$379,715	$379,715	$736,120
70	20	$0	$36,772	$404,891	$366,170	$697,399

TP: $15,893

$36,772

Illustration C

Illustration C, shown above, uses exactly the same assumptions as illustration B, with the exception that C assumes that the distributions will be provided by loans only. This difference generates a projected non-guaranteed retirement income of $36,772 annually. This is more than another $500 of income each month than if the retirement income was provided by withdrawn basis before the loans started (when compared to illustration B).

The reason for the difference is that the withdrawal of basis is not a cash value loan. There is no interest charged when the basis in the policy is withdrawn, and there is no interest credited on the amount representing the basis that is withdrawn.

When a fixed "wash" loan is used to provide distributions, there will be little impact on the amount of retirement income, regardless of whether the basis is withdrawn first or the distributions are made up of only loans. The fixed "wash" loan credits a net of zero percent on loans. The effect of withdrawing basis is also a net of zero percent, meaning that once basis is withdrawn, it is no longer credited with interest, but there is also no interest charged on that portion.

When basis is withdrawn first, the result will continue to reflect that the amount withdrawn will *not be credited* interest, and will *not be charged* interest, resulting in a net of zero percent. However, if *loans only* are taken, the amount borrowed *could be credited* with a higher interest rate than the rate of interest charged on the loan. This is precisely what illustration C is reflecting. It is assumed that all of the money that has been distributed is in the form of loans, not basis, and because of this, all of the distributions are being credited with 7.5 percent interest each year while the interest rate charged on the total loan amount is 5.3 percent. In other words, the amount distributed is still being credited with a net positive interest rate of 2.2 percent.

If the difference is still unclear, it may help to think of it another way. Assume that a client is using a participating loan, and at the end of a certain number of years of taking distributions, the total amount that the client has received in the form of retirement income is $500,000. Further assume that the total amount that the client had paid into the policy was $100,000 (the basis). If basis had been withdrawn first, the total cash value loan would be $400,000 ($500,000 total distributions - $100,000 basis).

Now, assume that under the participating loan option, the $400,000 is credited with a gross amount of indexed interest of 7.5 percent in a given year, and that the loan interest charged was 5.3 percent. The result is that $400,000 would be credited with a net interest rate of 2.2 percent that year. Contrast this to the difference if *loans only* had been used. Assuming the same total amount of $500,000 of distributions, since the basis had not been withdrawn, the entire amount would be a loan. Under the same participating loan option, $500,000 is credited with 7.5 percent, and charged a loan rate of 5.3 percent. $500,000 would be credited with a net interest rate of 2.2 percent that year.

The difference between these two examples comes down to the impact of having an extra $100,000 credited with a net interest of 2.2 percent when *loans only* are used.

That is also the reason that the retirement income is greater in illustration C than it is in illustration B.

However, as stated earlier, there is also a potential risk when using the participating loan option. If the stock market performs poorly for an extended period of time while there is an outstanding cash value loan, the amount of interest credited could be less than the loan interest rate charged. This would mean that the accumulated cash value would be drained by an amount greater than the distributions taken for retirement income. In addition to those distributions, the accumulated cash value would also be reduced by the negative net interest that would need to be absorbed.

IULs have the potential to be tremendous wealth-accumulation vehicles for clients. But these policies must be designed properly so that they can perform to their full potential. A skillful and knowledgeable agent is the key to unlocking this potential.

Chapter 7

Roth IRAs and Conversions

With regards to the tax treatment of the resulting income, Roth IRAs
and cash value loans from life insurance contracts have the potential to
share two common attributes under current law. The first is that it is
possible to avoid income taxes on their distributions. The second is that
it is possible that distributions from neither will be included in the
provisional income calculations to determine the amount of Social
Security that is subject to taxation. These two attributes make both
Roth IRAs and properly-structured permanent life insurance contracts
extremely powerful tools for boosting spendable retirement income
when combined with the right Social Security claiming strategy.

In addition, both of these financial instruments offer significant
advantages when it comes to estate planning. The leveraged income
tax-free death benefit of life insurance can create a legacy where one
might not have otherwise existed. A beneficiary inheriting a Roth IRA

can choose to stretch distributions over his or her lifetime, potentially receiving decades of tax-free growth on the remaining balance.

In some regards, Roth IRAs and life insurance contracts could be used interchangeably when attempting to reduce the taxable income and Social Security taxation during retirement. But taxes aren't the only consideration when choosing a financial instrument.

There may be many situations in which a client could benefit by having both a Roth IRA and a life insurance contract. But there are at least five primary questions that should be considered when determining the degree to which one of these instruments might be more appropriate than the other:

1. Will the *source of money* available to fund the instrument be from non-qualified or qualified retirement plan accounts?
2. Does the owner need, and can he qualify for a *death benefit*?
3. Is the high-cap *crediting method* structure currently available with IULs attractive to the owner?
4. Does the owner want to avoid the *loads, fees and charges* of life insurance?
5. Is pre-retirement *access to accumulated funds* a consideration?

Source of Money

The source of money is an important consideration because, generally speaking, a life insurance contract cannot be held in a qualified retirement plan like an IRA or 401(k). This means that in order for an individual to use the money that is currently in her qualified accounts to purchase a life insurance contract, she must first take a distribution, pay the tax on that distribution and use the remainder to pay premiums. An additional problem with using these funds to purchase an IUL will be the 10 percent IRS penalty if the individual is under the age of 59½.

Compare this to the alternative of converting a traditional IRA to a Roth IRA. In this case, the resulting "conversion tax" would be identical to the tax on any distribution, assuming that the conversion amount in any given year was the same as the distribution. The problem that can be avoided by converting to a Roth IRA has to do with the 10 percent early withdrawal penalty. There is no IRS penalty imposed when converting to a Roth IRA, regardless of the individual's age (there could be a penalty if future distributions from the converted Roth IRA did not meet certain requirements). For this reason, it may be more advantageous for a client to convert to a Roth IRA than to take distributions for the purpose of paying life insurance premiums when the individual is under the age of 59½.

When other circumstances, such as a person's need for a life insurance death benefit, might influence the decision, and the client is close to age 59½, the advisor should keep in mind that the requirements imposed by TAMRA's 7-pay test are *cumulative*. This could allow a person to start a policy prior to age 59½, for example at age 57, pay *minimum* premiums from non-qualified funds for the first few policy years, and then pay larger "catch up" premiums after reaching age 59½, using penalty-free withdrawals from an IRA or other qualified retirement plan. The IRA withdrawals would still be treated as taxable income, but the client could avoid the 10 percent IRA penalty by delaying the withdrawals.

When the money available is from qualified funds, and reasons or preferences exist that favor converting to a Roth IRA, a portion of that resulting Roth IRA could be used to purchase an annuity when suitable. During the period prior to retirement, the annuity might be an attractive option for the "safe money" portion of a portfolio for clients wishing to follow the "*100-minus age*" rule as outlined in chapter eight, which is devoted to annuities. After retirement, when the client needs income he might choose to use the annuity's *lifetime income* option to obtain the mortality credits to boost a payout that would be guaranteed to last for as long as he is alive. Any income coming from an annuity inside the client's Roth IRA would be tax-free, and would not be included in the *provisional income calculations* to determine the portion of the client's Social Security income that would be subject to taxation.

If a person has investments that she expects will significantly appreciate, she should consider placing those within the Roth IRA account. If a client thinks she will hit a "home run" with a particular stock or investment, placing it in a Roth IRA will be a great way to avoid a significant tax liability.

Death Benefit

Because life insurance contracts generally cannot be owned inside IRAs and 401(k)s, if a client needs a death benefit, the only choice will be to provide for that need using after-tax dollars to pay the required premiums.

In addition to having a need for life insurance, the insured must also be able to qualify.

When the client has insurability issues, a survivorship form of permanent life insurance might be considered. When dealing with a married couple, as long as one spouse is insurable, there should be little, if any, problem in obtaining a last-to-die survivorship insurance policy.

When a client isn't married, or when both spouses have insurability issues, there may be a possibility that the client could purchase and own a policy that insures the life of another person. In order for this to be a viable option, it would require that the owner have an insurable interest on the life of the insured.

A more important point here is that when the advisor has developed a strategy that relies on using an IUL specifically for its potential tax advantages, and then discovers that the client does not qualify for that strategy, the advisor should consider Roth IRAs as an alternative that can provide many of those same tax advantages.

The Crediting Method Structure of IULs

Generally speaking, because a Roth IRA cannot own a life insurance contract, the only option for a client who values the high-cap crediting method structure currently available with IULs will be to purchase one with after-tax money.

IULs can provide an attractive opportunity for upside potential for growth, but with protection from loss due to declines in the stock market, which can be particularly appealing to those people who are more risk-averse. Given the similarity of the potential tax advantages of an IUL compared to those of a Roth IRA, the crediting method structure might give an advantage to IULs for some individuals. But when pointing out any attractive feature of an IUL, it is only fair to consider that there are also additional costs that are unique to life insurance.

The Loads, Fees and Charges of Life Insurance

IULs, as with all forms of life insurance, have loads, fees and charges that are different than what you will find with traditional investments inside of a Roth IRA. The degree to which those life insurance loads, fees and charges might be greater than the fees associated with non-insurance alternatives can vary depending on the product selected, and the skill of the advisor in structuring that product to reduce the related insurance costs.

One expense that you will not find in any investments or other financial instruments other than life insurance is the *cost of insurance* (COI) or mortality charges.

Because these charges will always exist in a life insurance contract, any client who does not need or value the life insurance death benefit *might* be better off using a Roth IRA when the objective is solely one of obtaining tax advantages. Conversely, the more an individual values the availability of a death benefit in addition to tax advantages, the more attractive permanent life insurance will appear with respect to its *cost of insurance.*

Pre-Retirement Access to Funds

A person generally makes contributions to a Roth IRA for the purpose of accumulating wealth that can be used for retirement. And many people also pay premiums into IULs and other permanent life insurance contracts to create cash values that can be used during retirement. While the initial motivation for both instruments might be to help fund a future retirement, many people inevitably find themselves in a position in which they also have a need for a large amount of money prior to retirement.

Whether money will be needed to fund a child's college education, pay for a daughter's wedding, finance some major purchase, take advantage of a business opportunity, or for some other purpose, being able to access savings prior to retirement can be of extreme importance.

When it might be important for the owner to be able to borrow against, or use the accumulated value in his retirement savings as collateral for a loan, a life insurance contract provides some clear advantages over a Roth IRA and other qualified retirement plans.

As in traditional IRAs, the owner cannot borrow from a Roth IRA, nor can the Roth IRA be pledged as collateral for a loan. The IRS classifies this as a "prohibited transaction," and it results in the loan being treated as a distribution.

Roth IRAs do have an advantage over traditional IRAs in that the owner can withdraw his or her total contributions at any time without tax or penalty. *(Note that the rules are different with regards to the amounts converted from a traditional IRA to a Roth IRA where taxes and penalties might be charged.)*

A problem even with the "favorable" treatment of withdrawals of contributions is that once this money is taken, there is a very limited opportunity to put it back into the Roth IRA. This means that when you take a withdrawal from a Roth IRA, you likely "kill" the ability for that money to ever again benefit from tax-favored growth.

One distinct advantage of life insurance cash values is that they can be used as collateral for a loan from the insurer, or possibly from a bank or other lender.
401(k)s provide opportunities to borrow funds prior to retirement, but the amount of the loan can be based on qualifying for hardship exceptions, and there are strict rules concerning the repayment of those loans.

The ability to borrow on a life insurance policy's cash value is relatively simple and far less restrictive.

If the money is borrowed from the insurer using a *fixed loan* or "wash loan," in which the interest rate charged on the loan equals the interest rate credited to the cash value, no growth can occur on the borrowed portion, as long as the loan is outstanding. In the future, the contract owner could repay that loan, and the entire amount can once again benefit from tax-advantaged growth.

If the policy is an indexed universal life contract, and the owner uses the *participating loan* option, then tax-advantaged growth on the borrowed portion can continue as long as the interest *credited* to the cash values is *greater* than the loan interest rate *charged*.

Regardless of the loan option used, life insurance may have the potential to provide greater access to money on a more favorable basis than does a Roth IRA, particularly for individuals under the age of 59½.

It's Not One or the Other

Again, the above comparisons are not presented in order to suggest that one of these financial instruments is superior to the other. In spite of important similarities in tax treatment, Roth IRAs and life insurance are very different. And like all financial instruments, they are merely tools that can be used to different degrees and in a variety of situations by knowledgeable advisors.

Many clients already have qualified money accumulated in their IRAs and 401(k)s. Many more plan to continue to set aside a portion of their future earnings to build their retirement nest egg. Depending on the individual's circumstances and needs, it could make a great deal of sense to use a portion of the accumulations in any non-qualified accounts and/or divert a portion of planned future contributions (to a qualified plan) and instead use this money to fund an IUL. In addition, consideration should be given to strategically converting a portion of any money in qualified accounts to a Roth IRA. The point is that there may be good reasons to use both IULs and Roth IRAs to meet planning objectives.

The balance of this chapter will deal primarily with Roth IRAs. The content is organized into two sections, one discussing Roth IRAs created from *contributions*, and one discussing Roth IRAs created by *conversions* from traditional IRAs. The reason for presenting the information in this manner is that the taxation of withdrawals coming from a Roth IRA can be very different, depending on whether the Roth IRA was created by *contributions* or a *conversion*.

Roth IRAs Created by Contributions

The potential problem that people invite when contributing to any tax-deferred retirement plan is that they shift the tax liability from *today* to *tomorrow*. This might, in fact, prove to be a wise choice, but only if today's tax rate is greater than tomorrow's tax rate. If this does not prove to be the case, and an individual's tax rates turn out to be higher in the future, then the traditional recommendation to "max out your 401(k)" could prove to be a costly mistake for many participants. By following along with the mainstream and deferring taxation, people potentially reduce the value of their mortgage deduction while they are young and still paying large amounts of mortgage interest. Then if they retire with a large 401(k), their tax rates could not only be higher, but more of their Social Security could be included as taxable income as well.

If an employee can get a matching contribution from his employer, then he should probably take it, even if it means he will be deferring taxes. Free money is hard to beat!

But many people should consider using excess contributions to either fund a Roth IRA, or to purchase a properly-structured life insurance contract. One factor that might exist favoring the use of life insurance is that generally speaking, there are no contribution limits like those that exist with Roth IRAs.

Roth IRA Contribution Limits

The annual contributions that a person can make to a Roth IRA depend on his or her filing status, earned income and age. In 2013, the maximums are:

> $5,500 for people under the age of 50
> $6,500 for those who are 50 and over

These limits apply to both Roth IRAs and traditional IRAs. This means that a person can choose to contribute to a Roth IRA, to a traditional IRA, or to both in any amounts as long as he or she does not exceed the contribution limit.

These maximum contribution limits are reduced or *phased out* if the person exceeds certain earned income limits.

If a person files her tax return as a single, head of household or married filing separately *(note that the rules are different for married filing separately if the spouses lived together part of the year)* she can contribute up to the maximum, as long as her earned income does not exceed $112,000. If her earned income is $127,000 or more, the contribution is completely phased out, and she can't contribute anything to a Roth IRA in 2013. For earned income amounts between $112,000 and $127,000, her contribute limit is reduced or *phased out* based on a formula.

For example, assume a single person, Anne, who is under the age of 50, with earned income of $120,000. To calculate the reduced contribution, you start by taking the amount that Anne's income exceeds the $112,000 earned-income limit. In Anne's case, that is $8,000 (her earned income of $120,000 - $112,000 = $8,000). Next, you divide that $8,000 by the amount of the phase out *range*. The phase-out *range* is the difference between the $127,000 upper limit and the $112,000 lower limit, which is $15,000.

So the calculation for Anne would be $8,000 / $15,000 = 53.33 percent.

This means that for 2013, the maximum contribution limit would be reduced by 53.33 percent for Anne (a $2,933 reduction). Her maximum Roth IRA contribution that year would be only $2,567 ($5,500 - $2,933).

If a person files her tax return as married filing jointly or a qualifying widow(er) she can contribute up to the maximum as long has her earned income does not exceed $178,000. If her earned income is $188,000 or more, she cannot contribute to a Roth IRA in 2013. For earned income amounts between $178,000 and $188,000, her contribute limit is *phased out* based on the same formula.

For example, assume a married couple, the Thompsons, who are both under the age of 50 with a combined earned income of $183,000. To calculate their reduced contribution, you start by taking the amount that the Thompsons' income exceeds the $178,000 earned income limit. In their case, that is $5,000 ($183,000 - $178,000 = $5,000). Next, you divide that $5,000 by the amount of the phase-out *range*. For married couples filing a joint tax return, the phase-out range is the difference between the $188,000 upper limit and the $178,000 lower limit, which is $10,000.

For the Thompsons, the calculation would be $5,000 / $10,000 = 50 percent.

This means that for 2013, the maximum contribution limit ($5,500) is reduced by 50 percent for this couple. Their maximum Roth IRA contribution that year would be only $2,750.

In both of the phase-out examples shown above, the assumption was that someone under the age of 50 would make the contributions. Generally speaking, the *phase-out* calculation for someone age 50 and older and eligible to make catch-up contributions will always be 20 percent greater. In other words, you would use the same formulas as in the above two examples to do an initial calculation, and then you would add an extra 20 percent on top of that amount.

There are two additional rules that apply to the phase-out calculations. First, as long as the phase-out rule allows *some* contribution to be made, a person is allowed to round the contribution amount up to $200. For example, if the phase-out rule shows zero contribution, then the person can't make a contribution in any amount. But if it results in a maximum contribution of $125, the person can round their contribution up to $200. Second, all amounts above $200 can be rounded up to the next $10 interval. For example, if the phase-out calculation results in a maximum contribution of $1,433, the person could round this up to a contribution of $1,440.

Keep in mind that these income limits are specifically for Roth IRAs; the rules are different if the person is contributing to a traditional IRA. There is a penalty referred to as an *excise tax* in the amount of six percent that is imposed on contributions made to a Roth IRA (or traditional IRA) in excess of the contribution limits.

Withdrawals from a Roth IRA Created Through Contributions

There are two components that make up the balance of any Roth IRA that was created exclusively by contributions, as opposed to one created by a conversion. Those components are:

> The *contributions*
> The *growth and earnings*

This distinction is helpful, because the tax treatment and the possible application of the 10 percent IRS penalty on withdrawals are different depending on the component.

To understand this tax treatment, it is important to understand that Roth IRAs receive FIFO (First In, First Out) treatment with regards to the order in which the IRS views the money coming out. The contributions made to the Roth IRA will always be the first money that the IRS recognizes as coming out anytime withdrawals are taken.

Because Roth IRA contributions have already been taxed, there will be no additional tax or the IRS 10 percent penalty when those contributions are withdrawn. This is true regardless of the owner's age at the time of withdrawal. Specifically, a person can take a withdrawal from a Roth IRA prior to age 59½, and as long as the total cumulative withdrawals are less than the total cumulative contributions at that point in time, there will not be a 10 percent IRS penalty.

This treatment is much different when any earnings or growth that has occurred in the Roth IRA are withdrawn. Any withdrawals over and above the contributions can be taxed and penalized if they are not taken correctly.

If the growth and earnings is withdrawn prior to age 59½, it will be taxed *and* the IRS 10 percent penalty will be imposed. As is the case with traditional IRAs, the IRS does not impose the 10 percent penalty on any withdrawals after the age of 59½.

Whether the growth and earnings will be taxed when withdrawn after age 59½ will depend on how much time has passed since the person made his or her first contribution to the Roth IRA. If at least five years have passed since the initial contribution, then the withdrawal will be free of income tax. However, if it has been less than five years, these withdrawals will be taxed, but as long as the person is over the age of 59½, no IRS penalty will apply.

Using an example makes this easier to understand. On January 1, 2008, Mary opens her Roth IRA account and deposits $2,000. This will be the start of the five-year period referred to above. To make this example easier to follow, we will assume that she makes no additional contributions. In 2010, the Roth IRA has grown by $1,000, so that its total balance is $3,000. That year, Mary turned age 58, and she withdraws $2,000. Because Roth IRAs receive FIFO treatment, this entire $2,000 is considered a withdrawal of her contributions. Because Roth IRA contributions are made with after-tax dollars, Mary can withdraw those contributions at any time without tax or the 10 percent IRS penalty. By the year 2012, Mary has had her Roth IRA for four years, she is now age 60, and the total balance of her Roth IRA is now $1,500 because of additional earnings. Since she previously withdrew all of her contributions, this entire $1,500 is the result of growth and earnings. Because it has not yet been at least five years since she made her first contribution, any withdrawals will be taxable, but there won't be any IRS penalty because Mary is over the age of 59½. If Mary waits one more year, she could withdraw the entire balance, and it will be tax-free because the Roth IRA will have met the *five-year* requirement. This is a relatively simple, non-technical explanation for what is a confusing set of rules that relate to withdrawals from Roth IRAs. A more technical version will be used to explain the treatment of withdrawals from Roth IRAs that were created through conversion.

Roth IRAs Created by Conversion

Assuming that all of the contributions that were made to a traditional IRA were with dollars that had not yet been taxed, understanding the tax consequences of converting to a Roth IRA is pretty straightforward. The owner simply takes the amount converted and includes it as taxable income in the year of conversion. *(The owner does not include the portion of any non-deductible contributions that may have been made to a traditional IRA prior to the conversion.)*

The question facing anyone who is considering whether it is better to keep his or her traditional IRA or convert it to a Roth IRA essentially comes down to whether it will be better to pay the taxes *now*, or to pay them *later*.

But before continuing, it is important to say that the best possible outcome would be to not pay them either now or later! It may be timely to mention this, because due to the economic downturn and the high unemployment rates that have plagued this country since 2008, many people may find themselves in a position in which their current taxable income is low or nonexistent because they are not able to find employment, or, for business owners, because of a lack of profits. Advisors should be on the lookout for people in this situation, because some of them could be prime candidates for converting to a Roth IRA. Under the right circumstances, the taxes they pay today to do a conversion may be relatively small or perhaps nonexistent. But as their financial position improves in the future, they will have an asset with unparalleled tax advantages.

This is not the only situation in which converting to a Roth IRA can make a great deal of sense. This is especially true for the many people who are concerned that their personal tax rates could be much higher in the future than they are today.

How to Calculate the Tax on a Roth Conversion

Some clients may have made non-deductible contributions to their traditional IRAs with after-tax dollars. These dollars don't get taxed again when they are converted to a Roth IRA.

If 100 percent of the contributions to the traditional IRA were made with deductible or before-tax dollars, then the entire amount of the traditional IRA will be taxed upon conversion.

When the traditional IRA contains a combination of deductible and non-deductible contributions, the traditional IRA balance at the time of conversion, minus the total non-deductible contributions, will be included as taxable income in the year of the conversion.

Unfortunately, clients can't cherry-pick and only convert the non-deductible portion, while leaving the deductible contributions in the traditional IRA. Here is an example of how the calculations are done:

1. Total value of all traditional IRAs	$100,000
2. Total nondeductible contributions	$ 10,000
3. Divide line 2 by line 1.	0.1
4. Subtract line 3 from 1.00	0.9
5. Total amount to be converted	$ 50,000
6. Multiply line 5 by line 4	$ 45,000
7. Multiply line 6 by your tax rate *(This example assumes 33%)*	$ 14,850

Withdrawals From a Roth IRA Created by Conversion

The rules that determine if and when distributions from a Roth IRA will be free of penalties and income taxes are very complex. To navigate them safely, there are a lot of things you must know, and a lot of potential minefields you must avoid.

Fortunately, other than for estate tax purposes, people will generally only convert when they expect that the money will remain in the Roth IRA for at least five years, and until they are at least age 59½. Under these circumstances, understanding how withdrawals will be treated becomes much simpler, because there are only four *primary* things to understand:

> #1 – If you're over the age of 59½, you *never* pay the *10 percent penalty* on the Roth IRA distribution.

> #2 – If you're over the age of 59½, and it's a **qualified** distribution, you *never* pay income *taxes* on the Roth IRA distribution.

> #3 – If you're over the age of 59½, and it's **not** a **qualified** distribution, you *pay* income *taxes.*

> #4 – Regardless of your age, if you have to pay taxes on the distribution, only the portion representing the earnings will be taxed (not the conversion amount or contributions). And earnings are the *last* money coming out of a Roth IRA, because of FIFO treatment.

With the above four points in mind, advisors are able to tell their clients:

> *"As long as you are over the age of 59½ when you take the withdrawal, there will be no IRS penalty, and the most*

that will be subject to income tax is the earnings or
growth that occurred since conversion."

Or, the advisor could say:

"As long as you are over the age of 59½ and you limit
your total withdrawals to no more than the original
amount of the conversion, there will be no IRS penalty and
no income tax."

This last statement is very significant if the person just wants to make
sure that she can quickly get her hands on a large portion of her Roth
IRA money in the event of some emergency.

For example, assume she converted a $100,000 traditional IRA to a
Roth IRA when she was age 58. She is now age 60, and she wants to
help a family member with college expenses. She can withdraw the
$100,000 representing her original conversion amount without any *IRS*
penalty, and without any additional income taxes.

Suppose that, due to earnings that had accumulated since the
conversion, she has a total of $110,000 when she reaches the age of 60.
In other words, at age 60, her Roth IRA account balance reflects her
original conversion amount of $100,000, plus $10,000 in earnings.
Could she withdraw the entire $110,000 balance? Yes, but while she
would not be required to pay the 10 percent IRS penalty, she would
have to pay income taxes on the $10,000 of earnings.

That she is able to withdraw the original conversion amount without
any additional income tax makes sense, because this money had
already been taxed at the time of the conversion.

For situations in which withdrawals will be taken soon after converting
to a Roth, and/or a person is under the age of 59½, the layers of

complexity increase significantly, and a much higher level of understanding is required.

The Five-Year Rule: Qualified vs. Nonqualified Withdrawals

There are two types of withdrawals a person can take from a Roth IRA. One is a *qualified* withdrawal, and the other is a *nonqualified* withdrawal. The words "qualified" and "nonqualified" used here mean something different than they usually do with regards to retirement plans. In the context of Roth IRA withdrawals, the terms "qualified" and "nonqualified" distributions refer to the tax treatment of the withdrawal.

There are never income taxes or penalties on *qualified* distributions. There are possible income taxes and penalties on *nonqualified* distributions.

Qualified Distributions

A withdrawal will be considered a qualified distribution as long as any one of the following is true. The client must:

- Be age 59½ or older, and have had the Roth IRA for at least *five years*
- Be dead, and have had the Roth IRA for at least *five years*
- Be totally and permanently disabled, and have had the Roth IRA for at least *five years*
- Qualify as a first time-home buyer, and have had the Roth IRA for at least *five years*

Regardless of when the Roth IRA was started, the five-year requirement is always considered completed on January 1st of the final year. This means that you could start your Roth IRA late in one year and satisfy the five-year requirement early (January 1st) in the final year. If you started your Roth IRA on December 31 of any year, it would only take a total of four years and one day to satisfy this five-year requirement.

If one of the four above conditions are not met, then the distribution is considered *nonqualified*, and will be subject to income taxes and/or penalties.

Nonqualified Distributions and Income Taxes

All nonqualified distributions are subject to income taxes, but whether they will be taxed depends on the amount of the distribution. No taxes will be charged on distributions, no matter when they are taken, until the client has recovered all of her *basis* in the account.

The client's basis in the account is the total of her contributions and/or the amount of the conversion. Again, this money can be withdrawn at any time with no additional income taxes paid.

Only the earnings portion of a nonqualified distribution is subject to income tax.

When a Roth IRA is created by conversion, the first money that goes into it is the amount of the total dollar amount of the conversion. And because of FIFO treatment, this is also the first money that the IRS considers as coming out of the Roth IRA any time a distribution is taken. Again, none of this money is subject to additional income tax, because it was already taxed at the time of the conversion.

Assume you have a client age 59½ who converts $250,000 of her traditional IRA to a Roth. The $250,000 is considered the *basis* of her conversion. After three years, the Roth IRA has grown to $280,000. If the owner takes a withdrawal at this time, as long as she limits her withdrawal to her $250,000 basis, she will have no additional income taxes to pay, even though this is a nonqualified distribution because less than five years have passed since the conversion. If instead, she had withdrawn the entire $280,000 balance, the additional $30,000 of earnings would be subject to income taxes. If, however, she waited so that five years had passed since the conversion, this $30,000 would not be subject to income taxes.

Nonqualified Distributions and Penalties

In addition to possible income tax, *nonqualified* distributions will be subject to a 10 percent penalty unless any *one* of the following exceptions is met. To avoid this penalty, the owner must:

- Be age 59½ or older
- Be dead
- Be totally and permanently disabled
- Qualify as a first time-home buyer
- Receive distributions that are substantially equal periodic payments
  Or
- Use the distribution to pay for qualifying medical or education expenses

The 10 percent penalty on *nonqualified* distributions will apply not only to the earnings portion of any distributions, but also to any portion that is attributed to any conversion amount. In other words, if a person who is under the age of 59½ needs to withdraw the funds in his traditional IRA, he *cannot* avoid the 10 percent penalty by first converting to a Roth IRA.

However, the 10 percent penalty is *not* charged on any *contributions* that are withdrawn. Under FIFO, treatment contributions are always the first money that comes out of a Roth IRA. Contributions are never subject to the 10 percent penalty or income taxes when distributed. A conversion is not considered a withdrawal or distribution, so it does not trigger the IRS 10 percent penalty, regardless of the person's age.

Paying the Conversion Tax

Much of the potential advantage of a Roth IRA conversion is lost if the owner takes a taxable distribution from the IRA to pay the conversion tax:

> Our research suggests that the best conversion candidates are those who can afford to pay the cost of conversion from their taxable assets and fit any one of the following criteria:
>
> ■ They don't expect a significant decline in their effective tax rate in retirement.
> ■ They are making the conversion at a younger age.
> ■ They don't expect to spend meaningfully (or at all) from their IRA or will begin drawing from it only much later in their retirement.
> ■ They intend to transfer their IRA at death to beneficiaries who will then "stretch" it.[64]

Note that though the authors of the above quote mention several criteria for who make *the best conversion candidates,* what applies to them all is that they are able to pay the resulting tax from taxable assets as opposed to from a distribution from their IRAs. To understand why, it is important to realize that mathematically, there is *no* difference between paying taxes now and getting tax-free distributions in the future, or deferring taxes to some future date, assuming that ***everything else is equal.***

---

[64] Boyle, Patrick, and Litman, Warren. "The Roth Conversion Question" *The CPA Journal* May 2010.

Roth IRAs and Conversions

	Traditional IRA	Roth IRA
Contribution	$ 100	$ 100
30% Taxes Due *Today*	0	-30
Amount Remaining in IRA After Tax	$ 100	$ 70
Account Doubles	$ 200	$ 140
30% Taxes Due *Future*	$ 60	0
Spendable	**$140**	**$ 140**

Because of this mathematical equality, many people mistakenly conclude that in order to benefit by converting to a Roth IRA, future tax rates *must* be higher than current rates. And while there is a clear benefit if tax rates climb in the future, converting to a Roth IRA can also prove beneficial without a tax rate increase. But to get this benefit, a person must pay the conversion tax with funds outside his or her IRA:

> If an individual is unable (or unwilling) to pay the taxes from his taxable portfolio, conversion is not as compelling an option, and it becomes less compelling the lower his expected tax rate is in retirement.[65]

By paying the taxes with funds outside the IRA, the owner is in effect *grossing up* the value of the IRA. To see the impact of this, consider the example of Bob, who has $1,000,000 in a traditional IRA. Because the taxes have been deferred on this money, it would be a mistake for Bob to count the entire $1,000,000 as an asset. Depending on Bob's tax rates at the time he withdraws this money, it might net him a total of only $650,000 of spendable income. The reason, of course, is that Uncle Sam will take his share of $350,000 (in this example). If Bob converts his traditional IRA to a Roth IRA, Uncle Sam would also

---

[65] Boyle, Patrick, and Litman, Warren. "The Roth Conversion Question" *The CPA Journal* May 2010.

demand to be paid his share, so Bob might very well have to pay a tax on the conversion in the same amount ($350,000). The key is that if Bob uses money outside of the IRA to pay this tax, he effectively *grosses up* the value of the IRA from $650,000 to $1,000,000. It's almost as if Bob made a $350,000 additional contribution to the Roth IRA. He transformed $350,000 that was outside of his Roth IRA into a tax-free investment:

> Notwithstanding these principles, a Roth IRA will often yield greater economic benefits than a traditional retirement plan for an individual whose tax rate does not decline after retirement. Specifically, if the front-end tax is paid from outside sources, the benefits derived from a Roth IRA are greater than the benefits of a traditional retirement plan.[66]

Other Tax Considerations

If a person's adjusted gross income (AGI) for tax purposes would have been $85,000, and she made a $50,000 conversion, her new AGI for income tax purposes would be $135,000. Not only will she need to pay the income taxes on this higher total, but the conversion could also affect her itemized deduction thresholds that year.

This is one of many reasons that clients should always seek the advice of their tax professional prior to converting to a Roth IRA. The tax code is full of "gotchas" that can turn what might otherwise seem to be a good tax move into a bad one.

With Roth IRAs and permanent life insurance contracts, advisors have two powerful tools that can be combined with Social Security claiming strategies for structuring large amounts of retirement income that have

---

[66] Kwall, Jeffrey L. "The Value of Tax Deferral: A Different Perspective on Roth IRAs" *FPA Journal* 1998.

the potential to be extremely tax efficient. The choice of whether to use only one or both of these tools will depend entirely on the client's individual circumstances and objectives.

The advisor who understands both Roth IRAs and life insurance contracts is in a much better position to craft tax-favored strategies that simply can't be matched by those who lack this knowledge.

Find tools, articles, webinars, live training, case studies and more resources devoted to *the Synergy Effect*™ at ***Doug-Warren.com***

Chapter 8

Deferred Annuities
Reducing Portfolio Risk

There are a great number of baby boomers who face the challenge of trying to balance market risk, longevity risk and the many other risks that can interfere with the objective of positioning assets so that they will provide a stable and adequate retirement income for many years. For many, the much-maligned annuity contract may prove to be essential in order to have any chance at success.

After criticizing annuities for decades, financial commentators are starting to wake up to their unique power. Today, the media is starting to replace condemnation with actually encouraging people to consider annuities as a key part of their retirement plans.

In June of 2011, I was in an airport looking for reading material for a flight I was about to board. I was more than surprised to see a headline in Barron's magazine: "Best Annuities, Special Report – Retirement: With their steady income payments, annuities are suddenly hot."

Since there have been so many articles appearing in financial publications and newspapers in past years that practically accused any advisor recommending an annuity as being a cheat, crook or charlatan, imagine my surprise as I read the third paragraph of this article:

> Now, as baby boomers approach retirement with fresh memories of big market losses, many sharp financial advisors are recommending an annuity as an important part of an income plan.[67]

Now instead of being called con artists, annuity salespeople were suddenly elevated to "sharp financial advisors."

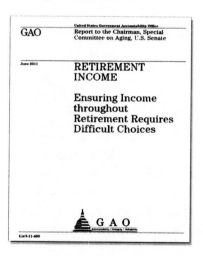

That same month, the US Government Accountability Office issued a report on the topic of meeting future retirement income needs. This report mentioned many challenges facing retirees, and it made two

---

[67] Hube, Karen. "Best Annuities: Special Report – Retirement: With their steady income payments, annuities are suddenly hot." *Barron's* 20 June 2011. < http://online.barrons.com/article/SB50001424053111904472004576392401608 661120.html#articleTabs_article%3D1>

recommendations as to the best way of meeting these challenges. One was that seniors should delay the start date of receiving their Social Security benefits, and the other was that "seniors should use a portion of their savings to purchase a lifetime income annuity to cover necessary expenses:"

> Experts we interviewed tended to recommend that retirees draw down their savings strategically and systematically and that they convert a portion of their savings into an income annuity to cover necessary expenses or opt for the annuity provided by an employer-sponsored DB pension, rather than take a lump sum. The experts also frequently recommended that retirees delay receipt of Social Security benefits until they reach at least full retirement age.[68]

Why is it that annuities are suddenly recognized as a superior solution to retirement income planning? The answer is that there are two strengths of annuities that have been largely misunderstood or underappreciated by consumers and the financial commentators who for years favored maligning annuities as high-cost gimmicks.

The first strength relates specifically to fixed indexed deferred annuities and the potential they provide for delivering returns that are greater than what might be provided by other safe-money alternatives. The second and perhaps most important of all is a unique feature exclusive to lifetime income annuities that is referred to as "mortality credits."

If you are a financial advisor and you do not thoroughly understand mortality credits, you will be crippled when it comes to your ability to help your clients. No other product, investment or savings vehicle besides annuities has the ability to provide your clients with mortality credits, and it is because of them that annuities beat every other option available for providing retirement income.

---

[68] "Ensuring Income throughout Retirement Requires Difficult Choices" *US Government Accountability Office Report GAO-11-400* June 2011. <http://www.gao.gov/new.items/d11400.pdf>

Deferred fixed rate annuities can be a great safe-money alternative accumulation vehicle for the conservative portion of a client's portfolio. *Lifetime income annuities* are an unbeatable tool for meeting the client's lifetime income needs.

This chapter will focus on deferred fixed indexed annuities and the following chapter will focus on income annuities.

It is important for the reader to understand that in this first part, we are specifically addressing the potential growth of a fixed indexed annuity's cash value accumulations, and not the guaranteed lifetime withdrawal benefit (GLWB) and the potential for growth within what is commonly referred to as the income account.

There is a great deal of misunderstanding surrounding annuities in general, and fixed indexed annuities in particular. Much of it is centered on what these products were designed to do and how they are intended to be used.

Fixed indexed annuities were never intended to compete with index investing or be a replacement for the portion of the client's portfolio that should be invested in equities. Instead, fixed indexed annuities are designed to compete with other safe-money products and accounts such as certificates of deposit, T-Bills, and — to a certain degree — low-to-moderate risk bonds.

In the world of retirement planning, there are many investment strategies and methods: modern portfolio theory, buy and hold, passive investing, market timing, dollar cost averaging, and asset allocation, to name only a few. This can be a rather intimidating array of concepts for the average client to deal with. However, there is one concept that is simple to understand, and highlights where annuities fit when it comes to dealing with risk. This concept is a popular rule of thumb known as the "100-minus age" rule.

Deferred Annuities

This rule dictates that the percentage of a person's retirement fund (assets in general) that is invested in equities should always equal 100 minus the person's age. For example, a person who is age 55 should limit his percentage of stock market investments to 45 percent of the total. At age 65, the portion invested in the stock market should be reduced to 35 percent of the total. And at age 75, there should be no more than 25 percent invested in stocks.

The concept behind the "100-minus age " rule can be seen applied to the recently-popular so-called "life-cycle funds" that mutual fund companies are currently promoting. It can also be seen in the relatively new "L Fund" plan that is now being offered as an option for federal employees in their version of the 401(k) plan, known as the Thrift Savings Plan. Both this government employee option and the life-cycle funds automatically reduce the participants' exposure to the risks of the stock market as they grow older.

No financial strategy is perfect, and there are many who criticize this life-cycle investing approach, but generally speaking, the concept of reducing risk as a person ages has proven to be popular among investors.

Agents who recommend using fixed indexed annuities as a replacement for stocks and other risk vehicles are incorrectly positioning that product in the wrong "slice" of the client's total "pie" of retirement assets.

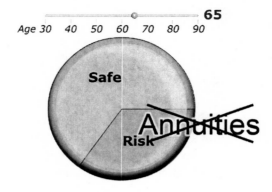

In addition to stocks, the investments that are traditionally viewed as appropriate for this risk portion of the pie are things like equity mutual funds, real estate, precious metals, and variable annuities.

In comparison to these risk-type investments, fixed indexed annuities simply are not designed in a way that provides the potential of matching the returns of these other investments over an extended period of time. Certainly, there may be periods when fixed annuities provide superior returns, but in the long run, it is more reasonable to assume that they will not.

Most clients will desire (and many will even desperately need) higher returns than what we can anticipate indexed annuities will provide in order to have a chance of dealing with inflation and many of the other challenges of retirement.

Where fixed indexed annuities become more appropriate is when they are allocated to the *safe-money* portion of the client's total "pie" of assets. Some of the financial instruments that logically belong in this section of the pie are things like certificates of deposit, T-Bills, money market funds, U.S. Government notes and bonds.

In addition, many advocates of the "100-minus age" rule would argue that corporate bonds and fixed income investments should also be included. The traditional view is that the reason for including them in this portion of the pie is in part due to the theory that during periods when stocks and equities perform poorly, bonds and fixed income investments would perform well. And conversely, when equities perform well, fixed income investments would perform poorly. This assumption was challenged during the economic collapse of 2008 and 2009, which saw the prices of the stock market and the bond market both fall dramatically and in unison.

The possibility that this could happen again might be too great of a concern for the risk-averse client, who might feel more comfortable moving corporate bonds from the safe-money portion to the risk portion of the pie.

The features and benefits of fixed indexed annuities can make them a great choice for the safe-money or "fixed" portion of the pie. One reason for this is that they can play a critical role in reducing the entire pie's exposure to market risk as well.

The following examples assume that the client wished to use the "100-minus age" rule to guide her in how to choose products and investments for her retirement portfolio. Each example also assumes that the individual is attempting to average an overall annual growth rate on the entire portfolio of six percent. For these examples, we will ignore the impact of taxes.

The first example is intended to highlight the problems created when the fixed indexed annuity is incorrectly positioning in the *equity* portion of the pie. For our example, we will use Mary, who is age 60 and has an investment portfolio of $500,000. By her own definition, Mary is very uncomfortable with and averse to the risks of the stock market. Based on her age, if she were to follow the "100-minus age" rule, she would allocate 60 percent of her portfolio to safe-money instrument, and only 40 percent to equities. She is comfortable placing $300,000 (60 percent) of her portfolio in CDs and T-Bills, but has a problem when it comes to risking any portion of her remaining money.

Aware of her attitude about market risk, Mary's financial advisor tells her that she can eliminated the "downside" risk of market losses to principal and still participate in the market's "upside" potential with a fixed indexed annuity. He advises using the 40 percent that the "100-minus age" rule calls for being allocated to equities to instead purchase an indexed annuity. This seems like the perfect solution to Mary, so she purchase the annuity with this $200,000 instead of investing it directly in to the stock market.

Unfortunately, instead of reducing risk, using the annuity in this manner could expose Mary to even greater market risk.

Remember that the goal is to average an overall return on the entire $500,000 portfolio of six percent. In dollar amounts, this means the total returns from the entire portfolio must average $30,000 per year. If in any year Mary's fixed indexed annuity caps the maximum gain that could be credited to the cash value at anything less than the six percent target, one of more of the other investments must earn more than six percent if this target overall return is to be achieved.

For example, assume that the FIA's annual return was capped at five percent. The most that could possibly be credited that year would be $10,000 ($200,000 X 5% = $10,000). In order for Mary to meet the six percent growth target for the entire $500,000 portfolio, the remaining $300,000 portion must grow by an additional $20,000. To do this, the return on the $300,000 must be a minimum of 6.67 percent ($300,000 X 6.67% = $20,000).

In the low interest rate environment that has existed in recent decades, it would be difficult — if not impossible — for Mary to accomplish this with the CDs and T-Bills that she wanted to use for the safe-money portion of the pie.

Consider the challenge if her CDs and T-Bills only grew at a rate of two percent. Over the course of a year, the $300,000 allocated to these instruments would generate only $6,000 in earnings. To hit the six percent growth target for the entire portfolio, Mary's fixed indexed annuity would need to earn $24,000 that year. That represents a required growth rate of 12 percent from the FIA ($200,000 X 12 percent = $24,000). This is not possible as long as the FIA's annual return is capped at anything under 12 percent (assuming an annual point-to-point crediting method). The cap rates provided by these products in recent years have been far below this level, and there is little reason to expect that that cap rates will increase this dramatically anytime soon.

Unless Mary is willing to reduce the overall target return to something less that six percent, she must attempt to increase the growth rates of the $300,000 that she allocated to the safe-money portion of the pie. The only way she could accomplish this would be to attempt to replace the CDs and T-Bills with some other vehicle that has the potential for higher returns. The problem is that if she does this with corporate bonds or most other investments, she is exposing her portfolio to a higher degree of risk, which is exactly what Mary was trying to avoid when she purchased her annuity.

Another choice Mary has is to keep her combination of CDs, T-Bills and annuity and simply accept a much lower growth rate than the six percent target. While this option may protect her nest egg from market risk, at the same time it subjects it to increased levels of the inflation risk. In the long run, inflation can prove to be just as devastating — if not more so — than losing money in the stock market.

Inflation Risk

A far better choice begins with the understanding that the fixed indexed annuity did not belong in the equity portion of the pie in the first place. It should only be considered appropriate when it is positioned in the fixed portion of the portfolio as a possible higher-earning replacement for the CDs, T-Bills and other safe-money vehicles.

Consider how things would change if the fixed indexed annuity is allocated this way. For the purpose of the following example, we will assume that the entire $300,000 fixed portion of the portfolio was used to purchase the fixed indexed annuity. That may not necessarily be appropriate or a good recommendation in Mary's situation, but it makes this example easier to follow.

If the average annual growth rate of the annuity is five percent, the earnings on the safe-money portion of the portfolio would instead be $15,000. This would mean that the portion allocated to equities would need to generate an additional $15,000 in order to meet the portfolio's overall six percent target ($15,000 + $15,000 = $30,000, which is 6% of $500,000). To do this, the $200,000 allocated to the equity portion of the pie would need to grow at the rate of 7.5 percent ($200,000 X 7.5 percent = $15,000).

$300,000
Annuity
If it earns
4.00%

60%
Safe

40%
Risk

$200,000
Must earn **9%**
to hit target

If the average annual growth rate of the fixed indexed annuity were a lower four percent, the earnings on the $300,000 would equal $12,000, which would mean that the $200,000 in equities would need to grow at the rate of nine percent to equal $18,000. In that case, the total combined earnings of the portfolio would be $30,000, which again equals the six percent target.

No one knows what returns will be possible with the stock market in the future, but 7.5 percent to nine percent might be considered reasonable based on past performance.

As these examples show, by positioning FIAs in the correct safe-money portion of the "pie," it may be possible to boost the total returns on the entire portfolio, and at the same time reduce the overall exposure to the risk of market volatility.

Of course, the four percent and five percent rates assumed for the fixed indexed annuities in these examples are entirely hypothetical. In the future, they may be higher or lower. If they are lower, this will place greater pressure on the equities portion of the pie to generate greater returns. That pressure will reduce if the future returns of annuities are higher.

The point is not the returns of FIAs versus the returns of equities, because they appropriately reside in different portions of the overall pie. Instead, the point is the returns of FIAs versus the returns of other safe-money investments that reside in the same safe-money portion of the pie. The more FIAs can boost the returns of the safe-money portion of the pie, the lower the risk that the individual might have to take with the investments in the equity portion of the pie.

A 2009 study of fixed index annuity returns indicated that: "From 1997 through 2007, the five-year annualized returns for FIA's averaged 5.79%."[69]

However, as the authors pointed out, there were several limitations regarding the data that they used to reach this 5.79 percent historical rate. Primarily, the data used came from only those insurance companies who wished to participate. The results might have been different had all companies participated. In addition, much has changed since this study was published. The stock market suffered a severe downturn in 2008-2009. Additionally, the cap rates of many fixed indexed annuities have fallen. These and other factors might indicate that future fixed indexed annuity rates could be lower.

What may be more significant than the future rates of return provided by FIAs is that historically, they have often exceeded the returns provided by certificates of deposit, T-Bills and other safe-money vehicles. If this continues to be true in the future, then annuities will continue to be a valid choice as safe-money instruments.

This may prove to be especially true with regards to any portion of the client's portfolio that is subject to current taxes. A 2008 study measuring the tax benefit of deferred annuities stated:

> If tax rates and interest rates both rise, the tax benefit of annuities will increase beyond its current levels.

The authors of this study concluded:

> The tax benefit can result in an annual yield spread of two percent or more, depending on how long the annuity is

---

[69] Babbel, David, Marrion, Jack, and VanderPal, Geoffrey. "Real World Index Annuity Returns" *Wharton Financial Institutions Center of Personal Finance* 5 October 2009.

held, how high the yields are, and whether annuitization occurs as one reaches the end of his or her accumulation period.[70]

The principle behind the popular rule of thumb known as the "100-minus age" rule is consistent with the actual portfolio choices that many individuals make.[71]

The protection fixed indexed annuities offer against market losses, along with their higher earnings potential when compared to other safe-money or lower risk instruments, can make them an appropriate addition to a client's retirement nest egg when properly positioned.

Find tools, articles, webinars, live training,
case studies and more resources devoted
to *the Synergy Effect*™
at ***Doug-Warren.com***

---

[70] Babbel, David F., and Reddy, Ravi. "Measuring the Tax Benefit of a Tax-Deferred Annuity" *Wharton Financial Institutions Center Policy Brief: Personal Finance* 4 October 2008.
<http://fic.wharton.upenn.edu/fic/Policy%20page/AnnuityTaxation1.pdf>
[71] Kintzel, Dale. "Portfolio Theory, Life Cycle Investing, and Retirement Income" *Social Security Administration, Policy Brief No. 2007-02* October 2007.

Chapter 9

Income Annuities
Reducing Longevity Risk and Other Risk

While deferred indexed annuities can be a great choice for the conservative portion of a client's portfolio, they are simply unbeatable when clients need income. This superiority is due the unique feature of lifetime income annuities known as mortality credits.

Just as Jack was able to use magical beans to grow a beanstalk much higher than an ordinary beanstalk, mortality credits will allow your client's retirement income to grow to levels that no other investment or account can come close to achieving. Fortunately, the power of mortality credits doesn't come from magic; it comes from math.

"It's better than beans, Jack.
It's mortality credits from income annuities."

The highest rate being offered on June 16, 2012 at the website www.bankrate.com on a one-year CD was 1.1 percent. Assuming such low rates, this CD would generate earnings of about $90 per month for a person with $100,000 to deposit.

Compare this with annuity payout rates. On the same day (June 16, 2012) there were several top-rated insurance companies that would provide a guaranteed single life income of about $550 per month for a male age 65 with this same $100,000 deposit. This income represents an annual payout rate of 6.6 percent. For a male age 75, many companies offered monthly income payments of about $760, representing an annual payout rate of 9.12 percent. And for a male age 85, there were several annuities available providing monthly income payments of about $1,220, a 14.64 percent annual payout rate.

Assume that we had three different clients, aged 65, 75 and 85, who went to the bank with $100,000 to purchase a CD with a one-year term. Do banks offer different CD interest rates based on the customer's age? In other words, would the bank give the 85-year-old a higher rate than it would give the customer who was age 75? Or, would the bank offer the 65-year-old a lower rate than they would give the customer who was 75? Of course not: the CD rates are the same regardless of the client's age.

What about treasury bills or money market funds? Are the rates different depending on the customer's age? No again. The rates offered are all the same.

What about stocks and bonds? Do they provide greater interest or dividends based on your client's age? No!

These may seem like silly questions, until you consider lifetime income annuities. With these annuities, the payout rate is directly tied to the customer's age. And at the older ages, the payout rate is significantly higher.

It is important to know that the reason for these different rates is mortality credits. Advisors who understand mortality credits have a powerful planning tool that many people — including many financial professionals — are not aware of.

A banker, stockbroker, bond salesman, or any other promoter of financial products cannot provide your client with mortality credits, because annuities are the only vehicle that has them. And this makes annuities the most powerful income-generating tool available to the advisor for helping clients deal with many of the challenges that they will face in the future.

The best way to understand mortality credits is to use an example:

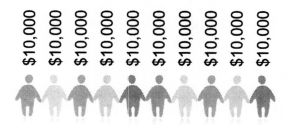

Assume there are 10 people age 65 who each have $10,000 to invest. They pool their money, and purchase a bank CD with a one-year term, paying two percent interest. At maturity, there will be a total of $102,000 in the pool.

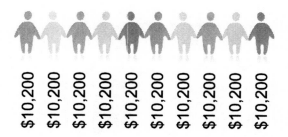

If divided equally, each of the ten would receive $10,200.

Now let's assume that one member of this group died before the distribution, and the members had previously agreed that only the surviving members would share in the pool.

MORTALITY CREDIT = $1,133

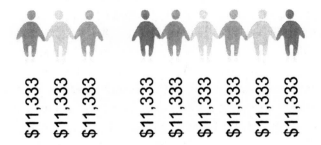

$11,333 $11,333 $11,333 $11,333 $11,333 $11,333 $11,333 $11,333 $11,333

The $102,000 now divided among the nine survivors would provide each with total of $11,333. This means that instead of a two percent return, each survivor received a payout rate of more than 13 percent. The difference between the two percent and 13 percent is the mortality credit.

What if the members of this group were older? It would be reasonable to expect that the amount of the mortality credit could be much greater. If each member was 85, the odds would increase that more members of the group might die prior to distributing the funds. If the $102,000 pool had been divided among only seven survivors, each would receive $14,571. That represents a return of more than 45 percent. This return is composed of two percent from interest earnings, plus an additional 43 percent mortality credit.

These examples are exaggerated. Statistically, you would not expect to have three out of ten 85-year-olds die before they reach age 86. But these examples are useful in illustrating why the payout rate of a lifetime income annuity varies based on age.

Jeffrey R. Brown, assistant professor of finance at the University of Illinois, offers another explanation of mortality credits. While Professor Brown calls them a "mortality premium," what he is referring to are the same mortality credits referenced in this chapter:

The extra rate of return that a life annuity can pay is sometimes called a "mortality premium" because it is essentially an extra rate of return that annuitants can earn in return for giving up their claim on their assets at death. To illustrate this concept in a simple, hypothetical example, suppose that at the beginning of the year 100 people each invest $1 in bonds earning 5 percent interest, and that 95 of them are still alive at the end of the year. Each of the 95 survivors would have $1.05 to consume, while the five decedents would leave $1.05 to each of their estates. If instead, each of these 100 individuals had pooled his or her money through an annuity contract, each of the 95 survivors would receive $105/95 = $1.10 to consume. Thus, the annuity contract provides an extra 5 percent rate of return – the mortality premium – in exchange for reducing the resources available for a bequest.[72]

What is interesting to consider is that life insurance companies know *exactly* how much of a mortality credit to include in the payout rate of their lifetime income annuities. They can calculate the payout rate to the penny, because they can predict with a great deal of accuracy the average age at which a large group of people will die.

Of course, they have no way of knowing how long you or I or any other individual will live, but it is possible to accurately predict how long a group of people will live, when those people share the same age, gender and approximately the same health.

---

[72] Brown, Jeffrey R. "The New Retirement Challenge" *Americans for Secure Retirement* September 2004.

If there are 100,000 relatively healthy men in a great big room who are all the same age, an insurance company might confidentially predict that five of them will die within the next 12 months. It just doesn't know which five it will be.

Because of the accuracy of this prediction, the insurance company is able to include mortality credits in the payout of their lifetime income annuities. And because of mortality credits, our clients can be *guaranteed* a payout rate that is significantly higher than what any other investment or product can provide, because no other financial vehicles have mortality credits.

I know that many readers are likely thinking: "Mortality credits are great, but only if the client lives long enough to collect them." The point is valid, because in their purest form, lifetime income annuities require that a person give up control of his or her principal, and this money is lost at the person's death.

Before going further, it may be important to consider that lifetime income annuities offer many options that provide protection against losing money if a person dies earlier than might be expected. A joint life annuity protects a spouse by providing the continuation of a payout for the lifetime of both the annuitant and the surviving spouse. Lifetime income annuities with 10, 20 or even 30 years of *certain* payments are another choice. And as most advisors are aware, these annuities provide

211

for the continuation of the payout for the certain period even if annuitant has died.

Some insurance companies offer *cash refund* annuities in which at the death of the annuitant (or the annuitant and spouse in the case of a joint life annuity) a lump sum is paid to the beneficiary in an amount that equals the initial premium paid, minus the total of all of the payouts received prior to death.

While there are many options available that effectively limit the potential losses the owner's estate might have from an early death, it is important to recognize that the use of any of these options will reduce the amount of mortality credits that a client will receive.

The older the client and the less money guaranteed to be paid out after death, the greater the mortality credits and the higher the income received from the lifetime income annuity.

It is precisely due to the power of mortality credits that lifetime income annuities might be the perfect vehicle for hedging against longevity risk. The longer a person lives, the greater the risk that she will exhaust her assets. But with the right annuity, the longer the annuitant lives, the more mortality credits she will collect.

Collecting these mortality credits does not require finding accounts with higher interest rates, picking the right stocks or finding a better investment advisor.

*"I can't put my finger on it, but
something doesn't seem right."*

For the rest of your client's life, the only thing she must do to collect mortality credits is to live. Contrast this with the only certain way to escape longevity risk when a person does not use a lifetime income annuity: she must die before she exhausts her assets.

The Illusion of Control

A major criticism of lifetime income annuities is the loss of control of a person's money. While it is certainly something that warrants consideration, control is somewhat of an illusion for the vast majority of people with limited assets available to adequately meet their future retirement income needs.

Consider a person with a retirement nest egg of one million dollars. Many people would view this as a great deal of money, but with regards to using it to fund the potentially large number of years that a person might be retired, it really is not a lot.

If this person told her broker, accountant or other financial advisor that she was considering using her money to purchase a lifetime income annuity, the criticism we might expect her to hear would likely center around the issue of loss of control of the $1 million.

In the name of retaining control, she might be advised to instead use an asset allocation strategy in which her money is divided between stocks and bonds. The theory is that such an allocation would allow her to withdraw some portion like 4.5 percent with a minimum risk that she would ever run out of money. Those advocating this approach would likely say that its advantage is that it not only provides the income she will need, but that it will also allow her to retain complete *control* of her $1 million nest egg.

But is this control real, or is it an illusion? If she needs every penny of the $45,000 that the 4.5 percent withdrawal will generate to pay her bills, then she can't touch any of the principal. If she spends an extra $50,000, or even an extra $500 of her principal, her future income will reduce, assuming she sticks to the 4.5 percent withdrawal rate.

However, assuming she was age 70, she would only need to use about $650,000 of the $1 million nest egg to purchase a lifetime income annuity that would guarantee her the same $45,000 of annual income. You could say that using the $650,000 to purchase the annuity would actually increase the amount of control she would have regarding how she might use the remaining $350,000.

She could use some of the money to help her grandchildren with college expenses, or to support her favorite charity, or for anything that is important to her.

If she is worried about the potential loss of the future purchasing power of her income due to inflation, she might want to invest a portion of these funds in the stock market or some other investment that provides the potential for greater returns.

She might feel more comfortable exposing a portion of her nest egg to the volatility of the stock market, knowing that regardless of what happens, her annuity will always provide a base amount of income that she can count on.

Many risk-averse people often make the mistake of investing too conservatively in an attempt to avoid the risk of losing money. While a 70-year-old widow with $1 million might see the logic of following the

"100-minus age" rule that would have her allocate 30 percent of her nest egg to equities, in practice, she might feel compelled to try to protect 100 percent of her money from market risk.

In today's low interest rate environment, it is difficult, if not impossible, to sustain a withdrawal rate of 4.5 percent without accepting some level of market risk. If the total return on the portfolio is less than 4.5 percent, she will be left with the quandary of either withdrawing less money than what she might need to sustain an adequate retirement lifestyle, or starting to consume part of the principal to meet her income needs.

Assume that in order to reduce market risk, she selects only safe-money vehicles that only generate a total return of three percent, as opposed to a lifetime income annuity. Her annual income, without using principal, would amount to only $30,000. Considering this shortfall in income, it is a good time to ask again if by avoiding the annuity, she truly retains control of her principal.

While it is true that she may have the ability to cash out any or all of those investments and use the proceeds in any way she might choose, control is somewhat of an illusion, if the entire $1 million is required to generate the income that she desperately needs. If she uses any portion of this principal to take a cruise, put a new roof on her house, pay medical bills or make up for a shortfall in income, then she has less principal to generate future income. If this reduction leads to additional shortfalls in future income, then she might need to withdraw even more principal to meet her income needs.

Most people understand that once they get on that "slippery slope" of consuming principal, it may never stop until they have exhausted it all and are broke. For this reason, many retirees become more and more frugal as they age, and as a result enjoy their retirement years less and less.

Now, consider that she could easily duplicate the $30,000 of income and enjoy all of the associated guarantees by devoting less than

$430,000 to the purchase of a lifetime income annuity. And by doing so, the annuity actually gives her greater control over the remaining $570,000. She sacrifices control of the smaller portion to gain control of the larger portion because she is now *guaranteed* to receive at least $30,000 for the rest of her life. All she needs is to find an insurance company that offers a lifetime income annuity with a payout rate of a little less than seven percent. At age 70, there are plenty available.

If she was age 80 when she made the purchase, she could easily use the $430,000 to purchase a lifetime income annuity with a payout rate of 9.76 percent, providing a guaranteed lifetime income of $42,000 per year. True, she must sacrifice control over the $430,000 used to purchase the annuity, but again, how much control does she really have over her entire $1 million if she attempts to generate the same income without using the annuity?

Let's examine this by using a comparison of hypothetical twin sisters whom we will call Betty and Barbara. Both are age 80 with identical $1 million nest eggs. Because both sisters insist on living extravagant lifestyles, they refuse to follow any advice that would limit their spending to a measly four or five percent of their portfolios. In their minds, they simply can't live on less than $100,000 per year.

Admittedly, this might be somewhat of an unrealistic example, but it is a simple way to make a valid point that can be applied to many circumstances.

To fund their extravagant lifestyles, they each invested in the stock market, but in different amounts. Betty placed her entire $1 million in stocks, believing that the market would give her the best opportunity to generate the $100,000 she needed annually.

Barbara took a different approach. She decided to split her nest egg between a lifetime income annuity and the stock market. $430,000 was used to purchase an annuity that provided a guaranteed payout of $43,000. (I did a search at the time of this writing and quickly found three annuities all with an A+ rating that offered even higher payout rates.) The remaining $570,000 was used to invest in the same stocks as her sister purchased.

Of course, no one can predict the future performance of the stock market, so it is impossible to know how Betty and Barbara will do with their strategies going forward. We can, however, get an idea of what might have happened had they used these strategies in the past. To give Betty's all-stock portfolio the best chance of doing well, we will assume that the stocks were purchased in 1970. From this date to 1999 was one of the best bull markets for stocks that any person alive today has ever lived through. Since both Betty and Barbara decided to use stocks for all, or in Barbara's case, a portion of their retirement income strategies, it is of particular interest to pick a period that we might assume is favorable to stocks.

The rate of increase in price of the S&P 500 Stock Index over this period is shown below.

1970	3.93%
1971	14.56%
1972	18.90%
1973	*-14.77%*
1974	*-26.39%*
1975	37.16%
1976	23.57%
1977	*-7.42%*
1978	6.38%
1979	18.20%
1980	32.27%
1981	*-5.01%*
1982	21.44%
1983	22.38%
1984	6.10%
1985	31.57%
1986	**18.56%**
1987	**5.10%**

1988	**16.61%**
1989	**31.69%**
1990	***-3.10%***
1991	**30.47%**
1992	**7.62%**
1993	**10.08%**
1994	**1.32%**
1995	**37.58%**
1996	**22.96%**
1997	**33.36%**
1998	**28.58%**
1999	**21.04%**

The actual stock market yield over this period of time as measured by the S&P 500 was 13.66 percent.

Again, both Betty and Barbara have an objective to withdraw $100,000 annually. Because the average annual yield during this period was actually 3.66 percent greater than their 10 percent desired withdrawal rate it would *appear* that there would be no problem meeting their annual income objective.

In fact, because Betty has her entire $1 million nest egg devoted to stocks, it might appear that if she limited her withdrawals to 10 percent, she would not only achieve her income requirement, but her nest egg would also experience some level of growth over time.

Again, Barbara only has $570,000 invested in stocks, because she used the rest to purchase the annuity. But because the annuity will provide her with a guaranteed lifetime income of $43,000, she only needs to withdrawal $57,000 from her stock portfolio to meet her income needs. Again, with an actual stock market yield of 13.66 percent, it might appear that she would also experience some growth in her stock portfolio even after taking her withdrawals.

Unfortunately, even though we picked an extremely favorable period of time for stocks, the sisters' results will be far different than might be expected because of the impact of market losses as they relate to the sequence of the returns generated by their stocks.

As the calculations below illustrate, Betty's $1 million nest egg would have been completely exhausted after only 14 years.

Betty's $1 Million Stock Portfolio

Yr		S&P 500	SOY Balance	Withdraw	Gain / Loss	EOY Balance
1	1970	3.93%	$1,000,000	-$100,000	$35,370	$935,370
2	1971	14.56%	$935,370	-$100,000	$121,630	$957,000
3	1972	18.90%	$957,000	-$100,000	$161,973	$1,018,973
4	1973	-14.77%	$1,018,973	-$100,000	-$135,732	$783,241
5	1974	-26.39%	$783,241	-$100,000	-$180,307	$502,933
6	1975	37.16%	$502,933	-$100,000	$149,730	$552,663
7	1976	23.57%	$552,663	-$100,000	$106,693	$559,356
8	1977	-7.42%	$559,356	-$100,000	-$34,084	$425,272
9	1978	6.38%	$425,272	-$100,000	$20,752	$346,024
10	1979	18.20%	$346,024	-$100,000	$44,776	$290,801
11	1980	32.27%	$290,801	-$100,000	$61,571	$252,372
12	1981	-5.01%	$252,372	-$100,000	-$7,634	$144,738
13	1982	21.44%	$144,738	-$100,000	$9,592	$54,330
14	1983	22.38%	$54,330	-$54,330	$0	$0
15	1984	6.10%	$0	$0	$0	$0

And likewise, the $570,000 that Barbara invested in stocks would have also disappeared after 14 years.

Barbara's $570,000 Stock Portfolio

Yr		S&P 500	SOY Balance	Withdrawal	Gain / Loss	EOY Balance
1	1970	3.93%	$570,000	-$57,000	$20,161	$533,161
2	1971	14.56%	$533,161	-$57,000	$69,329	$545,490
3	1972	18.90%	$545,490	-$57,000	$92,325	$580,815
4	1973	-14.77%	$580,815	-$57,000	-$77,367	$446,447
5	1974	-26.39%	$446,447	-$57,000	-$102,775	$286,672
6	1975	37.16%	$286,672	-$57,000	$85,346	$315,018
7	1976	23.57%	$315,018	-$57,000	$60,815	$318,833
8	1977	-7.42%	$318,833	-$57,000	-$19,428	$242,405
9	1978	6.38%	$242,405	-$57,000	$11,829	$197,234
10	1979	18.20%	$197,234	-$57,000	$25,523	$165,756
11	1980	32.27%	$165,756	-$57,000	$35,096	$143,852
12	1981	-5.01%	$143,852	-$57,000	-$4,351	$82,501
13	1982	21.44%	$82,501	-$57,000	$5,467	$30,968
14	1983	22.38%	$30,968	-$30,968	$0	$0
15	1984	6.10%	$0	$0	$0	$0

What killed both stock portfolios were the market large losses that were sustained in 1973 and 1974. During these years, both Betty and Barbara had continued to make withdrawals from their portfolios in order to meet their income needs. By selling stocks while market values were depressed, they ensured that the losses would be locked in, and would never benefit from the rebounds that occurred in future years.

While Betty was completely broke by the 14th year, sister Barbara still had her lifetime income annuity, so she has the peace of mind that comes with knowing that she would *at least* continue to receive its $43,000 annual payout for as long as she might live.

A legitimate argument can be made that the above example is not very realistic, and that few 80-year-olds would ever be advised to expose their entire nest eggs to market risk, or to attempt to take withdrawals in such large amounts. But while the example may not be entirely realistic, it does make some points that are valid. Many people who reject lifetime income annuities do so because they do not wish to lose control of their money. The problem is that it is difficult, if not impossible, to match the payout rates provided by the annuity by using other investments or savings vehicles. This will always be true, because no other vehicles except for lifetime income annuities benefit from mortality credits.

You could say that Betty was a person who chose to accept greater market risk in the name of having a chance of the greater returns needed to provide the income she desired. Barbara desired the same level of income, but she found that she could reduce her exposure to market risk by using a lifetime payout annuity to provide a portion of her income. Generally speaking, we can assume that the only reason that Betty wouldn't take the same annuity approach, with lower market risk, is because she did not want to lose control of her money. And most people believe that lifetime income annuities restrict or completely eliminate this control.

Barbara is a great example of how a lifetime income annuity can be used to actually increase the control a person has over his or her money. To illustrate how, it is important to distinguish between how much income a person *wants*, how much income a person needs, and how much income a person *must have*.

In the above example, both Betty and Barbara wanted $100,000 of income to live the lifestyle that they desired. Perhaps the reason they wanted income in this amount was that they wanted to take cruises, continue their membership at the country club, frequent fine restaurants, and lavish their grandchildren with gifts.

While these are all things that can make life more enjoyable, the question is: Do Betty and Barbara really need these things in the same way that they must have income each month to pay the cost of their housing, food, medical bills, debt and transportation?

Betty, Barbara and every one of us will decide how much of our retirement income we will spend on the things we *want* as opposed to the things that we *must have*. But most people, especially those who are retired, typically resist spending any money on things they want until after they have made sure that there is enough money to pay for all of the things they truly need.

Let's return to the example of Betty and Barbara and assume that both require a minimum annual income of $43,000 each year to pay for rent, groceries, medical insurance and co-payments, and the other things that they absolutely *must have* to live. In addition, they would like another $57,000 each year so they can really enjoy themselves with travel and the other things that they *want* to enjoy. In other words, they *must have* $43,000 to just get by, and *want* another $57,000 for pleasure.

Few 80-year-olds would be comfortable, or think it prudent, to expose their entire $1,000,000 life savings to the stock market to generate their incomes. Most would be too concerned that the possibility of market losses would expose them to the chance that they might one day find that they had no money left to pay for the things that they must have. So what do they do? Many people end up investing their money far too conservatively.

If Betty was a more typical risk-averse 80-year-old, instead of allocating 100 percent of her money in the stock market, it's far more likely that she might largely or completely avoid equities. In the name of avoiding market risk, like some retirees she might place the entire $1,000,000 in FDIC-insured certificates of deposit. The problem is that, even if she could find CDs paying a two-percent rate of return, her annual income would only be $20,000. Not only is this far short of the $100,000 of income she wants, it's less than half of the $43,000 she must have to pay just her basic living expenses.

The rate of return required in order to generate the income she must have is 4.3 percent. In recent years, this has been difficult, if not impossible to achieve. But let's assume for a minute that somehow she is able to find a CD offering this rate. Betty would still need to devote her entire $1,000,000 to generate the income that is absolutely required.

The important question to consider is: How much control would she truly have over her money? Unless she can find vehicles with even greater returns and equal guarantees against loss, she simply does not dare to touch any of her principal. If she spends any of it, her total income reduces, and she won't be left with enough money to meet her minimum living expenses. One way to look at this is that by using the CD, her entire nest egg is trapped.

Because Barbara knows that her basic living expenses will be met by the $43,000 payout guaranteed by her lifetime income annuity, she gains more control over the remaining portion of her nest egg. She could choose to avoid the risks of the stock market on her remaining $570,000, and instead use it to purchase a two percent CD and enjoy an extra $11,400 of income. As importantly, she has more freedom to spend that additional income however she might like, knowing that the annuity's payout will provide for her basic living expenses. In fact, she has more freedom to spend or use the $570,000 in any way she might like, because of the income guarantees provided by her annuity.

A valid argument can be made that by purchasing a lifetime income annuity, Barbara actually has greater control over a larger portion of her nest egg than her sister Betty will ever enjoy. And the primary reason this is true is because of the annuity's mortality credits. It is because of them and her age that the annuity's payout rate is boosted so dramatically. At Barbara's age, a nine to 10 percent payout rate is not only possible, but fairly typical.

When purchased by younger retirees, mortality credits won't be as large, but they will still boost the annuity's payout rates to 6.5 percent, 7.5 percent, or more.

Because of mortality credits, relatively small amounts of a person's nest egg can be allocated to a lifetime income annuity in order to provide relatively large amounts of guaranteed lifetime income. And by giving up control over the money used to purchase the annuity, a person might find that she increases the control over her remaining money.

Inflation and Lifetime Income Annuities

Another common criticism of lifetime income annuities is that their use can expose a person to a higher degree of the risk of loss of purchasing power due to the potential ravages of inflation.

Today, lifetime income annuities with inflation protection are more commonly available. The payout from these annuities will typically increase in some way so as to offset future inflation to some degree. The trade-off, however, is that the payout rate generally starts out at a lower level. Even still, annuities with this feature may be a great option for some clients.

But let's ignore this inflation protection option, and examine the validity of the "loss of purchasing power" criticism of the more traditional lifetime income annuities, in which the payout rate stays fixed.

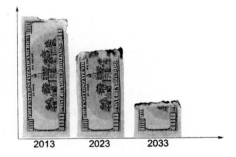

2013   2023   2033

One way to look at this is that mortality credits actually inflate the annuity's payout rate in a fairly significant way, starting the day that the client receives his or her first income check. An example of this is apparent with Barbara, who had $570,000 remaining after she purchased her annuity. Because of mortality credits, Barbara's annuity's payout was sufficient to generate all of the income she required to meet her basic living expenses. While there is no question that the annuity's fixed payout will be subject to the loss of purchasing power, it should be recognized that Barbara still has $570,000 available to use in ways that might help her offset at least some of the potential effects of inflation.

Because Barbara can count on always receiving a check each month from her annuity, she might feel comfortable subjecting all or a portion of the remaining $570,000 to vehicles that are exposed to greater market risk, in the hope that the return potential would be higher.

As previously stated, from the perspective of the inflation risk, too many retirees are far too conservative in their approach to investing. A person can focus so much attention on protecting his money from market risk that he unintentionally increases his exposure to what many consider an inevitable loss due to effects of inflation. Without the security of a guaranteed base amount of income, it's easy to understand how risk-averse people often feel compelled to make this mistake.

Because of mortality credits, less money needs to be allocated to an annuity to provide a base amount of income. This leaves more of the nest egg available for other investments, with a growth potential that can help offset inflation. And because of the guaranteed nature of the annuity's base income, it should allow the owner to expose some portion of the nest egg to a higher level of market risk for the purpose of combating inflation. One way to look at this is that the guarantees of a lifetime income annuity provide greater freedom to exchange inflation risk for market risk with regards to the client's remaining savings.

Sequence of Returns Risk

When retirees are drawing down their savings to provide retirement income, they are exposed to a significant risk often referred to as the "sequence of returns" risk. The risk is that if drawdowns begin after a period when the value of their investments had declined due to stock market fluctuations, the income draw would deplete a greater portion of their savings.

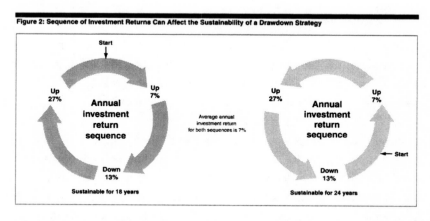

Figure 2: Sequence of Investment Returns Can Affect the Sustainability of a Drawdown Strategy

On page 16 of the Retirement Income report prepared by the US Government Accountability Office (GAO-11-400, June 2011) you will find the above chart and the following description:

If, for example, annual investment returns on retirement savings are up 7 percent in the first year, then down 13 percent in the following year, and then up 27 percent, with subsequent returns throughout retirement a repetition of the first 3 years, the average return would be 7 percent. If the sequence of returns in the second and third year were reversed, holding all else constant, the average annual return would be the same; yet if withdrawals are made each year, savings would be depleted sooner with the first sequence of returns.

Of particular interest to the financial advisor are the recommendations found in this same report for dealing with this sequence of returns risk:

Experts we spoke to generally recommended lifetime retirement income from DB plans, when DB plans are available to workers, and income annuities, in conjunction with systematic drawdown of other savings, to provide a greater level of retirement income security. Furthermore, they frequently recommend retirees delay Social Security to boost inflation adjusted lifetime retirement income.

With the first Betty and Barbara example used earlier in this chapter, we saw that both of sisters' stock portfolios were completely wiped out after 14 years of taking withdrawals. As mentioned, this occurred even though the period of time used could be viewed as a favorable time to be invested in the stock market.

Anyone who invests in the stock market must be prepared for the inevitable market volatility. But the impact of the ups and downs of the market can change radically once a person must make periodic withdrawals from his portfolio to provide retirement income.

To understand why, it helps to use the example of three different investors, each with $1,000,000 investment portfolios.

Year	1	2	3	4	5	6	7	8	9	10	11	12	13	14	15	16	17	18	19	20	Average	
Losses Early	-14	-10	8	8	8	8	8	8	8	8	8	8	8	8	8	8	8	8	8	8	6.00%	$3,092,919
Losses Late	8	8	8	8	8	8	8	8	8	8	8	8	8	8	8	8	8	8	-10	-14	6.00%	$3,092,919
Steady Growth	6	6	6	6	6	6	6	6	6	6	6	6	6	6	6	6	6	6	6	6	6.00%	$3,207,135

The first investor's portfolio ("Losses Early" in the graphic above) experiences losses of -14 percent in year one, -10 percent in the second year, and then enjoys annual gains of a consistent eight percent for the next 18 years. Considering these early losses, this portfolio's average growth rate would be six percent over a 20-year period of time.

The second investor has two years of losses that are identical to the first, except they occur at the end of the 20-year period instead of the beginning. The average growth rate for this investor is also six percent.

So regardless of whether the losses occur early or late, the annual growth rate is unaffected and stays at the same six percent.

For the third investor, we will assume that his portfolio experiences no losses. Instead it enjoys a steady gain each year of six percent.

The first two portfolios ended with exactly the same $3,092,919. The third portfolio, growing at a smaller rate of six percent, has a slightly higher ending balance of $3,207,135, because it experienced no years of loss.

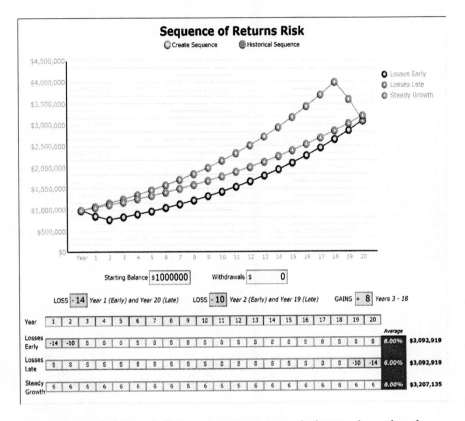

Sequence of Returns Risk

○ Create Sequence ● Historical Sequence

Year	1	2	3	4	5	6	7	8	9	10	11	12	13	14	15	16	17	18	19	20	Average	
Losses Early	-14	-10	8	8	8	8	8	8	8	8	8	8	8	8	8	8	8	8	8	8	6.00%	$3,092,919
Losses Late	8	8	8	8	8	8	8	8	8	8	8	8	8	8	8	8	8	8	-10	-14	6.00%	$3,092,919
Steady Growth	6	6	6	6	6	6	6	6	6	6	6	6	6	6	6	6	6	6	6	6	6.00%	$3,207,135

Starting Balance $1000000   Withdrawals $ 0

LOSS -14 Year 1 (Early) and Year 20 (Late)   LOSS -10 Year 2 (Early) and Year 19 (Late)   GAINS + 8 Years 3 - 18

The ending balances of all three are close enough that to show that the sequence of the returns had little impact.

Unfortunately, for many people this is not the case once they enter retirement and start taking withdrawals from their portfolios to provide needed income.

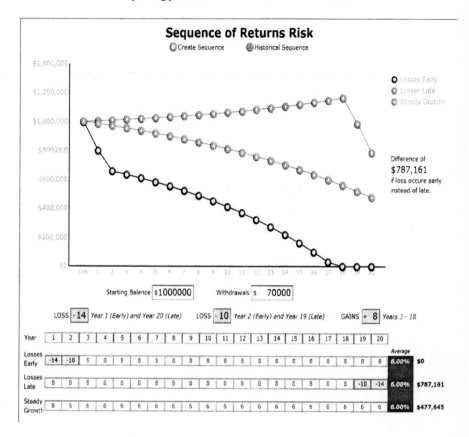

Assume that each of these three investors must take an annual withdrawal from their portfolios of $70,000. The investor whose portfolio experienced losses in the first two years would be out of money after only 18 years of withdrawals. Compare that to the investor with the portfolio that had two years of identical losses, but at the end of the 20-year period instead of the start. He would still have a $787,161 balance remaining after 20 years of withdrawals.

Again, the average annual growth rate is the same six percent in all of the portfolios. The reason that the outcomes are so different is due entirely to the sequence of the gains and the losses. When the losses come late, they create less of a problem because the portfolio has had time to grow. But when the losses come early, they are particularly destructive because each withdrawal "locks in" those losses, and the portfolio never has time to recover.

The financial meltdown in 2008 was painful for just about everyone invested in the stock market, but it was much worse for recently-retired people who were in the early years of taking withdrawals from their portfolios.

Bear markets resulting in a decline of 20 percent or more have occurred about every four years. This may not mean much for investors during the accumulation period prior to retirement, because historically, the markets generally rebound after these bear markets to not only recoup the losses but to rise to new heights. But a 20 percent loss just prior to retirement, or soon after a person starts making withdrawals, can have the devastating effect of reducing the number of years that the portfolio can support the withdrawals needed by the investor.

A lifetime income annuity can be an effective tool for helping a client reduce his or her exposure to the *sequence of returns* risk.

What Are Others Saying?

Today, we see a large number of financial commentators, prestigious academic scholars, and high-level government officials jumping on the annuity bandwagon:

> Equity-indexed annuities invest a fraction of the premium
> (e.g., 90 percent) in a fixed annuity, and use the remaining
> premium to purchase call options on a stock index, such as
> the Standard & Poor's 500. With this product, the
> individual is guaranteed never to receive less than the
> value of the fixed annuity portion, but can capture some of

the "upside" potential of equities if returns are high enough.[73]

The author of this brief, Jeffrey R. Brown, is the Assistant Professor of Public Policy at Harvard University's John F. Kennedy School of Government, and a Faculty Research Fellow of the National Bureau of Economic Research. He goes on to say that the fixed indexed annuity "preserves the longevity insurance feature that the individual will continue to receive payments for as long as he or she lives. "

"How did you do with those stocks I recommended?"

In his article "Rethinking the risk of stocks," *Money Magazine* senior editor Walter Updegrave refers to recent research from Morningstar that shows that the risks of future "big plunges" in the stock market might be more prevalent then the experts once thought. Among the advice he provides readers who are concerned about future stock market blowups is the following:

Next, give serious thought to putting some of your savings into an immediate annuity to generate income that will keep flowing even when the market dives.

---

[73] Brown, Jeffrey R. "How Should We Insure Longevity Risk in Pensions and Social Security?" *Center for Retirement Research at Boston College* August 2000, No. 4.

Those steady payments will give you more flexibility in drawing from your portfolio and give it a better shot at recovering from market slumps, no matter what the next decade (or two, or three) dishes out.[74]

James X Wiong, Ph. D, is a senior research consultant at the acclaimed Ibbotson Associates. In his article titled "Nailing Downside Risk," he has a suggestion for investors who are six years or less from retirement:

Advisors could decide to hedge against this extreme downside risk by using a portfolio insurance product— such as an appropriately-priced, equity-linked certificate of deposit with a maturity of six years or an insurance product that includes guaranteed minimum withdrawal benefits.[75]

An article appeared on June 17, 2011 on FOX Business online titled "Annuities the Next Big Retirement Option?" that stated:

So far, the likeliest candidate is an annuity within a 401(k) plan. Last September, the U.S. Department of Labor's Employee Benefits Security Administration and the Treasury Department sponsored a hearing on these lifetime income options. At the end of the sessions, it seemed clear that annuities within 401(k)s were a concept that employers, the government and -- especially insurance companies -- were happy to embrace.[76]

---

[74] Updegrave, Walter. "Rethinking the risk of stocks" *Money Magazine online* 9 June 2010.

[75] Xiong, James X. "Nailing Downside Risk" *Morningstar Advisor* February/March 2010. < http://corporate.morningstar.com/ib/documents/MethodologyDocuments/IBBAs sociates/NailingDownsideRisk.pdf>

[76] Phipps, Jennie. "Annuities the Next Big Retirement Option?" *FOX Business online* 17 June 2011. <http://www.foxbusiness.com/personal-finance/2011/06/17/annuities-next-big-retirement-option/#ixzz1efmADASn>

As more boomers move closer to and fall below the borderline of what is considered an adequate nest egg to meet their lifetime retirement needs, we can expect even greater focus on the benefits of using lifetime payout annuities in retirement planning.

Life annuities solve the consumption problem in retirement by insuring individuals against the risk of depleting all of their assets before they die. Moreover, actuarially fair annuities pay higher returns than other equally risky assets in exchange for the sacrifice of any residual asset value at death. As a result, simple theoretical models show that consumers should annuitize at least some of their retirement wealth. If they do not have a bequest motive, they should annuitize all of it.[77]

Today, there is a great deal of support for a strategy of combining Social Security retirement benefits with lifetime payout annuities to provide individuals with a guaranteed income sufficient to meet at least their minimum needs during retirement:

---

[77] Johnson, Richard W., Burman, Leonard E., and Kobes, Deborah I. "Annuitized Wealth at Older Ages: Evidence from the Health and Retirement Study" *Final Report to the Employee Benefits Security Administration U.S. Department of Labor* May 2004.

Income Annuities

> Given the difficulties in managing the decumulation of
> unannuitized wealth and the severe consequences of mis-
> steps, all households approaching retirement should
> consider annuitizing sufficient financial assets to secure at
> least their minimum required standard of living.[78]

Mortality credits are the unique ingredient only available with lifetime income annuities. They are a simple way to boost income that is guaranteed to be paid for as long as the annuitant lives. Their major weakness is that to benefit from mortality credits, the client must be willing to forfeit all or a portion of his or her principal at death. This is a difficult decision for clients who desire to leave a legacy to loved ones or a charitable organization.

Fortunately, the application of *the Synergy Effect*™ strategy will often include the use of life insurance. Properly structured, this life insurance may be able to provide both supplemental income during the life of the insured, and also a death benefit that could help fulfill the client's desire to leave a legacy behind.

For the legions of baby boomers faced with the multiple challenges of market risk, inflation risk, longevity and other risks, the skilled advisor who knows how to combine annuities properly with other financial vehicles can be the difference between failure and enjoying the retirement with dignity that clients deserve.

One final quote from the report prepared by the US Government Accountability Office that went to the chairman of the Special Committee on Aging, U.S. Senate in June 2011:

> For those that want a higher level of predictable income,
> an annuity can reduce the uncertainty that comes with
> managing a portfolio of investments and systematically
> drawing down income. The experts noted that retirees

---

[78] Webb, Anthony. "Making Your Nest Egg Last a Lifetime" *Insight on the Issues* 132, June, 2009.

235

might have more difficulty managing a portfolio of investments as they age.[79]

Find tools, articles, webinars, live training, case studies and more resources devoted to *the Synergy Effect*™ at ***Doug-Warren.com***

---

[79] 'Retirement Income: Ensuring Income throughout Retirement Requires Difficult Choices" *U.S. Government Accountability Office report number GAO-11-400* 1 July 2011. < http://www.gao.gov/assets/320/319390.html>

Chapter 10

The Synergy Effect™
In Action

This chapter presents projections of after-tax spendable income streams many years into the future. Even though the values shown appear to be exact dollar amounts, it is important to understand that in reality, the numbers are intended to be rough estimates at best. The further into the future, the more inexact the estimates will be.

Estimating future Social Security taxation is particularly challenging in the later years of the projections when it can be expected that Social Security will make up a larger percentage of a person's total income. While virtually all other provisions of federal income taxation are indexed to inflation, the thresholds for determining Social Security taxation are not. Because of this form of bracket creep, it is extremely difficult to make any estimates of taxable income and average tax rates as these benefit amounts rise due to inflation. Each case study will specify the tax assumptions used, but these assumptions should be viewed as very broad estimates only, which might prove to be highly inaccurate.

The case studies always assume that 100 percent of any distributions from tax deferred retirement plans will be included as taxable income. It is assumed that the growth occurring in non-qualified accounts is taxed at ordinary income tax rates in the year earned, and that withdrawals are taken annually from these accounts in amounts necessary to pay any resulting tax.

The decision to delay the start of Social Security benefits will not always be the best choice in every situation. Many factors, both financial and non-financial, must be taken into consideration when deciding on the most optimal time for people to claim their benefits.

This chapter will present a series of comparative scenario case studies for two hypothetical married couples. Each scenario will start with a summary of the basic assumptions, including average tax rates, investment growth rates and inflation rates that are used in each scenario.

In several of the scenarios, one or more of the assumptions will be changed so that the reader can see the impact that the change(s) will have on the couple's future spendable retirement income, and how long the retirement resources might be expected to last.

The scenarios titled *The Synergy Effect™* show how combinations of IULs, income annuities, Roth IRAs and Social Security claiming strategies can help manage risk while providing a greater amount of lifetime spendable retirement income.

The Synergy Effect™ *In Action*

Case Study 01 – Assumptions

Frank, DOB 1/2/1958 (Age 55 as of start of year 2013)
Mary, DOB 1/2/1958 (Age 55 as of start of year 2013)

Inflation Rate Assumption: **3 percent**

Starting Tax Rate Assumptions (unless otherwise noted):
　　Today's...　　Tax Bracket = **25%**　　Average Rate* = **17%**
　　Future...　　Tax Bracket = **25%**　　Average Rate* = **17%**
　　　　Average Tax Rate = Tax to Taxable Income

Non-Qualified Accounts:

Certificate of Deposit current balance = **$100,000**. Assumed annual return = **3 percent**. *(The current annual return is only 1.5 percent, but because Frank and Mary expect that interest rates will increase, they want to project a higher return.)* Assumed cost basis in this account = **$100,000**.

Tax-Deferred Qualified Retirement Accounts:

Frank's **401(k)** current balance = **$300,000**. Assumed annual return = **7 percent**. Contributions = **$15,000**. Company match = **$3,000** ($ for $ to $3,000). For this study we will assume that contributions continue at the same level until retirement.

Frank has an **IRA** that was a rollover from a 401(k) plan provided by a previous employer with a current balance = **$75,000**. Assumed annual return = **7 percent**. Contributions = **0**.

Liquidity Requirements:

This case study will assume that Frank and Mary have an additional amount of money sufficient to meet their liquidity needs, and will not take that money into consideration for the purpose of providing future retirement income.

Social Security:

> Frank's **SS** Primary Insurance Amount (PIA) at full retirement age (66yrs. 8mo.) = **$22,000**
>
> Mary's **SS** Primary Insurance Amount (PIA) at full retirement age (66yrs. 8mo.) = **$12,000**
>
> Assumed SS inflation factor = **2.3 percent**
> *(The inflation rate is used to inflate both wage-indexing factors as well as Cost of Living adjustments to Social Security benefit streams.)*
>
> *Important Notes:* Because both Frank and Mary were born in 1958, their full retirement age for Social Security would be age 66 and 8 months. In all but the final *Synergy Effect Scenario*, the assumption is that both Frank and Mary will start their Social Security worker's benefit once they reach age 65. Because this is earlier than their full retirement age, they will only receive 88 8/9 percent of their Primary Insurance Amount (PIA).
>
> Those projected amounts, including the penalty, would be:
>
> Frank's **SS** projected benefit if started at age 65 = **$23,448**
>
> Mary's **SS** projected benefit if started at age 65 = **$12,792**

Current Life Insurance:

> Frank's = **$500,000**. 20-year level term, recently purchased (at his age 54). Annual premium is $1,500.
>
> Mary's = **0**

Long-Term Care:

> The issue of providing for long-term care needs is critically important to a client's future financial security but this topic is beyond the scope of this book. This case study assumes that those

needs are addressed in some manner independent of what will be illustrated.

Planned Retirement Age:

Frank plans to work through age 64 and retire the year he turns age 65. Mary is not employed.

Case Study 01: Scenarios

While everyone's vision of an ideal retirement lifestyle is different, most people would be happy if they had the financial resources necessary to enjoy the same lifestyle during retirement that they enjoyed prior to retirement. The object of this scenario is to see if Frank and Mary have sufficient resources for their future after-tax spendable retirement to match their present after-tax spendable income.

Are Frank and Mary's Income Objectives Realistic?

For the purpose of this scenario, we will assume that Frank and Mary currently enjoy an annual spendable income of $75,000. This is the net amount of income that remains after they pay taxes, and does not include their mortgage payment, which is scheduled to be paid off prior to retirement, or any other expenses that they will no longer have after they retire.

Initially, this case study assumes that Frank and Mary's objective is to enjoy the same standard of living after they retire as they enjoy today. To do this, they will need to have the same $75,000 of spendable income that they enjoy today. If we adjust this income for inflation, the after-tax spendable income needed once Frank and Mary reach age 65 will be approximately $100,000.

The illustration below shows how close Frank and Mary can come to meeting this spendable retirement income objective, assuming they continue on their current path.

Version 201301

Current Position

Yr	Age	SSI Workers Frank	SSI Workers Mary	SSI Spousal Mary	Q-Plan IRA Frank	Q-Plan 401(k) Frank	Non-Q CD	Roth XYZ	Gross Income	Taxes Paid	Actual Spendable Income	Target Spendable Income	Over / Under Spendabl
11	65	23,448	12,792	0	83,129	0	0	0	120,021	20,021	100,000	100,000	0
12	66	23,987	13,086	0	68,916	16,968	0	0	123,626	20,626	103,000	103,000	0
13	67	24,539	13,387	0	0	88,728	0	0	127,339	21,249	106,090	106,090	0
14	68	25,103	13,695	0	0	91,664	0	0	131,164	21,891	109,273	109,273	0
15	69	25,680	14,010	0	0	94,694	0	0	135,104	22,553	112,551	112,551	0
16	70	26,271	14,332	0	0	97,821	0	0	139,162	23,234	115,927	115,927	0
17	71	26,875	14,662	0	0	101,049	0	0	143,342	23,936	119,405	119,405	0
18	72	27,493	14,999	0	0	104,380	0	0	147,647	24,659	122,987	122,987	0
19	73	28,126	15,344	0	0	107,818	0	0	152,081	25,404	126,677	126,677	0
20	74	28,773	15,697	0	0	111,366	0	0	156,649	26,172	130,477	130,477	0
21	75	29,434	16,058	0	0	115,028	0	0	161,354	26,962	134,392	134,392	0
22	76	30,111	16,427	0	0	118,807	0	0	166,200	27,777	138,423	138,423	0
23	77	30,804	16,805	0	0	122,707	0	0	171,192	28,616	142,576	142,576	0
24	78	31,513	17,192	0	0	126,731	0	0	176,333	29,480	146,853	146,853	0
25	79	32,237	17,587	0	0	130,885	0	0	181,629	30,370	151,259	151,259	0
26	80	32,979	17,991	0	0	48,753	68,965	0	168,688	13,378	155,797	155,797	0
27	81	33,737	18,405	0	0	0	108,328	0	160,471	0	160,471	160,471	0
28	82	34,513	18,829	0	0	0	10,962	0	64,303	0	64,303	165,285	-100,981
29	83	35,307	19,262	0	0	0	0	0	54,569	0	54,569	170,243	-115,675
30	84	36,119	19,705	0	0	0	0	0	55,824	0	55,824	175,351	-119,527

The Synergy Effect™   *Case Study 01 - Is $100,000 of Spendable Income Realistic?*

View ○ All Sources ○ This Acct | View ○ All Sources ○ This Acct | File | Print

Regarding the taxable portion of the Social
Security benefits, the above scenario assumes:

85 percent from start to year 26,
 0 percent from year 27 to end.

Regarding the average tax rate applied to all
taxable income, the above scenario assumes:

17 percent from year one to year 25,
14 percent in year 26,
 0 percent from year 27 to end.

If you refer to the projected values in the above illustration titled "Is
$100,000 of Spendable Income Realistic?" you can see that by starting
Social Security at age 65, the couple's current Primary Insurance
Amount (PIA) projects to a starting benefit of $23,448 for Frank and
$12,792 for Mary.

These amounts reflect a penalty because both Frank and Mary wish to
start their benefits at age 65, as opposed to their full retirement age,
which would be age 66 and 8 months based upon their birth dates.

Subtracting their combined projected Social Security income of
$36,240 from their spendable retirement income target of $100,000
(column labelled "Target Spendable Income"), it would appear that
they would only need to withdraw $63,760 from one of their accounts
to meet their income needs. However, if they withdraw this money
from one of their tax-deferred accounts, the entire withdrawal will be
considered taxable income. What is worse is that the entire withdrawal
from a tax-deferred account would also then be included in the
provisional income formula used to calculate the amount of Frank and
Mary's Social Security income, which must also be included as taxable
income.

In spite of this exposure to taxes, this scenario assumes that they will
initially take the needed withdrawal from Frank's traditional IRA. This

is identical to what so many people entering into retirement are forced to do because they have relied so much on using 401(k)s, IRAs and other traditional tax-deferred retirement plans to accumulate their retirement savings.

As a result, 85 percent of their $36,240 of combined Social Security income is taxable. This amounts to $30,804 of additional taxable income.

Based on the assumed average tax rate of 17 percent, the gross amount of the withdrawal from Frank's IRA would need to be $83,129 in order to net the additional needed spendable income needed after paying the tax on the IRA withdrawal and the tax on the taxable portion of their Social Security income.

As the column labeled "Gross Income" shows, their total gross income that year is projected to be $120,021. *(Note that the total from Social Security and the IRA is $119,369. The projections assume that an additional $652 is withdrawn from the CD that year to pay the tax on the growth in that account.)*

Based upon the assumption that the average tax rate for Frank and Mary would be 17 percent, the assumed total estimated tax would be $20,021. The breakdown of taxes at their age 65 is as follows:

Certificate of Deposit
      Projected Balance at the start of year…$127,884
(Assumes a 3 percent annual taxable growth rate, but with amounts withdrawn each year to pay the income tax due on these earnings.)

Annual Taxable Growth…	$ 3,837
Taxes on Annual Growth…	*$ 652*

Social Security

His Total Benefit…	$ 23,448
His Taxable Portion…	$ 19,931
Taxes…	*$ 3,388*

Her Total Benefit...	$ 12,792
Her Taxable Portion...	$ 10,873
Taxes...	*$ 1,848*

IRA Withdrawal

Gross Amount...	$ 83,129
Taxable Portion...	$ 83,129
Taxes...	*$ 14,132*

Total Taxes...	**$ 20,021**

After paying this tax, Mary and Frank will be left with the $100,000 of inflation-adjusted spendable income that was their target.

(At best, the 17 percent average tax rate is a rough estimate, and does not take into account any itemized deductions that Mary and Frank might be able to use to reduce their taxable income.)

While the illustration shows that Frank and Mary's spendable retirement income is projected to be met at age 65, the looming problem is that they must consume a large portion of the balance in the IRA account to accomplish this.

Using the 3 percent assumed rate of inflation, the spendable income needed the following year climbs to $103,000.

After considering their combined Social Security benefit that year, an additional $85,884 would need to be withdrawn from the IRA and 401(k) accounts to continue to meet their spendable income need. This would require withdrawing $68,916 from Frank's IRA, which would exhaust the balance, and an additional $16,968 from the 401(k).

Their total gross annual income in that year would be $123,626. *(Note that the projections assume that an additional $669 is withdrawn from the CD that year to pay the tax on the growth in that account.)*

As the projections in this example show, if Frank and Mary continue to withdraw the amounts neccesary to meet their spendable retirement income objective, Frank's 401(k) account would also be completely exhausted by the time they reach the age of 80.

At their age 80, withdrawing the remaining balance of $48,753 from Frank's 401(k) would not be sufficent to meet their spendable income objective. To make up the difference, an additional $68,965 would need to be withdrawn from their CD.

The illustration assumes that this CD had been left intact and growing at a rate of 3 percent with taxes on the growth deducted annually. This would result in a total projected balance at age 80 of $184,943.

Prior to age 80, the tax calculations have assumed an average tax rate of 17 percent. Starting at age 80, the tax rate has been lowered to 14 percent due to the reduced taxable income from Frank's 401(k). And from age 81 on, it is assumed that Frank and Mary's taxable income would be so low that they would pay no income tax.

There is a high probability that at least one of them will live into their 90s or beyond, which means that the likelihood is that there could be many years when Social Security would be the only remaining source of income.

One way that Frank and Mary could make their savings last longer would be to reduce their target spendable income objective and adjust to a lower standard of living during their retirement years.

The Reduced Lifestyle Scenario

If we assume that the objective is to make Frank and Mary's savings last at least until they reach age 90, projections can be made to show the level of spendable income they might be able to receive.

The Synergy Effect™ *In Action*

Yr	Age	SSI Workers Frank	SSI Workers Mary	SSI Spousal Mary	Q-Plan IRA Frank	Q-Plan 401(k) Frank	Non-Q CD	Roth XYZ	Gross Income	Taxes Paid	Actual Spendable Income	Target Spendable Income	Over/Under Spendable
11	65	23,448	12,792	0	59,387	0	0	0	96,164	13,164	83,000	83,000	0
12	66	23,987	13,086	0	61,429	0	0	0	99,053	13,563	85,490	85,490	0
13	67	24,539	13,387	0	35,194	28,344	0	0	102,028	13,974	88,055	88,055	0
14	68	25,103	13,695	0	0	65,715	0	0	105,093	14,397	90,696	90,696	0
15	69	25,680	14,010	0	0	67,965	0	0	108,250	14,833	93,417	93,417	0
16	70	26,271	14,332	0	0	70,289	0	0	111,502	15,282	96,220	96,220	0
17	71	26,875	14,662	0	0	72,689	0	0	114,851	15,745	99,106	99,106	0
18	72	27,493	14,999	0	0	75,167	0	0	118,301	16,222	102,080	102,080	0
19	73	28,126	15,344	0	0	77,727	0	0	121,855	16,713	105,142	105,142	0
20	74	28,773	15,697	0	0	80,370	0	0	125,515	17,219	108,296	108,296	0
21	75	29,434	16,058	0	0	83,100	0	0	129,286	17,741	111,545	111,545	0
22	76	30,111	16,427	0	0	85,920	0	0	133,169	18,278	114,891	114,891	0
23	77	30,804	16,805	0	0	88,831	0	0	137,169	18,831	118,338	118,338	0
24	78	31,513	17,192	0	0	91,837	0	0	141,289	19,401	121,888	121,888	0
25	79	32,237	17,587	0	0	94,942	0	0	145,533	19,988	125,545	125,545	0
26	80	32,979	17,991	0	0	98,147	0	0	149,904	20,593	129,311	129,311	0
27	81	33,737	18,405	0	0	101,457	0	0	154,407	21,216	133,191	133,191	0
28	82	34,513	18,829	0	0	104,875	0	0	159,045	21,858	137,186	137,186	0
29	83	35,307	19,262	0	0	108,403	0	0	163,822	22,520	141,302	141,302	0
30	84	36,119	19,705	0	0	112,047	0	0	168,742	23,201	145,541	145,541	0
31	85	36,950	20,158	0	0	115,809	0	0	173,810	23,903	149,907	149,907	0
32	86	37,800	20,621	0	0	119,692	0	0	179,031	24,626	154,404	154,404	0
33	87	38,669	21,096	0	0	123,702	0	0	184,408	25,371	159,037	159,037	0
34	88	39,559	21,581	0	0	127,842	0	0	189,946	26,138	163,808	163,808	0
35	89	40,468	22,077	0	0	72,698	51,099	0	186,343	18,396	168,722	168,722	0
36	90	41,399	22,585	0	0	0	109,799	0	173,784	0	173,784	173,784	0
37	91	42,351	23,105	0	0	0	81,928	0	147,384	0	147,384	178,997	-31,613
38	92	43,325	23,636	0	0	0	0	0	66,961	0	66,961	184,367	-117,406

The Synergy Effect ™   *Case Study 01 - The Reduced Lifestyle Scenario*

Regarding the taxable portion of the Social
Security benefits, the above scenario assumes:

85 percent from start to year 36,
50 percent from year 37 to end.

Regarding the average tax rate applied to all taxable income, the above scenario assumes:

17 percent from year one to year 10,
14 percent from year 11 to year 35,
0 percent from year 36 to end.

The illustrated values in the above "Case Study 01 – The Reduced Lifestyle Scenario" shows that if the inflation-adjusted spendable retirement income objective was adjusted downward to $83,000, instead of the original $100,000 their savings balances would not be total exhausted until the year that they would reach age 91.

Because the withdrawals from the taxable IRA and 401(k) have reduced, it is logical to assume that the average tax rate would reduce as well once retirement begins. In this scenario, the assumed average tax rate has been reduced to 14 percent starting at age 65. Further, this illustration assumes that they pay no income taxes from age 90 on.

An argument might be made that the tax rates used in both the *$100,000 Income* and the *Reduced Lifetstyle* scenarios may be unrealistically low. While that may or may not prove to be true, the purpose in presenting these scenarios is so that we can ultimately compare them to one that relies on the tax-advantaged synergistic approach detailed in this book. If that recommended scenario proves to be attractive based on conservate tax rate assumptions, then we would expect it to look even better if future tax rates were higher.

Reducing their spendable retirement income objective would make their savings last longer, but Frank and Mary would continue to be exposed to many other pontential risks.

The Sequence of Returns Risk Scenario

In chapter nine, a risk was explored that is commonly referred to as the sequence of returns risk. This risk is of particular concern to retirees who are drawing down their savings to provide retirement income from accounts that are exposed to stock market fluctuations.

Yr	Age	SSI Workers Frank	SSI Workers Mary	SSI Spousal Mary	Q-Plan IRA Frank	Q-Plan 401(k) Frank	Non-Q CD	Roth XYZ	Gross Income	Taxes Paid	Actual Spendable Income	Target Spendable Income	Over/Under Spendabl
11	65	23,448	12,792	0	59,387	0	0	0	96,164	13,164	83,000	83,000	0
12	66	23,987	13,086	0	61,429	0	0	0	99,053	13,563	85,490	85,490	0
13	67	24,539	13,387	0	5,200	58,338	0	0	102,028	13,974	88,055	88,055	0
14	68	25,103	13,695	0	0	65,715	0	0	105,093	14,397	90,696	90,696	0
15	69	25,680	14,010	0	0	67,965	0	0	108,250	14,833	93,417	93,417	0
16	70	26,271	14,332	0	0	70,289	0	0	111,502	15,282	96,220	96,220	0
17	71	26,875	14,662	0	0	72,689	0	0	114,851	15,745	99,106	99,106	0
18	72	27,493	14,999	0	0	75,167	0	0	118,301	16,222	102,080	102,080	0
19	73	28,126	15,344	0	0	77,727	0	0	121,855	16,713	105,142	105,142	0
20	74	28,773	15,697	0	0	80,370	0	0	125,515	17,219	108,296	108,296	0
21	75	29,434	16,058	0	0	83,100	0	0	129,286	17,741	111,545	111,545	0
22	76	30,111	16,427	0	0	85,920	0	0	133,169	18,278	114,891	114,891	0
23	77	30,804	16,805	0	0	88,831	0	0	137,169	18,831	118,338	118,338	0
24	78	31,513	17,192	0	0	91,837	0	0	141,289	19,401	121,888	121,888	0
25	79	32,237	17,587	0	0	94,942	0	0	145,533	19,988	125,545	125,545	0
26	80	32,979	17,991	0	0	98,147	0	0	149,904	20,593	129,311	129,311	0
27	81	33,737	18,405	0	0	101,457	0	0	154,407	21,216	133,191	133,191	0
28	82	34,513	18,829	0	0	104,875	0	0	159,045	21,858	137,186	137,186	0
29	83	35,307	19,262	0	0	108,403	0	0	163,822	22,520	141,302	141,302	0
30	84	36,119	19,705	0	0	31,876	68,947	0	156,647	11,688	145,541	145,541	0
31	85	36,950	20,158	0	0	0	92,800	0	149,907	0	149,907	149,907	0
32	86	37,800	20,621	0	0	0	50,802	0	109,223	0	109,223	154,404	-45,181
33	87	38,669	21,096	0	0	0	0	0	59,765	0	59,765	159,037	-99,272
34	88	39,559	21,581	0	0	0	0	0	61,139	0	61,139	163,808	-102,668
35	89	40,468	22,077	0	0	0	0	0	62,546	0	62,546	168,722	-106,176
36	90	41,399	22,585	0	0	0	0	0	63,984	0	63,984	173,784	-109,799
37	91	42,351	23,105	0	0	0	0	0	65,456	0	65,456	178,997	-113,541
38	92	43,325	23,636	0	0	0	0	0	66,961	0	66,961	184,367	-117,406

The Synergy Effect™   Case Study 01 - The Sequence of Returns Risk Scenario

Regarding the taxable portion of the Social Security benefits, the above scenario assumes:

85 percent from start to year 30,
50 percent from year 31 to end.

Regarding the average tax rate applied to all
taxable income, the above scenario assumes:

17 percent from year one to year 10,
14 percent from year 11 to year 30,
0 percent from year 31 to end.

The above illustration titled "The Sequence of Returns Risk Scenario,"
shows the potential devastating impact that market losses can have if
they occur just prior to or early in retirement. In this scenario, the
spendable income objective is the same as was used previously in "The
Reduced Lifestyle Scenario." The primary difference is that the above
illustration changes the assumptions relating to the annual total returns
on both Frank's IRA and 401(k). Instead of assuming a constant annual
return of seven percent, those qualified plan accounts are now assumed
to suffer a *negative* return of **-12** percent in the year before retirement
(age 64) and a *positive* return of **+12** percent in the year that they turn
age 68. The assumed annual return for all other years remains at a
constant seven percent.

Note that instead of their money lasting to age 91, because of this
single loss, Frank and Mary are now projected to run out of money five
years earlier when they would be age 86. And consider that this is in
spite of the fact that the illustration also assumes a positive return in the
same 12 percent amount, occuring only four years after the loss. The
point is that even though the "market" rebounded, this did little to
offset the impact of the earlier loss, because the withdrawals taken that
year effectively *lock in* the loss forever.

When considering the potential impact of the sequence of returns risk,
anyone approaching retirement must consider the wisdom of
withdrawing retirement income from accounts that are exposed to
market volatility.

The Longevity Risk Scenario

As medical advances increase life expectancy, more attention must be given to one of the most potentially devastating risks of all, the *longevity risk*. And because women tend to outlive their husbands, this is a risk that should be of particular concern to married couples.

Yr	Age	SSI Workers Frank	SSI Workers Mary	SSI Spousal Mary	Q-Plan IRA Frank	Q-Plan 401(k) Frank	Non-Q CD	Roth XYZ	Gross Income	Taxes Paid	Actual Spendable Income	Target Spendable Income (Version 2013.01)	Over/Under Spendable
11	65	23,448	12,792	0	59,387	0	0	0	96,164	13,164	83,000	83,000	0
12	66	23,987	13,086	0	61,429	0	0	0	99,053	13,563	85,490	85,490	0
13	67	24,539	13,387	0	35,194	28,344	0	0	102,028	13,974	88,055	88,055	0
14	68	25,103	13,695	0	0	65,715	0	0	105,093	14,397	90,696	90,696	0
15	69	25,680	14,010	0	0	67,965	0	0	108,250	14,833	93,417	93,417	0
16	70	26,271	14,332	0	0	70,289	0	0	111,502	15,282	96,220	96,220	0
17	71	26,875	14,662	0	0	72,689	0	0	114,851	15,745	99,106	99,106	0
18	72	27,493	14,999	0	0	75,167	0	0	118,301	16,222	102,080	102,080	0
19	73	28,126	15,344	0	0	77,727	0	0	121,855	16,713	105,142	105,142	0
20	74	28,773	15,697	0	0	80,370	0	0	125,515	17,219	108,296	108,296	0
21	75	29,434	16,058	0	0	83,100	0	0	129,286	17,741	111,545	111,545	0
22	76	30,111	16,427	0	0	85,920	0	0	133,169	18,278	114,891	114,891	0
23	77	30,804	16,805	0	0	88,831	0	0	137,169	18,831	118,338	118,338	0
24	78	31,513	17,192	0	0	91,837	0	0	141,289	19,401	121,888	121,888	0
25	79	32,237	17,587	0	0	94,942	0	0	145,533	19,988	125,545	125,545	0
26	80	0	0	32,979	0	116,578	0	0	150,344	21,032	129,311	129,311	0
27	81	0	0	33,738	0	93,601	0	0	128,320	21,768	106,552	106,552	0
28	82	0	0	34,514	0	96,653	0	0	132,172	22,423	109,749	109,749	0
29	83	0	0	35,308	0	99,801	0	0	136,139	23,098	113,041	113,041	0
30	84	0	0	36,120	0	103,050	0	0	140,226	23,793	116,432	116,432	0
31	85	0	0	36,951	0	106,402	0	0	144,435	24,509	119,925	119,925	0
32	86	0	0	37,800	0	109,861	0	0	148,770	25,247	123,523	123,523	0
33	87	0	0	38,670	0	113,430	0	0	153,236	26,007	127,229	127,229	0
34	88	0	0	39,559	0	117,111	0	0	157,835	26,790	131,046	131,046	0
35	89	0	0	40,469	0	120,910	0	0	162,573	27,596	134,977	134,977	0
36	90	0	0	41,400	0	18,989	78,638	0	139,026	0	139,026	139,026	0
37	91	0	0	42,352	0	0	100,845	0	143,197	0	143,197	143,197	0
38	92	0	0	43,326	0	0	67,167	0	110,493	0	110,493	147,493	-37,000
39	93	0	0	44,323	0	0	0	0	44,323	0	44,323	151,918	-107,595

Tax Rates | View | All Sources | This Acct | View | All Sources | This Acct | File | Print

The Synergy Effect ™

Case Study 01 - The Longevity Risk Scenario

In the above illustration titled "The Longevity Risk Scenario," it is assumed that Frank dies at the beginning of the year when he would turn age 80. And it is also assumed that he did not have any life insurance coverage in force at that time.

In addition to dealing with the loss of her companion, Mary must also cope with several financial losses as well. One such loss will be the reduction of income from Social Security. As a widow, Mary has the right to receive the greater of her own worker's benefit based on her own earnings history with Social Security, or Frank's worker's benefit. "The Longevity Risk Scenario" illustrates the continuation of Frank's higher benefit and the loss of Mary's lower benefit. Instead of receiving a total of $50,971 inflation adjusted dollars from Social Security at age 80, as they would have if Frank had not died that year, Mary will now receive only $32,979.

An argument can be made that Mary should be able to live on less income than the amount that was required to pay the joint expenses while Frank was alive. But as is often the case, the reduction in expenses actually experienced when a spouse dies are surprisingly less then what many people expect. In addition, it can take time for the surviving spouse to adjust to a lower income. During this adjustment period, account balances can be drained more than might be expected.

The "Longevity Risk Scenario" illustration assumes that Mary experiences no reduction in expenses in the year of Frank's death. Again, this is often the case because of immediate expenses due to medical bills, funeral and the other bills that generally occur following a spouse's death. However, the following year (age 81), the inflation-adjusted desired spendable income amount has been reduced to $106,552. This reduction represents 80 percent of what was projected to have been needed if Frank were alive.

Keep in mind that Frank and Mary had already reduced their withdrawals from their retirement accounts in order to make their money last longer. So at Frank's death, the numbers in the projections would require that Mary further reduce withdrawals by an additional 20 percent. Her total inflation adjusted income at age 81 is $128,320. *(Note that the total from Social Security and the 401(k) is $127,339. The projections assume that an additional $981 is withdrawn from the CD that year to pay the tax on the growth in that account.)*

What is often a shock to many surviving spouses who find themselves in Mary's position is to learn that tax rates often increase after the loss of a spouse, even as income declines.

Mary is a good example of how this can happen. First, instead of filing tax returns as *married filing jointly*, she must now file as a single taxpayer. For 2013, married joint filers could have taxable income of up to $72,500 and be taxed at a maximum of 15 percent. But a single filer would be taxed at the rate of 25 percent on every dollar of taxable income above $36,250. In addition, the standard deduction rates in 2013 are $12,200 for married taxpayers but only $6,100 for individual taxpayers (plus $1,200 for the aged or the blind). If that wasn't bad enough, the thresholds for determining the percentage of Social Security that must be included in taxable income are lower for individuals. So even though Mary's Social Security benefit is less then the total combined benefit received while Frank was alive, she must still include 85 percent of her reduced benefit as taxable income.

As previously stated, virtually all other provisions of federal income taxation are indexed to inflation, with the exception of the thresholds for determining Social Security taxation. So along with Mary, many other widows, widowers and married couples can eventually expect to have 85 percent of their Social Security included as taxable income due to this form of bracket creep.

Even though she must now get by on a lower income, Mary can expect that her tax rates would go up as the deductions she claims go down.

The assumed average tax rates used in "The Longevity Risk Scenario" are 14 percent from the beginning of retirement, up to and including the year of Frank' death. Starting at age 81 and continuing through age 89, this illustration reflects an increase in the tax rate to 17 percent to reflect Mary's changed tax filing status. Starting at age 90, it is assumed that Mary no longer has enough taxable income to require the payment of any tax.

Note that the 17 percent average tax rate and other tax assumptions used in this illustration were arrived at by taking the present value of the future income streams and using those amounts to do tax calculations based on today's tax rates. At best this is a rough estimate, and it does not take into account any exemptions or tax deductions that Mary might be able to use to reduce her taxable income.

Based upon these assumptions, Mary will have exhausted all of her resources at age 92. From that point on, her only remaining source of income is her Social Security.

This is precisely the situation that many widowed spouses find themselves in today. And while women may have greater exposure to longevity risk, it has the potential to destroy the financial future of anyone, regardless of gender or marital status.

The Inflation Risk Scenario

The prior scenario illustrations have all assumed that the spendable retirement income objective increases each year by a rate of three percent in order to account for cost of living increases due to inflation.

Three percent was chosen because that has been the average yearly rate of inflation as measured by the Consumer Price Index for All Urban Consumers (CPI-U) for the past 100 years. Inflation has also averaged three percent since 1982.

The prior scenario illustrations have also assumed a Social Security COLA of 2.3 percent. The logic behind using a lower COLA for Social Security is that it understates the inflation experienced by older people who spend more of their money on health care costs, which have historically increased at a greater rate then what is reflected by the Consumer Price Index.

While inflation has been under control in recent years, there is no guarantee that this will be the case in the future.

Yr	Age	SSI Workers Frank	SSI Workers Mary	SSI Spousal Mary	Q-Plan IRA Frank	Q-Plan 401(k) Frank	Non-Q CD	Roth XYZ	Gross Income	Taxes Paid	Actual Spendable Income	Target Spendable Income	Over / Under Spendable
11	65	23,448	12,792	0	59,387	0	0	0	96,880	13,880	83,000	83,000	0
12	66	24,855	13,560	0	62,949	0	0	0	102,693	14,713	87,980	87,980	0
13	67	26,346	14,374	0	33,567	33,159	0	0	108,855	15,596	93,259	93,259	0
14	68	27,927	15,236	0	0	70,730	0	0	115,386	16,532	98,854	98,854	0
15	69	29,603	16,150	0	0	74,974	0	0	122,310	17,524	104,786	104,786	0
16	70	31,379	17,119	0	0	79,472	0	0	129,649	18,576	111,073	111,073	0
17	71	33,262	18,146	0	0	84,240	0	0	137,428	19,691	117,737	117,737	0
18	72	35,257	19,235	0	0	89,295	0	0	145,674	20,873	124,801	124,801	0
19	73	37,373	20,389	0	0	94,652	0	0	154,415	22,126	132,289	132,289	0
20	74	39,615	21,613	0	0	100,332	0	0	163,680	23,453	140,227	140,227	0
21	75	41,992	22,909	0	0	106,351	0	0	173,501	24,861	148,640	148,640	0
22	76	44,512	24,284	0	0	112,733	0	0	183,912	26,353	157,559	157,559	0
23	77	47,182	25,741	0	0	119,497	0	0	194,947	27,935	167,012	167,012	0
24	78	50,013	27,285	0	0	126,666	0	0	206,645	29,611	177,033	177,033	0
25	79	53,014	28,923	0	0	134,266	0	0	219,044	31,389	187,655	187,655	0
26	80	56,195	30,658	0	0	142,322	0	0	232,187	33,273	198,914	198,914	0
27	81	59,566	32,497	0	0	150,862	0	0	246,119	35,270	210,849	210,849	0
28	82	63,140	34,447	0	0	159,913	0	0	260,887	37,386	223,500	223,500	0
29	83	66,929	36,514	0	0	52,945	100,245	0	256,632	22,329	236,910	236,910	0
30	84	70,945	38,705	0	0	0	141,475	0	251,125	0	251,125	251,125	0
31	85	75,201	41,027	0	0	0	149,964	0	266,192	0	266,192	266,192	0
32	86	79,713	43,489	0	0	0	465	0	123,667	0	123,667	282,164	-158,497
33	87	84,496	46,098	0	0	0	0	0	130,594	0	130,594	299,094	-168,499
34	88	89,566	48,864	0	0	0	0	0	138,430	0	138,430	317,039	-178,609
35	89	94,940	51,796	0	0	0	0	0	146,736	0	146,736	336,062	-189,326
36	90	100,636	54,904	0	0	0	0	0	155,540	0	155,540	356,225	-200,685
37	91	106,674	58,198	0	0	0	0	0	164,872	0	164,872	377,599	-212,727
38	92	113,075	61,690	0	0	0	0	0	174,765	0	174,765	400,255	-225,490

Case Study 01 - The Inflation Risk Scenario

The Synergy Effect ™

Regarding the taxable portion of the Social
Security benefits, the above scenario assumes:

85 percent from start to end.

Regarding the average tax rate applied to all
taxable income the above scenario assumes:

17 percent from year one to year 10,
14 percent from year 11 to year 29,
0 percent from year 30 to end.

"Case Study 01 – The Inflation Risk Scenario" illustration uses the
same assumptions as were used in "The Reduced Lifestyle Scenario"
with these exceptions: the spendable retirement income objective is
increased by an annual rate of six percent instead of three percent, the
assumed COLA increase in Social Security benefits starting at age 65
was also increased to six percent annually as opposed to the original 2.3
percent, and the assumed interest rate earned on Frank and Mary's CD
was increased from three percent to seven percent starting at age 65.

Increasing the Social Security COLA to six percent may be unrealistic,
but if a smaller COLA was used to project future Social Security
income, or if a lower earnings rate on the CD were assumed, then the
impact of inflation would have been even worse. As it is, it's bad
enough. At this rate of inflation, Frank and Mary would run out of
money by age 86 instead of age 91.

The Tax Risk Scenario

Another important consideration is the risk that tax rates might increase
in the future. This can have a particularily damaging effect on
retirement resources that rely heavily on traditional tax-deferred
retirement accounts like IRAs and 401(k) plans.

The Synergy Effect™ *In Action*

Yr.	Age	SSI Workers Frank	SSI Workers Mary	SSI Spousal Mary	Q-Plan IRA Frank	Q-Plan 401(k) Frank	Non-Q CD	Roth XYZ	Gross Income	Taxes Paid	Actual Spendable Income	Target Spendable Income	Over / Under Spendabl
11	65	23,448	12,792	0	66,151	0	0	0	103,158	20,158	83,000	83,000	0
12	66	23,987	13,086	0	68,399	0	0	0	106,258	20,768	85,490	85,490	0
13	67	24,539	13,387	0	19,991	50,730	0	0	109,451	21,396	88,055	88,055	0
14	68	25,103	13,695	0	0	73,118	0	0	112,739	22,043	90,696	90,696	0
15	69	25,680	14,010	0	0	75,593	0	0	116,127	22,710	93,417	93,417	0
16	70	26,271	14,332	0	0	78,149	0	0	119,616	23,396	96,220	96,220	0
17	71	26,875	14,662	0	0	80,788	0	0	123,210	24,104	99,106	99,106	0
18	72	27,493	14,999	0	0	83,514	0	0	126,912	24,832	102,080	102,080	0
19	73	28,126	15,344	0	0	86,328	0	0	130,725	25,583	105,142	105,142	0
20	74	28,773	15,697	0	0	89,233	0	0	134,652	26,356	108,296	108,296	0
21	75	29,434	16,058	0	0	92,233	0	0	138,698	27,153	111,545	111,545	0
22	76	30,111	16,427	0	0	95,330	0	0	142,865	27,974	114,891	114,891	0
23	77	30,804	16,805	0	0	98,528	0	0	147,157	28,819	118,338	118,338	0
24	78	31,513	17,192	0	0	101,830	0	0	151,578	29,690	121,888	121,888	0
25	79	32,237	17,587	0	0	105,239	0	0	156,132	30,587	125,545	125,545	0
26	80	32,979	17,991	0	0	108,758	0	0	160,823	31,512	129,311	129,311	0
27	81	33,737	18,405	0	0	112,390	0	0	165,654	32,464	133,191	133,191	0
28	82	34,513	18,829	0	0	116,141	0	0	170,631	33,445	137,186	137,186	0
29	83	35,307	19,262	0	0	120,012	0	0	175,757	34,455	141,302	141,302	0
30	84	36,119	19,705	0	0	124,009	0	0	181,037	35,496	145,541	145,541	0
31	85	36,950	20,158	0	0	120,728	5,925	0	183,761	35,051	149,907	149,907	0
32	86	37,800	20,621	0	0	0	95,983	0	154,404	0	154,404	154,404	0
33	87	38,669	21,096	0	0	0	99,272	0	159,037	0	159,037	159,037	0
34	88	39,559	21,581	0	0	0	12,733	0	73,872	0	73,872	163,808	-89,935
35	89	40,468	22,077	0	0	0	0	0	62,546	0	62,546	168,722	-106,176
36	90	41,399	22,585	0	0	0	0	0	63,984	0	63,984	173,784	-109,799
37	91	42,351	23,105	0	0	0	0	0	65,456	0	65,456	178,997	-113,541
38	92	43,325	23,636	0	0	0	0	0	66,961	0	66,961	184,367	-117,406

The Synergy Effect ™

Case Study 01 - The Tax Risk Scenario

Regarding the taxable portion of the Social Security benefits, the above scenario assumes:

85 percent from start to year 31,
50 percent from year 32 to end.

Regarding the average tax rate applied to all
taxable income, the above scenario assumes:

17 percent from year one to year 10,
20 percent from year 11 to year 31,
0 percent from year 32 to end.

"The Tax Risk Scenario" illustration uses the same assumptions as were
used in "The Reduced Lifestyle Scenario" except that the assumed tax
rates are different. In "The Reduced Lifestyle Scenario," it was
assumed that Frank and Mary would pay an average tax rate of 17
percent from their current age of 55 until retirement, starting at age 65
they would pay an average tax rate of 14 percent until age 89, and from
age 90 on they would pay no income taxes. These assumptions have
been changed in "The Tax Risk Scenario." Starting at age 65, instead of
14 percent, the it is assumed that their average tax rate would increase
to 20 percent. They would continue to be taxed at this rate until no
income taxes would be paid from age 86 on.

The primary impact of this higher tax assumption is that Frank and
Mary would need to increase the withdrawals from their taxable IRA
and 401(k) in order to net the same amount of after-tax spendable
income. These increased withdrawals cause them to exhaust their
resources by age 88, as opposed to age 91 if those tax rates had
remained lower.

The Synergy Effect™ **Scenario**

In the *Synergy Effect™* scenario major changes are made to the types of
products and financial instruments Mary and Frank will use to provide
their future spendable retirement income. These changes will be
explained in detail later in this chapter. For now, it is very important to
explain the changes assumed in this scenario as they relate to the
strategies used with regards to when Mary and Frank claim their Social
Security retirement benefits.

Current Position

Yr	Age	SSI Workers Frank	SSI Workers Mary	SSI Spousal Mary	Q-Plan IRA Frank	Q-Plan 401(k) Frank	Non-Q CD	Roth XYZ	Gross Income	Taxes Paid	Actual Spendabl e Income	Target Spendabl e Income	Over/Under Spendabl
11	65	23,448	12,792	0	59,387	0	0	0	96,164	13,164	83,000	83,000	0
12	66	23,987	13,086	0	61,429	0	0	0	99,053	13,563	85,490	85,490	0
13	67	24,539	13,387	0	35,194	28,344	0	0	102,028	13,974	88,055	88,055	0
14	68	25,103	13,695	0	0	65,715	0	0	105,093	14,397	90,696	90,696	0
15	69	25,680	14,010	0	0	67,965	0	0	108,250	14,833	93,417	93,417	0
16	70	26,271	14,332	0	0	70,289	0	0	111,502	15,282	96,220	96,220	0
17	71	26,875	14,662	0	0	72,689	0	0	114,851	15,745	99,106	99,106	0
18	72	27,493	14,999	0	0	75,167	0	0	118,301	16,222	102,080	102,080	0
19	73	28,126	15,344	0	0	77,727	0	0	121,855	16,713	105,142	105,142	0
20	74	28,773	15,697	0	0	80,370	0	0	125,515	17,219	108,296	108,296	0

Revised Position

Yr	Age	SSI Workers Frank	SSI Workers Mary	SSI Spousal Mary	Q-Plan Inc. Ann. IRA Frank	Q-Plan 401(k) Frank	Non-Q CD	Roth XYZ	IUL	Gross Income	Taxes Paid	Actual Spendabl e Income	Target Spendabl e Income	Over/Under Spendabl
11	65	0	0	0	0	96,512	0	0	0	96,512	13,512	83,000	83,000	0
12	66	0	0	4,496	0	94,801	0	0	0	99,297	13,807	85,490	85,490	0
13	67	0	0	13,800	0	88,252	0	0	0	102,052	13,998	88,055	88,055	0
14	68	0	0	14,117	0	90,999	0	0	0	105,116	14,420	90,696	90,696	0
15	69	0	0	14,442	0	93,830	0	0	0	108,272	14,855	93,417	93,417	0
16	70	37,428	20,412	0	0	52,631	0	0	0	110,471	14,251	96,220	96,220	0
17	71	38,289	20,881	0	0	54,625	0	0	0	113,795	14,689	99,106	99,106	0
18	72	39,170	21,361	0	0	56,688	0	0	0	117,219	15,140	102,080	102,080	0
19	73	40,071	21,853	0	0	58,823	0	0	0	120,746	15,604	105,142	105,142	0
20	74	40,992	22,355	0	0	61,032	0	0	0	124,379	16,083	108,296	108,296	0

The Synergy Effect ™   Case Study 01 - *The Synergy Effect™ Scenario (age 65 - 74)*

Regarding the taxable portion of the Social Security benefits, the revised position section in the above scenario assumes:

85 percent from year one to end.

(Note: To an extent, the advantages of the Synergy Effect™ scenario are due to the significant increase in lifetime Social Security benefits that are the result of delaying the starting age of these benefits. Because the thresholds for determining Social Security taxation are not indexed to inflation, it is assumed that the larger benefits will result in the requirement to include 85 percent of the amounts as taxable income.)

Regarding the average tax rate applied to all taxable income, the above scenario assumes:

17 percent from year one to year 10,
14 percent from year 11 to 23,
10 percent from year 24 to end.

The top portion Current Position of the above illustration shows the Social Security benefits that Frank and Mary can expect to receive if they started those benefits at their age 65. These benefit amounts are the same as have been used in all of the prior illustrations. And the withdrawals from the IRA and 401(k) that are need to meet the inflation-adjusted spendable income object of of $83,000 are also the same as were used in several of the prior illustrations.

The bottom portion ("Revised Position") will allow us to see the *Synergy Effect™* that is gained, in part, by Frank and Mary using a different Social Security claiming strategy.

Social Security Claiming Strategies

Chapter three presented techniques for synergizing Social Security. In large part, those techniques revolve around delaying the start of Social Security in order to benefit from delayed retirement credits to boost the amount of lifetime income.

Because both Frank and Mary were born in 1958, their *full retirement age* under the Social Security rules is age 66 and 8 months. All of the prior scenarios assume that they start their Social Security at age 65. Because this is earlier than their normal retirement age, they are penalized and will only receive 88 and 8/9 percent of their *primary insurance amount.*

If they both delayed the start of their Social Security worker's benefit until age 70, they would each receive delayed retirement credits as well as additional credits for any COLAs that might be declared prior to the start of their benefits.

This can make a significant difference in the potential amounts of those benefits. For Frank, instead of the reduced Social Security benefit of $23,448 (year 11 under "Current Position") that he is projected to receive if he started it at age 65, his projected increased benefit by waiting until age 70 would be $37,428 (year 16 under "Revised Position"). For Mary, the projected reduced benefit is $12,792 (year 11 under "Current Position") compared to the projected delayed benefit of $20,412 (year 16 under "Revised Position").

Both the current and revised Social Security benefits assume the same 2.3 percent COLA.

In all of the prior scenarios, the total combined income from Social Security at age 65 is $36,240 ($23,448 + $12,792), as opposed to a total combined income of $57,840 ($37,428 + 20,412) if started later at age 70.

This is too large of a difference in income to ingore. Yet as was pointed out earlier, the majority of Americans do ignore it as is evidenced by the fact that most people start their Social Security benefits even earlier then age 65.

By starting their Social Security early at age 65, Frank and Mary lose more then just the additional income. Any future COLAs that are declared are applied to the larger base income that they would receive by delaying the start of their benefits. For example, a 2.3 percent COLA applied to the smaller starting combined base income of $36,240 is $834 compared to the same percentage COLA applied to the larger delayed starting combined base income of $57,840 or $1,330. The difference is almost $500 more in annual income. This additional annual income might go a long way in offsetting inflation or in making Frank and Mary's retirement more enjoyable. In addition, the *promise* of Social Security is that it will provide a lifetime income. Assuming it fullfills this promose, it will play a critically important role in helping Frank and Mary deal with *longevity risk.*

As is shown in the revised position section of the illustration, the assumption that Frank and Mary will retire at age 65 has not changed. Because the retirement age is unchanged, in order for them to be able to delay the start of their Social Security benefit, they would need to initially withdraw a greater amount of money from their qualified retirement plans to meet their income needs between the ages of 65 to 70. In effect, they would need to consume a larger portion of their qualified plan balances in the early years of their retirement in order to receive more Social Security dollars in the later years of their retirement. This is the concept of *trading IRA dollars for more Social Security dollars* that was described in chapter three.

Referring to the revised position section of the above illustration, you see that because Frank and Mary have no Social Security benefit at age 65, they would need to meet their entire spendable income need of $83,000 by taking a withdrawal from Frank's 401(k). Again, the assumption is that any withdrawal would be taxed at an average rate of 14 percent. This would require them to withdrawal a pre-tax amount of $96,512 (year 11 under "Revised Position") so that after taxes, $83,000 would be available for them to spend. Compare this to the smaller withdrawal of $59,387 needed if they started their Social Security at age 65 (year 11 under "Current Position").

Again, the strategy used under the *Synergy Effect™* is to trade traditional IRA, 401(k) and other tax deferred retirement plan dollars for more Social Security dollars. This is done by consuming more of the qualified plan balances early in retirement, so that the start of Social Security can be delayed and get boosted from the delayed retirement credits.

Referring to the revised position section of the above illustration you will see a column labelled "SSI Spousal Mary." It shows an annual income of $4,496 at age 66, $13,800 at age 67, $14,117 at age 68 and $14,442 at age 69 (years 12 - 15 under "Revised Position"). These benefit amounts represent Mary's *spousal benefit* that would be available through Social Security. The total, $46,855, represents *free* additional money that is available to many spouses who use the *file and suspend* strategy.

To use this strategy, once Frank reaches his full retirement age (66 years and 8 months) he would file a restricted application with the Social Security Administration to start his worker's benefit. This allows Mary to apply for her spousal benefit that is based on Frank's work history. Frank then immediately suspends his worker's benefit so that it can earn delayed retirement credits prior to the benefit's permanent starting age of 70 (year 16 under "Revised Position"). At that same age, Mary's spousal benefit will be replaced by her larger worker's benefit, which also would receive delayed retirement credits (year 16 under "Revised Position").

So while Frank and Mary will need to withdraw more from their IRA and 401(k) while they are waiting to claim their larger worker's benefit at age 70, those withdrawals will be lessened by this *free* additional $46,855 that they would receive by using the file and suspend strategy (years 12 - 15 under "Revised Position").

Repositioning Assets

In addition to the changes with regards to Social Security, *the Synergy Effect*™ scenario reflects major and immediate repositioning of Frank and Mary's savings and investments.

The first change assumes that Frank immediately uses the current $75,000 balance in his IRA to purchase a *deferred income annuity* (DIA). This is a single life annuity with income payments scheduled to start when Frank is age 78 and guaranteed for a ten-year *period certain*. To add protection against the inflation risk, this annuity provides a three percent annual increase in income. The starting guaranteed annual payment provided by a highly-rated insurance company from this annuity is $16,015.

It is important to understand that this particular annuity does not include a death benefit option. This means that if Frank dies prior to the start of the deferred payments, there would not be anything paid to the beneficary. Frank could have opted for a deferred-income annuity with a death benefit, but the annual payment would have been approximately $3,000 less.

This higher $16,015 of lifetime income is an example of the mortality credits examined in chapter nine.

In order to obtain this higher lifetime income, Frank and Mary must accept the risk that the money placed into the annuity would be forfeited if Frank dies prior to the payment start date. In addition, they must accept that if Frank dies after the payment start date, the payments would only continue for a period of ten years (from the payment start date).

To help manage this risk as well as for other benefits, Frank and Mary decide to purchase an indexed universal life insurance policy on Frank's life. Currently, Frank has $500,000 of term life insurance which will be replaced by this new permenant coverage. This will help protect Mary from the longevity risk described earlier in this chapter as well as offset the risks associated with the purchase of the deferred-income annuity. In addition, both Frank and Mary are attracted to the ability of the IUL's cash values to grow tax-deferred and to possibly access those values tax-free to provide additional income, if needed, during Frank's life.

Frank and Mary will use the money accumulated in their certificate of deposit to partially fund the purchase of this IUL. In addition, it is assumed that Frank will immediately reduce his 401(k) contributions in excess of his employer's matching contributions. So instead of contributing at the prior level of $15,000, he will only contribute $3,000 annually until he retires. He uses these excess contributions as a source of additional premiums to pay into his IUL.

Unfortunatly he will not have the entire $15,000 available to pay into his IUL because he will lose a good portion of the tax deductions that he would have received had he continued contributing the larger amounts to his 401(k).

The Synergy Effect™ scenario illustration uses an assumed marginal tax rate of 25 percent to calculate the amount of the tax deduction that will be lost with the reduced 401(k) contributions. The reason that this higher 25 percent tax rate is used, as opposed to the lower *average* tax rate that has been used in the prior illustrations, is that the lost tax deduction will be felt at the higher marginal tax rate.

For example, the tax rates in 2013 for *married filing jointly* tax income between $72,501 up to $146,400 at the rate of 25 percent. Any deductions that offset taxable income within this range will reduce the taxes paid by 25 percent. This means that a married couple with $100,000 of taxable income would reduce their current tax bill by $3,000 by making a tax deductible 401(k) contribution of $12,000 ($12,000 X 25% = $3,000).

Because of the lost tax deduction due to the reduced 401(k) contribution and the assumed 25 percent marginal tax rate, *the Synergy Effect*™ scenario illustration assumes that Frank will only have a net of $9,000 remaining to divert to his IUL after paying the increased taxes.

Using the $100,000 in their certificate of deposit, the net $9,000 annual amount from the diverted 401(k) contributions and the $1,500 annual premium payment for the term insurance that will be replaced, the IUL premium payment schedule over Frank' remaining working years would be as follows:

Year	Total Premium
1	$35,500
2	$35,500
3	$35,500
4	$35,500
5	$10,500
6	$10,500
7	$10,500
8	$10,500
9	$10,500
10	$10,500
11+	0

Assuming a non-guaranteed annual index interest rate of seven percent, a preferred nontobacco risk classification and the use of the increasing death benefit option, this policy's initial death benefit would be slightly above $533,000. This death benefit is scheduled to increase each year until year 13. The assumption is that in that year, the death benefit option would be changed from *increasing* to the minimum *level* death benefit in order to reduce future mortality charges and enhance cash value accumulation.

The illustration below is a continuation of the prior "Synergy Effect™ Scenario" illustration, except that it shows projections of what we might expect to occur while Frank and Mary are between the ages of 75 and 84.

The Synergy Effect™ *In Action*

Current Position

Yr	Age	SSI Workers Frank	SSI Workers Mary	SSI Spousal Mary	Q-Plan IRA Frank	Q-Plan 401(k) Frank	Non-Q CD	Roth XYZ	Gross Income	Taxes Paid	Actual Spendable Income	Target Spendable Income	Over / Under Spendable
21	75	29,434	16,058	0	0	83,100	0	0	129,286	17,741	111,545	111,545	0
22	76	30,111	16,427	0	0	85,920	0	0	133,169	18,278	114,891	114,891	0
23	77	30,804	16,805	0	0	88,831	0	0	137,169	18,831	118,338	118,338	0
24	78	31,513	17,192	0	0	91,837	0	0	141,289	19,401	121,888	121,888	0
25	79	32,237	17,587	0	0	94,942	0	0	145,533	19,988	125,545	125,545	0
26	80	32,979	17,991	0	0	98,147	0	0	149,904	20,593	129,311	129,311	0
27	81	33,737	18,405	0	0	101,457	0	0	154,407	21,216	133,191	133,191	0
28	82	34,513	18,829	0	0	104,875	0	0	159,045	21,858	137,186	137,186	0
29	83	35,307	19,262	0	0	108,403	0	0	163,822	22,520	141,302	141,302	0
30	84	36,119	19,705	0	0	112,047	0	0	168,742	23,201	145,541	145,541	0

Revised Position

Yr	Age	SSI Workers Frank	SSI Workers Mary	SSI Spousal Mary	Taxable Annuity	Q-Plan IRA Frank	Q-Plan 401(k) Frank	Non-Q CD	Roth XYZ	IUL	Gross Income	Taxes Paid	Actual Spendable Income	Target Spendable Income	Over / Under Spendable
21	75	41,935	22,869	0	0	0	63,317	0	0	0	128,121	16,576	111,545	111,545	0
22	76	42,899	23,395	0	0	0	65,681	0	0	0	131,976	17,084	114,891	114,891	0
23	77	43,886	23,933	0	0	0	68,127	0	0	0	135,946	17,608	118,338	118,338	0
24	78	44,896	24,484	0	16,015	0	1,178	0	0	42,933	129,505	7,617	121,888	121,888	0
25	79	45,928	25,047	0	16,495	0	0	0	0	45,757	133,227	7,682	125,545	125,545	0
26	80	46,985	25,623	0	16,990	0	0	0	0	47,584	137,182	7,871	129,311	129,311	0
27	81	48,065	26,212	0	17,500	0	0	0	0	49,477	141,254	8,064	133,191	133,191	0
28	82	49,171	26,815	0	18,025	0	0	0	0	51,437	145,448	8,261	137,186	137,186	0
29	83	50,302	27,432	0	18,566	0	0	0	0	53,466	149,766	8,464	141,302	141,302	0
30	84	51,459	28,063	0	19,123	0	0	0	0	55,568	154,213	8,672	145,541	145,541	0

The Synergy Effect ™   Case Study 01 - The Synergy Effect™ Scenario (age 75 - 84)

The "revised position" section of this illustration shows that Frank's 401(k) plan balance would be completely exhausted by his age 78 (year 24 under Revised Position). This should be expected because immediately after retiring, Frank and Mary need to take larger withdrawals from the 401(k) because they delayed the start of their of their Social Security. In addition, there would not be as much money in the 401(k) at retirement because Frank diverted a good portion of the contributions he had been making to this plan to pay a portion of the premium payments for the IUL.

In the year the 401(k) balance was exhausted (year 24 under "Revised Position") Frank and Mary are scheduled to receive much larger delayed retirement benefits from Social Security of $44,896 and $24,484 respectively. In addition, the $16,015 annual payout from the deferred income annuity that Frank purchased with his IRA money would begin. When these income amounts are added to the final withdrawal of $1,178 from the 401(k), the total equals $86,573. Their spendable income objective that year (year 24 under Revised Position) is $121,888. In order to meet that income need, Frank and Mary would take a loan from the accumulated cash value in their IUL of $42,933.

Their total gross income that year (year 24 under "Revised Position") is $129,505. Of this amount, only $76,166 is taxable (85 percent of Social Security, the 401(k) withdrawal and the payout from the annuity). Net of a 10 percent assumed average tax rate, the amount remaining meets their spendable income target of $121,888.

The illustration below advances the period viewed to show from the 31st year when Frank and Mary would each be age 85, through the 40th year.

Version 201301

Current Position

Yr	Age	SSI Workers Frank	SSI Workers Mary	SSI Spousal Mary	Q-Plan IRA Frank	Q-Plan 401(k) Frank	Non-Q CD	Roth XYZ	Gross Income	Taxes Paid	Actual Spendable Income	Target Spendable Income	Over / Under Spendabl
31	85	36,950	20,158	0	0	115,809	0	0	173,810	23,903	149,907	149,907	0
32	86	37,800	20,621	0	0	119,692	0	0	179,031	24,626	154,404	154,404	0
33	87	38,669	21,096	0	0	123,702	0	0	184,408	25,371	159,037	159,037	0
34	88	39,559	21,581	0	0	127,842	0	0	189,946	26,138	163,808	163,808	0
35	89	40,468	22,077	0	0	72,698	51,099	0	186,343	18,396	168,722	168,722	0
36	90	41,399	22,585	0	0	0	109,799	0	173,784	0	173,784	173,784	0
37	91	42,351	23,105	0	0	0	81,928	0	147,384	0	147,384	178,997	-31,613
38	92	43,325	23,636	0	0	0	0	0	66,961	0	66,961	184,367	-117,406
39	93	44,322	24,180	0	0	0	0	0	68,501	0	68,501	189,898	-121,397
40	94	45,341	24,736	0	0	0	0	0	70,077	0	70,077	195,595	-125,518

Revised Position

Yr	Age	SSI Workers Frank	SSI Workers Mary	SSI Spousal Mary	Taxable Annuity	Q-Plan IRA Frank	Q-Plan 401(k) Frank	Non-Q CD	Roth XYZ	IUL	Gross Income	Taxes Paid	Actual Spendable Income	Target Spendable Income	Over / Under Spendabl
31	85	52,642	28,708	0	19,696	0	0	0	0	57,745	158,792	8,884	149,907	149,907	0
32	86	53,853	29,369	0	20,287	0	0	0	0	59,998	163,507	9,103	154,404	154,404	0
33	87	55,091	30,044	0	20,896	0	0	0	0	62,331	168,363	9,326	159,037	159,037	0
34	88	56,359	30,735	0	21,523	0	0	0	0	64,746	173,363	9,555	163,808	163,808	0
35	89	57,655	31,442	0	22,169	0	0	0	0	67,247	178,512	9,790	168,722	168,722	0
36	90	58,981	32,165	0	22,834	0	0	0	0	69,835	183,814	10,031	173,784	173,784	0
37	91	60,337	32,905	0	23,519	0	0	0	0	40,900	157,661	10,277	147,384	178,997	-31,613
38	92	61,725	33,662	0	24,224	0	0	0	0	20,869	140,480	10,530	129,950	184,367	-54,417
39	93	63,145	34,436	0	24,951	0	0	0	0	20,869	143,401	10,789	132,611	189,898	-57,287
40	94	64,597	35,228	0	25,699	0	0	0	0	20,869	146,394	11,055	135,339	195,595	-60,256

The Synergy Effect ™   Case Study 01 - The Synergy Effect™ Scenario (age 85 - 94)

You can see that the non-guaranteed projections based on the current assumptions from the IUL illustration show that the policy should be able to support a continuation of cash value loans in amounts neccesary to fully meet Frank and Mary's spendable income objective until year 37 when they each reach the age of 91.

Note that this is the same age at which the current position projections show that they would have exhausted all of their savings.

Both their current position, or *the Synergy Effect™* as is reflected in the revised position, would meet the spendable income target through their age 90. But if Mary or Frank or both live beyond this age, *the Synergy Effect™* scenario could prove to be the greatly superior position.

Neither their current position nor *the Synergy Effect™* revised position will provide 100 percent of the spendable income Frank and Mary desire after age 90, but the revised position is projected to provide significantly more. For example, in year 38, the actual spendable income projected in their current position is only $66,961, compared to $129,950 under the revised position. That is almost twice the spendable income.

Much of the increase comes from the larger Social Security benefits. The rest comes from the annuity and the IUL.

The IUL cash value loan amounts were reduced to $20,869 starting in year 38 (age 92), because this was the maximum amount of income that the policy would support for the balance of Frank's life based upon the non-guaranteed assumptions.

In preparing the IUL illustration, the objective was to borrow cash value in amounts nessecary to meet Frank and Mary's spendable income objective for at least as long as their current position would provide that income (age 91). To accomplish this, you simply schedule cash value loans in the amounts needed using the insurance company's illustration software. Starting at age 92, you would use the insurance company's illustration software to "solve for" the maximum non-guaranteed cash value loan amounts that the policy would be able to support for the balance of the insured's life. In Frank's example, the illustration software calculated this amount to be $20,869.

It is also important to consider how the death of either spouse would impact the survivor. Under their current position, if either death occurred after age 91, the survivor would only be left with the benefit amount received from Social Security. While the death of a spouse might created many problems under *the Synergy Effect™* revised position, the survivor would still be better off than under the current position if for no other reason than the fact that their Social Security benefit would be much larger.

For example, under *the Synergy Effect™* revised position if Frank died at age 92, Mary would "inherit" his $61,725 Social Security benefit (as the surviving spouse, Mary receives the greater of her own worker's benefit or Frank's benefit). Compare this to the much lower $43,325 benefit she would "inherit" under the current position.

And upon Frank's death, Mary would also receive any net death benefit from the IUL. For example, if Frank died at age 91, the non-guaranteed death benefit is projected to be approximately $160,000. (This death benefit amount assumes that they had not yet taken a cash value loan from the policy in the year of Frank's death.)

On an inflation-adjusted basis, this death benefit may not be a lot of money, but at least it is more than Mary would receive under the current position, which projects that all of their savings would have been exhausted by this age.

Frank's financial situation would be more secure if he was the survivor. In addition to his $61,725 Social Security benefit, he would continue to receive the lifetime payout from the annuity ($24,224 at age 92) as well as the non-guaranteed cash value loans from the IUL ($20,869 at age 92).

Changes could be made in how assets were initially repositioned under *the Synergy Effect™* that might make Mary's future more secure as the surviving spouse. Death benefit options or a longer *period certain* payout could have been added to Frank's annuity, a larger death benefit could have been added to the IUL, or a second IUL could have been purchased on Mary's life. While these and other options would likely improve her financial situation as the surviving spouse, it can be expected that they might also reduce the income provided while both were alive.

Determining the proper combination of Social Security claiming strategies with income annuities and IULs to obtain *the Synergy Effect™* will depend upon the client's objectives and what is most important to them. It will be up to the advisor to use his or her skills in assessing those objectives, modifing the strategy and presenting alternatives to the client.

In addition to boosting spendable income in the later years of Frank and Mary's lives, valid arguments can be made *the Synergy Effect™* scanario puts them in a better position to deal with the sequence of returns risk, the longevity risk, the inflation risk, the tax risk and many other risks that people should expect to face throughout retirement.

The Synergy Effect™ *In Action*

Case Study 02 – Assumptions

Fred, DOB 1/2/1951 (Age 62 as of start of year 2013)
Betty, DOB 1/2/1953 (Age 60 as of start of year 2013)

Inflation Rate Assumption: **3 percent**

Tax Rate Assumptions (unless otherwise noted):

Today's...	Tax Bracket = **25%**	Average Rate* = **18%**
Future...	Tax Bracket = **25%**	Average Rate* = **18%**

*Average Tax Rate = Tax to Taxable Income

Non-Qualified Accounts:

Money Market Account current balance = **$270,000**. Assumed annual return = **0.005 percent** years one through three and **4 percent** from year four and beyond. *(This money had been invested in stocks and mutual funds, which were sold in 2009 because of market volatility. Under their current plan Fred and Betty are waiting for interest rates to increase and then use this money to purchase a bank certificate of deposit.)*

Tax-Deferred Qualified Retirement Accounts:

Fred's **IRA** current balance = **$750,000**. Assumed annual return = **6 percent**. Contributions = **0**.

Betty's **IRA** current balance = **$650,000**. Assumed annual return = **6 percent**. Contributions = **0**

Tax-Free Qualified Retirement Accounts:

Betty's **Roth IRA** current balance = **$70,000**. Assumed annual return = **5 percent**. Contributions = **0**

Liquidity Requirements:

This case study will assume that Fred and Betty have an additional amount of money sufficient to meet their liquidity needs, and will not take that money into consideration for the purpose of providing future retirement income.

Social Security:

Fred's **SS** Primary Insurance Amount (PIA) at full retirement age (66yrs. 0 mo.) = **$30,000**

Betty's **SS** Primary Insurance Amount (PIA) at full retirement age (66yrs. 0 mo.) = **$24,000**

Assumed SS inflation factor = **2.3 percent**
(The inflation rate is used to inflate both wage-indexing and Cost of Living adjustments to Social Security benefit streams.)

Important Notes: Because both Fred and Betty where born prior to 1954, their full retirement age for Social Security would be age 66. Their current plan is for Fred to start his Social Security worker's benefit at his current age of 62, and Betty will start her Social Security worker's benefit in two years when she reaches age 62. Because this is earlier than their full retirement age, they will only receive 75 percent of their Primary Insurance Amount (PIA).

Those projected amounts, including the penalty would be:

Fred's **SS** projected benefit if started at age 62 = **$22,500**

Betty's **SS** projected benefit if started at age 62 = **$18,000**

Current Life Insurance:

Fred = **$500,000**. 20-year level term, purchased five years earlier (at his age 57). Annual premium is $2,000.

Betty = **0**

Long-Term Care:

The issue of providing for long-term care needs is critically important to a client's future financial security, but this topic is beyond the scope of this book. This case study assumes that those needs are addressed in some manner independent of what will be illustrated.

Planned Retirement Age:

Both Fred and Betty recently retired so they could travel and start enjoying their retirement years.

Is Fred and Betty's Income Objective Realistic?

In this case study we will assume that Fred and Betty need a spendable income in the amount of $100,000. This income needs to start immediately because Fred has recently retired and Betty has not worked for several years.

Because Fred and Betty have accumulated a retirement nest egg of over $1.7 million, they have assumed that they can afford to take their Social Security benefits early and start enjoying their retirement.

But as the illustration below shows, meeting their inflation-adjusted spendable income objective over a long period of time might be more difficult than they have anticipated.

Yr	Age	SSI Workers Fred	SSI Workers Betty	SSI Spousal Betty	Q-Plan IRA Fred	Q-Plan IRA Betty	Non-Q Money Market	Roth Betty	Gross Income	Taxes Paid	Actual Spendable Income	Target Spendable Income	Over/ Under Spendabl Income
1	62	22,500	0	0	98,710	0	0	0	121,453	21,453	100,000	100,000	0
2	63	23,016	0	0	101,836	0	0	0	125,096	22,096	103,000	103,000	0
3	64	23,545	18,000	0	86,465	0	0	0	128,255	22,165	106,090	106,090	0
4	65	24,087	18,408	0	89,365	0	0	0	133,828	24,555	109,273	109,273	0
5	66	24,641	18,831	0	92,353	0	0	0	137,858	25,307	112,551	112,551	0
6	67	25,208	19,265	0	95,438	0	0	0	142,010	26,082	115,927	115,927	0
7	68	25,787	19,708	0	98,623	0	0	0	146,286	26,881	119,405	119,405	0
8	69	26,381	20,161	0	101,911	0	0	0	150,691	27,704	122,987	122,987	0
9	70	26,987	20,625	0	105,305	0	0	0	155,229	28,552	126,677	126,677	0
10	71	27,608	21,099	0	93,582	15,226	0	0	159,903	29,426	130,477	130,477	0
11	72	28,243	21,584	0	0	112,424	0	0	164,718	30,327	134,392	134,392	0
12	73	28,893	22,081	0	0	116,157	0	0	169,678	31,255	138,423	138,423	0
13	74	29,557	22,588	0	0	120,011	0	0	174,788	32,212	142,576	142,576	0
14	75	30,237	23,108	0	0	123,988	0	0	180,051	33,197	146,853	146,853	0
15	76	30,932	23,640	0	0	128,093	0	0	185,472	34,213	151,259	151,259	0
16	77	31,644	24,183	0	0	132,331	0	0	191,057	35,260	155,797	155,797	0
17	78	32,372	24,739	0	0	136,704	0	0	196,809	36,339	160,471	160,471	0
18	79	33,116	25,308	0	0	141,218	0	0	202,735	37,450	165,285	165,285	0
19	80	33,878	25,891	0	0	145,877	0	0	208,839	38,596	170,243	170,243	0
20	81	34,657	26,486	0	0	150,686	0	0	215,127	39,777	175,351	175,351	0
21	82	35,454	27,095	0	0	155,649	0	0	221,604	40,993	180,611	180,611	0
22	83	36,270	27,718	0	0	107,684	43,531	0	215,203	38,908	186,029	186,029	0
23	84	37,104	28,356	0	0	0	129,424	0	194,883	23,564	191,610	191,610	0
24	85	37,957	29,008	0	0	0	133,742	0	200,707	4,182	197,359	197,359	0
25	86	38,830	29,675	0	0	0	138,199	0	206,705	3,736	203,279	203,279	0
26	87	39,723	30,358	0	0	0	80,533	58,763	209,378	0	209,378	209,378	0
27	88	40,637	31,056	0	0	0	0	143,966	215,659	0	215,659	215,659	0
28	89	41,572	31,770	0	0	0	0	45,391	118,733	0	118,733	222,129	-103,396
29	90	42,528	32,501	0	0	0	0	0	75,029	0	75,029	228,793	-153,764

The Synergy Effect ™   *Case Study 02 - Is $100,000 of Spendable Income Realistic?*

Regarding the taxable portion of the Social Security benefits, the above scenario assumes:

85 percent from year one to year 22,
50 percent from year 23 to year 35,
85 percent from year 36 to end.

276

Regarding the average tax rate applied to all taxable income the above scenario assumes:

18 percent from year one to year 22,
10 percent from year 23 to year 25,
* 0 percent from year 26 to end.*

If you refer to the illustrated values in "Case Study 02 – Is $100,000 of Spendable Income Realistic?" you can see that by starting Social Security at age 62, the couple's current Primary Insurance Amount (PIA) projects to a starting benefit of $22,500 for Fred, and $18,000 when Betty starts her benefit two years later (when she will turn age 62).

In the first year, after subtracting Fred's $22,500 (net of taxes) from their spendable retirement income target of $100,000 (column labelled "Target Spendable Income") the illustration assumes that a total of $98,710 would need to be withdrawn from Fred's taxable IRA to meet their after-tax spendable income need.

The entire withdrawal will be considered taxable income and would also then be included in the *provisional income formula* used to calculate the amount of Fred's Social Security income, which must also be included as taxable income. As a result, 85 percent of the $22,500 Social Security income is taxable. This amounts to $19,125 of additional taxable income.

As the column labeled "Gross Income" shows, their total gross income the first year is projected to be $121,453. *(Note that the total from Social Security and the IRA is $121,210. The projections assume that an additional $243 is withdrawn from the Money Market account that year to pay the tax on the growth in that account.)*

Based upon the assumption that the average tax rate for Fred and Betty would be 18 percent, the assumed total estimated tax would be $21,453. The breakdown of taxes at Fred's age 62, Betty's age 60 are as follows:

Money Market
>   Projected Balance at the start of year...$270,000

(Assumes a .005 percent annual taxable growth rate, but with amounts withdrawn each year to pay the income tax due on these earnings.)

Annual Taxable Growth...	$ 1,350
Taxes on Annual Growth...	*$ 243*

Social Security

His Total Benefit...	$ 22,500
His Taxable Portion...	$ 19,125
Taxes...	*$ 3,442*

IRA Withdrawal

Gross Amount...	$ 98,710
Taxable Portion...	$ 98,710
Taxes...	*$ 17,768*

Total Taxes...	**$ 21,453**

After paying this tax, Fred and Betty will be left with the $100,000 of spendable income that was their target.

Note that at best, the 18 percent is a rough estimate and does not take into account any itemized deductions that Fred and Betty might be able to use to reduce their taxable income.

Using the three percent assumed rate of inflation, the spendable income needed the following year climbs to $103,000.

After receiving Social Security of $23,016 (assuming a 2.3 percent COLA), Fred will now need to withdraw a total of $101,836 from his IRA so that after taxes, he and Betty can continue to meet their spendable income need that year.

In year three, Betty turns age 62 and would start her $18,000 Social Security worker's benefit.

With a combined $41,545 income from Social Security and a withdrawal from Fred's IRA in the amount of $86,465, their total gross income in the third year would be $128,255. *(Note that the total from Social Security and the IRA is $128,010. The projections assume that an additional $245 is withdrawn from the Money Market account that year to pay the tax on the growth in that account.)*

Based on their total income, 85 percent of their Social Security ($35,313) would be included as additional taxable income. This, along with the taxes due on the IRA withdrawal, would require the payment of $22,165 in taxes.

Money Market
>Projected Balance at the start of year...$272,219
(Assumes a .005 percent annual taxable growth rate but with amounts withdrawn each year to pay the income tax due on these earnings.)

Annual Taxable Growth...	$ 1,361
Taxes on Annual Growth...	*$ 245*

Social Security

His Total Benefit...	$ 23,545
His Taxable Portion...	$ 20,013
Taxes...	*$ 3,602*

Social Security

His Total Benefit...	$ 18,000
His Taxable Portion...	$ 15,300
Taxes...	*$ 2,754*

IRA Withdrawal

Gross Amount...	$ 86,465
Taxable Portion...	$ 86,465

Taxes...   *$ 15,564*

      Total Taxes...   **$ 22,165**

As the projections in this illustrate show, if Fred and Betty continue to withdraw the amounts neccesary to meet their spendable retirement income objective, they will completely exhaust Fred's IRA by the time Fred is age 71 (Betty would be age 69).

At this time, their inflation-adjusted spendable income need would have grown to $130,477. That year, the final $93,582 withdrawal from Fred's IRA would not be enough to meet this income objective. To make up the difference, they would need to start taking withdrawals from Betty's IRA.

By taking withdrawals from her IRA in amounts necessary to keep up with inflation, the entire balance would be exhausted by the time Fred turns age 83 and Betty turns age 81.

At this time, the illustration assumes that Fred and Betty start taking withdrawals from their Money Market account.

This would cause two changes in Fred and Betty's exposure to income taxes. Both changes are due to the fact that once both of their tax-deferred IRA balances are exhuasted (in year 22), their remaining taxable income will be from only the taxable portion of their Social Security and any interest earnings from their Money Market account.

The illustration assumes that the taxable portion of their Social Security drops to 50 percent, and their average tax rate drops to 10 percent starting in year's 23. Then, starting with year 26, it is assumed that their tax rate drops to zero because they would have exhausted their Money Market account and their only remaining money is in Betty's tax-free Roth IRA.

Based upon the withdraws they would need to meet their inflation-adjusted spendable income objective, Betty's Roth IRA would be completely exhausted in the 28th year, when Fred is age 89 and Betty is age 87.

As was the case in the prior study, there is a chance that either Betty or Fred, or possibly both, will live into their 90s or beyond, which means that the likelihood is that Social Security will be their only source of income.

It might be more prudent for Betty and Fred to lower their spendable income objective in the hope that their resources will last longer, but before taking that step, let's see if they might benefit from *the Synergy Effect™*.

The Synergy Effect™ **Scenario**

As with any scenario using *the Synergy Effect™*, at the foundation is the strategy of delaying the age at which Social Security benefits are claimed so that the amount of those lifetime benefits can be significantly boosted due to the impact of delayed retirement credits and COLAs.

Current Position

Yr	Age	SSI Workers Fred	SSI Workers Betty	SSI Spousal Betty	Q-Plan IRA Fred	Q-Plan IRA Betty	Non-Q Money Market	Roth Betty	Gross Income	Taxes Paid	Actual Spendable Income	Target Spendable Income	Over/Under Spendable
1	62	22,500	0	0	98,710	0	0	0	121,453	21,453	100,000	100,000	0
2	63	23,016	0	0	101,836	0	0	0	125,096	22,096	103,000	103,000	0
3	64	23,545	18,000	0	86,465	0	0	0	128,255	22,165	106,090	106,090	0
4	65	24,087	18,408	0	89,365	0	0	0	133,828	24,555	109,273	109,273	0
5	66	24,641	18,831	0	92,353	0	0	0	137,858	25,307	112,551	112,551	0
6	67	25,208	19,265	0	95,438	0	0	0	142,010	26,082	115,927	115,927	0
7	68	25,787	19,708	0	98,623	0	0	0	146,286	26,881	119,405	119,405	0
8	69	26,381	20,161	0	101,911	0	0	0	150,691	27,704	122,987	122,987	0
9	70	26,987	20,625	0	105,305	0	0	0	155,229	28,552	126,677	126,677	0
10	71	27,608	21,099	0	93,582	15,226	0	0	159,903	29,426	130,477	130,477	0
11	72	28,243	21,584	0	0	112,424	0	0	164,718	30,327	134,392	134,392	0

Revised Position

Yr	Age	SSI Workers Fred	SSI Workers Betty	SSI Spousal Betty	Tax Free Annuity	Q-Plan IRA Fred	Q-Plan IRA Betty	Non-Q Money Market	Roth Betty	IUL	Gross Income	Taxes Paid	Actual Spendable Income	Target Spendable Income	Over/Under Spendable
1	62	0	0	0	0	121,951	0	0	0	0	121,951	21,951	100,000	100,000	0
2	63	0	0	0	0	125,610	0	0	0	0	125,610	22,610	103,000	103,000	0
3	64	0	0	0	0	129,378	0	0	0	0	129,378	23,288	106,090	106,090	0
4	65	0	0	0	0	133,259	0	0	0	0	133,259	23,987	109,273	109,273	0
5	66	0	0	0	0	137,257	0	0	0	0	137,257	24,706	112,551	112,551	0
6	67	0	0	0	0	141,375	0	0	0	0	141,375	25,447	115,927	115,927	0
7	68	0	0	17,184	0	96,675	31,192	0	0	0	145,050	25,645	119,405	119,405	0
8	69	0	0	17,580	0	0	131,826	0	0	0	149,406	26,418	122,987	122,987	0
9	70	47,484	0	17,984	0	0	86,860	0	0	0	152,328	25,651	126,677	126,677	0
10	71	48,576	0	18,398	0	0	89,939	0	0	0	156,913	26,436	130,477	130,477	0
11	72	49,693	37,992	0	0	0	73,320	0	0	0	161,005	26,613	134,392	134,392	0

The Synergy Effect™ Case Study 02 - The Synergy Effect™ Scenario (age 62 - 72)

Regarding the taxable portion of the Social Security benefits, the revised position section of the above scenario assumes:

85 percent from year one to end.

*(Note: To an extent, the advantages of the
Synergy Effect™ scenario are due to the
significant increase in lifetime Social Security
benefits that are the result of delaying the
starting age of these benefits. Because the
thresholds for determining Social Security
taxation are not indexed to inflation, it is
assumed that the larger benefits will result in the
requirement to include 85 percent of the amounts
as taxable income.)*

Regarding the average tax rate applied to all
taxable income, the above scenario assumes:

*18 percent from year one to year 16,
12 percent from year 17 to end.*

The top portion ("Current Position") of the above illustration titled
"*The Synergy Effect* Scenario (age 62 – 72)" projects what can be
expected if Fred and Betty continue with their current plan of taking the
reduced Social Security benefits as well as the distributions from their
exiting retirement accounts. The bottom portion ("Revised Position")
will allow us to see *the Synergy Effect™* that is gained by Fred and
Betty using a different Social Security claiming strategy as well as
repositioning some of their assets.

Social Security Claiming Strategies

Because both Fred and Betty were born before 1954, their *full
retirement age* under the Social Security rules is age 66 and zero
months. Instead of receiving only 75 percent of their *primary insurance
amount* as they would if they started their Social Security benefits at
age 62, by delaying the start to age 70 the benefit amounts are boosted
by delayed retirement credits. In addition, any COLAs that might be
declared prior to the start of their benefits would provide further

increases in the lifetime income they would receive from Social Security.

Again, it is important to stress that the revised position scenario does not require that Fred and Betty delay the start of their retirement, only the date they claim their Social Security worker's benefit. Since the revised position scenario assumes that the retirement age is unchanged, the only way that they can meet their income needs until Social Security does start is to initially withdraw a greater amount of money from their IRAs between the ages of 62 to 70.

For example, in year one ("Revised Position") Fred would need to take a gross withdrawal of $121,951 from his IRA so that after taxes, they would have the $100,000 of spendable income they desire. In fact, all of their income in the first six years would come solely from withdrawals from Fred's IRA. Because of this, he is exhausting the balance of that account more rapidly than would have been the case if he had started a reduced Social Security benefit at an earlier age. Again, this is the concept described in Chapter Three, regarding the strategy of trading IRA dollars for more Social Security dollars.

The benefit of consuming more of the qualified plan balances early in retirement is the significant boost in lifetime Social Seurity income.

Referring to the revised position section of the above illustration, you will see a column labeled "SSI Spousal Betty." By referring to years seven – 10 under "Revised Position," you see annual income amounts of $17,184 at Fred's age 68 (Betty's age 66), $17,580 at age 69, $17,984 at age 70 and $18,398 at Fred's age 71 (Betty's age 69). These benefit amounts represent Betty's *spousal benefit* that would be available through Social Security. The total, $71,146, represents *free* additional money that is available to many spouses who use the *file and suspend* strategy.

As with the first case study, to use this strategy Fred would file a restricted application with the Social Security Administration to start his worker's benefit. This allows Betty to apply for her spousal benefit, which is based on Fred's work history. Fred then immediately suspends his worker's benefit so that it can earn delayed retirement credits prior to the benefit's permanent start at his age 70 (year nine under "Revised Position"). Two years later, Betty is age 70 and applies for her worker's benefit based on her own work and earnings history with Social Security. This results in a benefit of $37,992 (year 11 under "Revised Position"), which would replace the spousal benefit that she had been receiving.

So while Fred and Betty will need to exhaust more of their IRA balances while they are waiting until age 70 to claim their larger worker's benefit, the extent of the withdrawals that they must take to meet their income needs will be lessened by the *free* additional $71,146 that they would receive by using the file and suspend strategy (years seven - 10 under "Revised Position").

All of the Social Security benefits shown in both the *current* and *revised* position in the above illustration assume the same 2.3 percent annual COLA.

Consider the total projected income that Fred and Betty might expect to receive from Social Security in year 11 based on the assumptions reflected in both the current and revised positions. The total of Fred and Betty's benefit that year in the current position is $49,827 ($28,243 + $21,584). In the revised position, the total from Social Security in year 11 is $87,685 ($49,693 + $37,992). Delaying the start of Social Security provides Fred and Betty with an increase in income of $37,858 for that year alone.

As mentioned, to get this increase Fred and Betty would need to initially take much greater withdrawals from their IRAs. Again, this is the strategy of trading IRA dollars for more Social Security dollars.

Is this a good deal for them? The answer to that question depends a lot on their attitude towards *risk*.

Some people have the view that it is too risky to trade their IRA dollars for more Social Security dollars, because they fear that the program cannot be sustained and that ultimatly, these promised benefits won't be delievered. This can be referred to as a *politcal risk,* or a risk that politicians will change Social Security. And certainly there is evidence to support this position. Still other people have the view that this is too risky because they might not live long enough to take advantage of the higher Social Security benefits they *might* receive if they delayed the start of those benefits. And certainly this is a legitimate concern, especially if that person is in poor health or has a family history of reduced longevity.

These and other concerns might be justifiable reasons to support Fred and Betty or anyone else's decision to take Social Security at an earlier age. However, the potential of enjoying an *extra* $37,858 of income in a single year should not be ignored. By rejecting such a large amount of income, Fred and Betty might be exposing themselves to many other risks that might prove to be more certain than the political risk associated with Social Security.

For example, there is a different kind of political risk that should be considered. That is the risk that the government will increase future taxes. Under current law, at least 15 percent of every dollar received from Social Security is tax-free. This means that of the combined total delayed benefit of $87,685 that Fred and Betty might expect in year 11, at least $13,152 is tax-free under current law. Contrast this to their tax-deferred IRA dollars that are 100 percent taxable.

What about longevity risk? Again, some people decide to take Social Security benefits as early as possible because they fear that they might not live a long time. But what about the risk that either Fred or Betty or both might live much longer than the typical life expectancy? The longer they live, the greater the chance that they might exhaust all of their savings and be left with only their Social Security to see them through. The extra $37,858 of income in year 11, for example, might be an important factor when considering the longevity risk.

What about the inflation risk? The value of Social Security cost of living adjustments might end up being an important way to combat inflation. A 2.3 percent COLA applied to Fred and Betty's combined $49,827 reduced early benefit in year 11 ("Current Position") amounts to an increase of $1,146. But the same COLA percentage applied to their larger combined $87,685 delayed benefit that same year ("Revised Position") is an increase of $2,016. That amounts to an extra $870 of income in a single year to help offset the impact of the potentially higher cost of food, housing, medical and other expenses that Fred, Betty and all of us might one day face.

What about investment risk? Sure, Fred and Betty *might* be able to invest the money in their IRAs so that they provide them with a greater amount of inflation-adjusted lifetime income. But then again, the possibility exists that they might also need to live through the challenges of another financial meltdown or two in the process. The older they get, the likelihood is that they would prefer to expose their savings to less investment risk, which means that it may be more difficult for their investments to provide the growth and income they need to match what a higher delayed Social Security benefit might provide.

The point is that while there certainly are risks associated with a strategy that relies on trading IRA dollars for more Social Security dollars, there are also many, perhaps even greater, risks involved if Fred and Betty take reduced Social Security benefits early.

Repositioning Assets

In order to see the impact of repositioning some of Fred and Betty's assets, it helps to refer to the illustration on the next page titled "*The Synergy Effect* Scenario (age 73 – 83)."

Version 201301

Current Position

Yr	Age	SSI Workers Fred	SSI Workers Betty	SSI Spousal Betty	Q-Plan IRA Fred	Q-Plan IRA Betty	Non-Q Money Market	Roth Betty	Gross Income	Taxes Paid	Actual Spendable Income	Target Spendable Income	Over / Under Spendabl
12	73	28,893	22,081	0	0	116,157	0	0	169,678	31,255	138,423	138,423	0
13	74	29,557	22,588	0	0	120,011	0	0	174,788	32,212	142,576	142,576	0
14	75	30,237	23,108	0	0	123,988	0	0	180,051	33,197	146,853	146,853	0
15	76	30,932	23,640	0	0	128,093	0	0	185,472	34,213	151,259	151,259	0
16	77	31,644	24,183	0	0	132,331	0	0	191,057	35,260	155,797	155,797	0
17	78	32,372	24,739	0	0	136,704	0	0	196,809	36,339	160,471	160,471	0
18	79	33,116	25,308	0	0	141,218	0	0	202,735	37,450	165,285	165,285	0
19	80	33,878	25,891	0	0	145,877	0	0	208,839	38,596	170,243	170,243	0
20	81	34,657	26,486	0	0	150,686	0	0	215,127	39,777	175,351	175,351	0
21	82	35,454	27,095	0	0	155,649	0	0	221,604	40,993	180,611	180,611	0
22	83	36,270	27,718	0	0	107,684	43,531	0	215,203	38,908	186,029	186,029	0

Revised Position

Yr	Age	SSI Workers Fred	SSI Workers Betty	SSI Spousal Betty	Tax Free Annuity	Q-Plan IRA Fred	Q-Plan IRA Betty	Non-Q Money Market	Roth Betty	IUL	Gross Income	Taxes Paid	Actual Spendable Income	Target Spendable Income	Over / Under Spendabl
12	73	50,836	38,868	0	0	0	76,151	0	0	0	165,855	27,432	138,423	138,423	0
13	74	52,005	39,762	0	0	0	79,084	0	0	0	170,852	28,276	142,576	142,576	0
14	75	53,202	40,676	0	0	0	82,120	0	0	0	175,998	29,145	146,853	146,853	0
15	76	54,425	41,612	0	0	0	85,263	0	0	0	181,300	30,041	151,259	151,259	0
16	77	55,677	42,569	0	0	0	86,360	0	1,767	0	186,373	30,576	155,797	155,797	0
17	78	56,958	43,548	0	0	0	0	0	70,216	0	170,722	10,252	160,471	160,471	0
18	79	58,268	44,550	0	0	0	0	0	72,955	0	175,772	10,487	165,285	165,285	0
19	80	59,608	45,574	0	31,055	0	0	0	12,401	32,333	180,972	10,729	170,243	170,243	0
20	81	60,979	46,623	0	31,987	0	0	0	0	46,738	186,326	10,975	175,351	175,351	0
21	82	62,381	47,695	0	32,946	0	0	0	0	48,816	191,839	11,228	180,611	180,611	0
22	83	63,816	48,792	0	33,935	0	0	0	0	50,973	197,515	11,486	186,029	186,029	0

The Synergy Effect™ — Case Study 02 - The Synergy Effect™ Scenario (age 73 - 83)

The first change to note assumes that Betty converts $200,000 of the money in her traditional tax-deferred IRA to a Roth IRA. Prior to converting, Betty should go to her tax advisor to not only get a complete understanding of the ramifications of converting to a Roth IRA, but also to determine if the best strategy might be to convert smaller portions of the total over a number of years in an effort to possibly reduce the total tax resulting from the conversion.

To keep this illustration simple, the assumption is that the conversion would be completed over two years and that the total amount of the resulting conversion tax would be $60,000.

Fred and Betty decide to use $60,000 of the $270,000 in their money market account to pay the conversion tax.

In addition to a reduction in their money market account balance, the impact of this Roth conversion is that the remaining balance in Betty's traditional tax-deferred IRA is reduced from the initial balance of $650,000 to $450,000. But of course, there is now $200,000 more in a new Roth IRA account.

The revised position assumes that Fred and Betty will take withdrawals from the remaining balance in Betty's traditional IRA to meet their income needs after Fred's IRA balance has been exhausted (year 10). Because there is only $450,000 in Betty's IRA, they will exhaust this account balance more rapidly. The projections show this occuring in year 16 ("Revised Position").

At that time, it is assumed that Fred and Betty would start taking withdrawals from one of Betty's Roth IRAs. Remember, Betty now has two Roth IRAs. She has her original Roth IRA that had a balance of $70,000 just prior to retirement, and a new Roth IRA created from the conversion that had an initial balance of $200,000.

The illustration assumes that in year 16, withdrawals would be taken from the original Roth IRA. It is assumed that over the past 16 years, this Roth IRA's balance would have grown to $145,525.

This Roth IRA was not repositioned to another financial vehicle. The assumption is that it was left in the same investment that Fred and Betty had initially selected, and grew at the annual rate of five percent that they had expected it to.

With withdrawals starting in year 16 in amounts nessecary to meet their remaining income objective, the balance of this Roth IRA would be completely exhausted in year 19.

From year 17 on, it is assumed that the only taxable income that Fred and Betty will receive is from their combined Social Security benefits, which due to the anticipated COLAs, are projected to total $100,506.

As mentioned previousely, the thresholds for determining Social Security taxation are not indexed to inflation. Because of this, it is assumed that 85 percent of this income would be included as taxable income. However, since this is their only taxable income, the projections assume that from this year (17) and beyond, their average tax rate would reduce to 12 percent.

If that seems low considering they would have more than $85,000 of taxable income (from Social Security), remember that federal income taxes are indexed to inflation. The present value of $85,000 of income after 17 years, assuming a three percent inflation rate, would be about $54,000. The average tax rate today for a married couple over the age of 65 claiming the standard deduction would be about 12 percent.

Again, in year 19 ("Revised Position") the projections show that Betty's original Roth IRA would be exhausted. This is also the year in which we can see the impact of the other changes assumed with regards to repositioning assets.

The first relates to how the $200,000 Roth IRA conversion money is invested. At the time of the conversion, the assumption was that Betty used this money to purchase a *deferred income annuity* (DIA). She had received a quote from a highly-rated insurance company providing a guaranteed annual payment of $31,055 starting 19 years from the date of purchase.

This is a single life annuity with income payments guaranteed for a ten year *certain period*. To add protection against the inflation risk, this annuity provides a three percent annual increase in income.

Because this annuity is "inside" Betty's Roth IRA, the lifetime income it provides will be free of income taxes.

It is important to understand that this particular annuity does not include a death benefit option. This means that if Betty dies prior to the start of the deferred payments, there would not be anything paid to the beneficiary. Betty could have opted for a deferred income annuity with a death benefit, but the payment she would receive while alive would be approximately $4,500 less annually.

This higher $31,055 of lifetime income is an example of mortality credits.

As was the situation in the first case study, in order to obtain this higher lifetime income, Betty and Fred must accept the risk that the money placed into the annuity would be forfeited if Betty dies prior to the payment start date. In addition, they must be willing to accept that if Betty dies after the payment start date, the payments would only continue for a period of ten years (from the payment start date).

This is a risk that the illustration assumes they are willing to accept, because in their situation, both Betty and Fred are primarily concerned about the possibility of Fred predeceasing Betty, and the longevity risk assocated with her living long past her normal life expectancy.

The next change in assets regards repositioning the remaining money in their money market account.

The assumption was that of the original $270,000 balance, only $210,000 remains after using $60,000 to pay the added income tax that resulted from Betty's $200,000 Roth IRA conversion.

Fred and Betty use this entire $210,000 balance to fund the purchase of a life insurance policy on Fred's life. They select a policy with a "blend" of $300,000 of indexed universal life and an additional $300,000 of term life insurance for a total death benefit of $600,000.

This policy uses the level death benefit option for the indexed universal life portion and the term "blend" is scheduled to remain level for 15 years, at which time the intention is to drop it from the policy.

As was outlined in the assumptions at the beginning of this case study, Fred is currently insured under a 20-year term life insurance policy that he had purcashed five years earlier (at his age 57). This policy has a $500,000 level death benefit with an annual premium payment of $2,000.

Because Fred intends to replace this older term policy with the new policy, he can apply the $2,000 that he had been paying as additional premium on the new policy.

Using the $210,000 from the money market account along with the net $2,000 annual premiums that Fred had been paying for his term insurance, the IUL premium payment schedule would be as follows:

Year	Total Premium
1	$40,256
2	$40,256
3	$40,256
4	$40,256
5	$40,256
6	$20,936
7	$ 2,000
8	$ 2,000
9	$ 2,000
10	$ 2,000
11	$ 2,000
12	$ 2,000
13	$ 2,000
14	$ 2,000
15	$ 2,000
16+	$ 0

Because Fred and Betty have a more conservative outlook with regards to the future performance of the financial markets, the projections used in the IUL illustration assume a non-guaranteed annual index interest rate of six percent. In addition, it is assumed that Fred would qualified for the preferred nontobacco risk classification.

Based upon these assumptions, the IUL would support the series of cash value loans starting in year 19, when Fred is age 80, as is shown in the above "Synergy Effect™ Scenario age 73 – 83" illustration under the revised position.

In year 19 of that illustration the amount of the cash value loan is projected to be $32,333. This, along with the tax free $31,055 that would be received that same year from the annuity inside Betty's Roth IRA and the combined Social Security benefits, provide a total gross income of $180,972. Only 85 percent of the Social Security benefits are considered taxable income, so the assumed amount of income taxes paid would be $10,729. After the payment of these taxes, Fred and Betty have the spendable income that they desired.

The illustration below advances the period viewed to show from the 23rd year, when Fred and Betty would be age 84 and 82 respectively, through the 33rd year.

View | All Sources | This Acct | File | Print | Version 201301

Current Position

Yr	Age	SSI Workers Fred	SSI Workers Betty	SSI Spousal Betty	Q-Plan IRA Fred	Q-Plan IRA Betty	Non-Q Money Market	Roth Betty	Gross Income	Taxes Paid	Actual Spendable Income	Target Spendable Income	Over/Under Spendable
23	84	37,104	28,356	0	0	0	129,424	0	194,883	23,564	191,610	191,610	0
24	85	37,957	29,008	0	0	0	133,742	0	200,707	4,182	197,359	197,359	0
25	86	38,830	29,675	0	0	0	138,199	0	206,705	3,736	203,279	203,279	0
26	87	39,723	30,358	0	0	0	80,533	58,763	209,378	0	209,378	209,378	0
27	88	40,637	31,056	0	0	0	0	143,966	215,659	0	215,659	215,659	0
28	89	41,572	31,770	0	0	0	0	45,391	118,733	0	118,733	222,129	-103,396
29	90	42,528	32,501	0	0	0	0	0	75,029	0	75,029	228,793	-153,764
30	91	43,506	33,249	0	0	0	0	0	76,754	0	76,754	235,657	-158,902
31	92	44,506	34,013	0	0	0	0	0	78,520	0	78,520	242,726	-164,206
32	93	45,530	34,796	0	0	0	0	0	80,326	0	80,326	250,008	-169,682
33	94	46,577	35,596	0	0	0	0	0	82,173	0	82,173	257,508	-175,335

Revised Position

Yr	Age	SSI Workers Fred	SSI Workers Betty	SSI Spousal Betty	Tax Free Annuity	Q-Plan IRA Fred	Q-Plan IRA Betty	Non-Q Money Market	Roth Betty	IUL	Gross Income	Taxes Paid	Actual Spendable Income	Target Spendable Income	Over/Under Spendable
23	84	65,284	49,914	0	34,953	0	0	0	0	53,210	203,361	11,750	191,610	191,610	0
24	85	66,785	51,062	0	36,001	0	0	0	0	55,530	209,379	12,020	197,359	197,359	0
25	86	68,321	52,237	0	37,081	0	0	0	0	57,937	215,576	12,297	203,279	203,279	0
26	87	69,893	53,438	0	38,194	0	0	0	0	60,433	221,958	12,580	209,378	209,378	0
27	88	71,500	54,667	0	39,340	0	0	0	0	63,021	228,528	12,869	215,659	215,659	0
28	89	73,145	55,925	0	40,520	0	0	0	0	3,242	172,831	13,165	159,666	222,129	-62,463
29	90	74,827	57,211	0	41,735	0	0	0	0	3,242	177,015	13,468	163,547	228,793	-65,245
30	91	76,548	58,527	0	42,987	0	0	0	0	3,242	181,304	13,778	167,527	235,657	-68,130
31	92	78,309	59,873	0	44,277	0	0	0	0	3,242	185,700	14,095	171,606	242,726	-71,120
32	93	80,110	61,250	0	45,605	0	0	0	0	3,242	190,207	14,419	175,788	250,008	-74,220
33	94	81,952	62,659	0	46,973	0	0	0	0	3,242	194,826	14,750	180,076	257,508	-77,432

The Synergy Effect™   Case Study 02 - The Synergy Effect™ Scenario (age 84 - 94)

By referring to the current position section of the above illustration, you will see that Fred and Betty are projected to exhaust all of their savings by the 28th year if they continue on their current path.

The revised position section illustrates *the Synergy Effect™*, which in the same 28th year, projects a continuation of income from both Betty's income annuity inside her Roth IRA and an additional $3,242 provided by Fred's IUL.

The annuity income is guaranteed to continue for the balance of Betty's life (or a minimum of ten years from the start of the income payments, which in this example is year 19). The continuation of the $3,242 from the IUL is the non-guaranteed projected amount that the illustration shows as being available based on the assumption that the policy is credited annually with an assumed interest rate of six percent. In other words, based on the non-guaranteed current assumptions, the maximum amount of cash value loans that the IUL would support in year 28 and beyond is $3,242.

In preparing the illustration, cash value loans were scheduled in the amounts needed to meet Fred and Betty's spendable income objective from year 19 through year 27. Again, in the 28th year, all of Fred and Betty's savings are projected to be exhausted if they continue on their current path. Any income from any financial instrument that *the Synergy Effect™* might provide in that year and beyond is an improvement. Specifically, in the 28th year under their current plan, the only income they have would be Fred's $41,572 Social Security, Betty's $31,770 Social Security and the remaining $45,391 balance in Betty's Roth. This equals a total $118,733 of spendable income compared to their objective of $222,129. This means that they have $103,396 less income than they had wanted. The following year (year 29) their situation gets worse. That year, Fred's Social Security is $42,528 and Betty's is $32,501. Since all of their other accounts are projected to be exhausted, this $75,029 equals their total income. That year, their spendable income objective is $228,793, so they have a shortage of $153,764.

Compare this to what is projected to occur with *the Synergy Effect™* as is illustrated in the "Revised Position" section of the above illustration. In year 28, the projections show Fred and Betty receiving $73,145 and $55,925 respectively from Social Security. In addition, they have a tax-free payout of $40,520 from the annuity and the loans of $3,242 from the IUL. Considering that the only taxable portion of this income is 85 percent of their Social Security, they are left with an after-tax spendable income of $159,666.

While it is true that this is $62,463 less then their spendable income objective, it is still a $40,933 improvement ($159,666 - $118,733). In year 29, Fred and Betty are projected to receive payments of $74,827 and $57,211 respectively from Social Security, as well as $41,735 and $3,242 from the annuity and the IUL. The total after-tax spendable income that year is projected to be $163,547. They are $65,245 short of meeting their income objective, but they have $88,518 more spendable income ($163,547 - $75,029) than what is projected to be provided under the current position.

The IUL's Annual Index Interest Rate's Potential Impact on Performance

Again, the assumption used to arrive at the IUL projections is that the annual index interest rate that would be credited is six percent. It may be of interest to note how these projections would be impacted if that assumed crediting rate was increased to seven percent.

Current Position

Yr	Age	SSI Workers Fred	SSI Workers Betty	SSI Spousal Betty	Q-Plan IRA Fred	Q-Plan IRA Betty	Non-Q Money Market	Roth Betty	Gross Income	Taxes Paid	Actual Spendable Income	Target Spendable Income	Over / Under Spendabl
23	84	37,104	28,356	0	0	0	129,424	0	194,883	23,564	191,610	191,610	0
24	85	37,957	29,008	0	0	0	133,742	0	200,707	4,182	197,359	197,359	0
25	86	38,830	29,675	0	0	0	138,199	0	206,705	3,736	203,279	203,279	0
26	87	39,723	30,358	0	0	0	80,533	58,763	209,378	0	209,378	209,378	0
27	88	40,637	31,056	0	0	0	0	143,966	215,659	0	215,659	215,659	0
28	89	41,572	31,770	0	0	0	0	45,391	118,733	0	118,733	222,129	-103,396
29	90	42,528	32,501	0	0	0	0	0	75,029	0	75,029	228,793	-153,764
30	91	43,506	33,249	0	0	0	0	0	76,754	0	76,754	235,657	-158,902
31	92	44,506	34,013	0	0	0	0	0	78,520	0	78,520	242,726	-164,206
32	93	45,530	34,796	0	0	0	0	0	80,326	0	80,326	250,008	-169,682
33	94	46,577	35,596	0	0	0	0	0	82,173	0	82,173	257,508	-175,335

Revised Position

Yr	Age	SSI Workers Fred	SSI Workers Betty	SSI Spousal Betty	Tax Free Annuity	Q-Plan IRA Fred	Non-Q Money Market	Roth Betty	IUL	Gross Income	Taxes Paid	Actual Spendabl e Income	Target Spendabl e Income	Over / Under Spendabl
23	84	65,284	49,914	0	34,953	0	0	0	53,210	203,361	11,750	191,610	191,610	0
24	85	66,785	51,062	0	36,001	0	0	0	55,530	209,379	12,020	197,359	197,359	0
25	86	68,321	52,237	0	37,081	0	0	0	57,937	215,576	12,297	203,279	203,279	0
26	87	69,893	53,438	0	38,194	0	0	0	60,433	221,958	12,580	209,378	209,378	0
27	88	71,500	54,667	0	39,340	0	0	0	63,021	228,528	12,869	215,659	215,659	0
28	89	73,145	55,925	0	40,520	0	0	0	31,827	201,416	13,165	188,251	222,129	-33,878
29	90	74,827	57,211	0	41,735	0	0	0	31,827	205,600	13,468	192,132	228,793	-36,660
30	91	76,548	58,527	0	42,987	0	0	0	31,827	209,889	13,778	196,112	235,657	-39,545
31	92	78,309	59,873	0	44,277	0	0	0	31,827	214,285	14,095	200,191	242,726	-42,535
32	93	80,110	61,250	0	45,605	0	0	0	31,827	218,792	14,419	204,373	250,008	-45,635
33	94	81,952	62,659	0	46,973	0	0	0	31,827	223,411	14,750	208,661	257,508	-48,847

The Synergy Effect™   Case Study 02 - The Synergy Effect™ Scenario IUL at 7%

As the above illustration shows, increasing the assumed index crediting rate on the IUL to seven percent boosts the projected non-guaranteed amount of cash value loans that the policy would support starting in year 28 to beyond Fred's age of 100 to $31,827.

How a Spouse's Death Impacts the Survivor

In discussing the impact that either Fred or Betty's death would have on the survivor, it is important to recognize that under their current position, it is assumed that Betty has no life insurance and that Fred only has a term policy that is scheduled to terminate once he reaches age 77.

In the revised position, the assumption is that Fred purchases a $300,000 IUL that has been blended with an additional $300,000 of term. This initially provides a total death benefit of $600,000 for 15 years and $300,000 thereafter, assuming Fred decides to drop the term portion of this policy as planned.

Upon Fred's death, Betty will receive the IUL death benefit, the continuation of the annual payment amounts from her annuity and Social Security. As a surviving spouse, she is entitled to receive the larger of Fred's worker's benefit or her own worker's benefit. For example, if Fred died at age 85, then his $66,785 benefit would be paid to Betty, and would replace her lower $51,062 benefit (year 24 in the revised section). Her income that year would be $36,001 from the annuity, plus the $66,785 from Social Security (Fred's worker's benefit) for a total of $102,786. Since Fred was the insured on the IUL policy, the cash value loans would stop but as the beneficiary, she would receive the remaining non-guaranteed net death benefit. In this example, the non-guaranteed death benefit is projected to be $232,183 based upon an annual six percent assumed index interest rate or a higher $364,150 if the assumed rate was seven percent. (Both death benefit amounts assume that they had not yet taken a cash value loan that year from the policy.)

Contrast this to Betty's situation if Fred's death occurred that same year under their current position. Fred's worker's benefit would replace Betty's Social Security benefit, but because it had been started it at Fred's age 62, the COLA adjusted amount is projected to be only $37,957 at his death.

298

Betty would also have the remaining balances in the money market account and her Roth IRA that could be used to provide a continuation of some income.

Under the revised position scenario, Fred's situation could be more precarious if Betty predeceased him, primarily due to the impact on Betty's annuity. As was previously mentioned, to increase the payout amount, it is assumed that this annuity was purchased without adding the death benefit option. This would mean that Fred would receive nothing from the annuity if Betty died prior to the payment start date (year 19). Even if Betty dies after the payment start date, the payments provided by this particular annuity were for a period of Betty's life, or at least a ten-year *period certain.*

If annuity payments started in year 19, and Betty's death occurred in the 24th year, Fred would only receive payments for four more years. After that, his only income would be from Social Security and any policy loans that could be supported by the remaining cash value in his IUL.

To make Fred's future more certain, he and Betty might consider purchasing a smaller IUL on his life and using some of the premium payments to purchase an IUL on Betty's life. That way, the death benefit that Fred would receive if Betty predeasesed him could make up for a portion of the future annuity payments that would be lost.

Another option would be for Betty to purchase an annuity with a longer *period certain.* Instead of a 10-year period certain, selecting an annuity that guaranteed a continuation of 20 years (from the start of payments) would provide Fred with more security. However, the annuity's payment would drop from the initial amount of $31,055 (when started in year 19) down to $26,579 if the payment certain period was increased to 20 years.

Fred and Betty must decide the best course of action based upon the objectives that are important to them. While no strategy or retirement plan will be perfect, *the Synergy Effect™* provides important advantages that should not be ignored.

There is no perfect strategy that can magically eliminate all risk. The challenges of investment volitiliy, inflation, taxation and other risks only add to the difficulty of providing adaquate spendable income throughout what might prove to be many decades of retirement years.

The Synergy Effect™ provides new opportunities to provide clients with the retirement dignity that they deserve.

Find tools, articles, webinars, live training, case studies and more resources devoted to *the Synergy Effect™* at ***Doug-Warren.com***

CPSIA information can be obtained at www.ICGtesting.com
Printed in the USA
LVOW12s0548120813

347426LV00002B/4/P